Advance Praise

Quite a few of the recent commentaries on 1 Corinthians provide too much recycled information from older commentaries on this letter. It is with much delight, then, that I am able to commend Dr. Brookins's commentary as an important exception to the rule. His focus on stoic and ancient philosophical aspects of the letter is a much-needed addition to Corinthian studies, not only for a fresh reading of the correspondence but also because the philosophical ideas addressed in this work are indeed important elements influencing this congregation. This is an impressive commentary that will engage students, ministers, and scholars alike.

—*B. J. Oropeza*
Professor of Biblical and Religious Studies
Azusa Pacific University

Timothy Brookins is among the most qualified people currently writing in English on 1 Corinthians for his familiarity with the Greek text of the letter, understanding of philosophies and social mores in the milieu of first-century-CE Corinth, and sense for how we Christians can apply this letter to our lives. In academic settings, this commentary will prove to be accessible and valuable for undergraduates through graduate students, as well as for their professors. In church settings, it will be a very useful resource for lay people, seminarians, and pastors who desire to engage at a deeper level with 1 Corinthians.

—*Mark Reasoner*
Marian University

In a crowded field, Brookins cuts a clear and sensible path to understanding Paul's first letter to the Corinthians. This is more than a sure-footed guide, for *Reading 1 Corinthians* is a brilliant treatment that time and time again generously rewards the reader for their effort. Especially significant is Brookins's extensive knowledge of the Greco-Roman world and his mastery of the secondary literature. This is truly a treasure trove of learning. Disappoint? Hardly. Students need the best. So the next time I teach 1 Corinthians, this will be required reading.

—*Jay Smith*
Department Chair and Professor of New Testament Studies
Dallas Theological Seminary

READING 1 CORINTHIANS

Smyth & Helwys Publishing, Inc.
6316 Peake Road
Macon, Georgia 31210-3960
1-800-747-3016
© 2020 by Timothy A. Brookins
All rights reserved.

Library of Congress Cataloging-in-Publication Data

Names: Brookins, Timothy A., author.
Title: Reading 1 Corinthians : a literary and theological commentary / by
    Timothy A. Brookins.
Description: Macon, GA : Smyth & Helwys Publishing, 2020. | Series: Reading
    The New Testament, second series | Includes bibliographical references.
Identifiers: LCCN 2020037651 (print) | LCCN 2020037652 (ebook) | ISBN
    9781641732703 (paperback) | ISBN 9781641732710 (ebook)
Subjects: LCSH: Bible. Corinthians, 1st--Commentaries.
Classification: LCC BS2675.53 .B76 2020 (print) | LCC BS2675.53 (ebook) |
    DDC 227/.2077--dc23
LC record available at https://lccn.loc.gov/2020037651
LC ebook record available at https://lccn.loc.gov/2020037652

Reading 1 Corinthians

A Literary and Theological Commentary

Timothy A. Brookins

SMYTH&HELWYS
PUBLISHING INCORPORATED   MACON, GEORGIA

Reading the New Testament
2nd Series

Also by Timothy A. Brookins

Corinthian Wisdom, Stoic Philosophy, and the Ancient Economy

1 Corinthians 1–9: A Handbook on the Greek Text
(co-authored with Bruce W. Longenecker)

1 Corinthians 10–16: A Handbook on the Greek Text
(co-authored with Bruce W. Longenecker)

To my mom and dad
for giving me opportunities

Contents

Acknowledgments

I must credit my initial interest in 1 Corinthians to a seminar I took with Dr. Charles Talbert during my first year of graduate school at Baylor University. I am grateful to have learned from him and honored to author, in this book, the partial re-issue of his earlier commentary, *Reading Corinthians*. For the opportunity to take on this volume, I thank the general editor of the series, Dr. Todd Still. Many individuals have helped me in various ways to complete and to improve upon the final product. I owe thanks to Adam Winn and Mark Reasoner, as well as my colleagues Ben Blackwell, Randy Hatchett, Chris Kugler, and Jason Maston at Houston Baptist University, for offering feedback on portions or the entirety of the manuscript. I owe a special debt of gratitude to B. J. Oropeza, who read the entire manuscript and offered extensive and very helpful feedback. I also benefited greatly from engagement with the students in my Greek exegesis seminars on 1 Corinthians in the Spring of 2018 and the Spring of 2019. These students included Christopher Atkins, Michael Birdwell, Kailey Gregory, Nick Hadsell, Farah Helgerson, Tay Lawson, Michael Liga, Hannah McDermett, Phil Morrow, Jade Myers (now Jade Yang), Chris Nation, Matt Phillips, Twan Pullen, Kyle Smith, Eric Solorio, Rachel Sweet, Charlie Tracy, Andrew Wittmeier, Wesley Young, and Beth Zimmerman (now Beth White). Special thanks goes to Christopher Atkins, Phil Morrow, and Charlie Tracy, who volunteered to work on an annotated bibliography. Finally, I thank my parents, for the nurture and support that has given me the opportunity to do what I do. I dedicate this book to them.

Editor's Foreword

Like its predecessor (Reading the New Testament) and its companion series (Reading the Old Testament), Reading the New Testament: Second Series seeks to help readers—whether students or scholars, ministers or laypeople—gain a greater understanding of and appreciation for biblical texts in their original contexts. To this good end, commentaries in this series attend not only to lexical, historical, and critical concerns but are also attuned to and interested in, as the subtitle of each volume signals, literary matters and theological meaning.

Whereas some commentaries are committed to the necessary and salutary task of commenting on every jot and tittle (see Matthew 5:18), works in this series seek to trace the thought and observe the craft of biblical authors in a less atomistic manner. While attending to various trees, they are also intent on not missing the forest. Relatedly, while technically undergirded and academically informed, the commentaries within this series are intended for and are meant to be accessible and valuable to a broad readership. The seventeen volumes that will make up Reading the New Testament: Second Series, then, are written *by* scholars but are not exclusively, or even primarily, *for* scholars.

Contributors to this commentary series are accomplished academics, experienced teachers, capable communicators, and professing Christians who are committed to explicating Scripture thoughtfully, clearly, and sympathetically. To the extent that this series results in people reading the twenty-seven New Testament documents with greater skill, care, insight, devotion, and joy, the contributors and editor of Reading the New Testament: Second Series will be grateful and gratified.

—Todd D. Still
Baylor University
George W. Truett Theological Seminary
Waco, Texas

Introduction

From its infancy, the Corinthian church was a troubled church. Founded by the Apostle Paul but left shortly thereafter to manage its own affairs, the church quickly fell into disorder and division. The letter that we call 1 Corinthians is Paul's attempt to put things right again.

As a letter directed not to a universal, much less a modern, audience but to a specific church in a specific place with a specific set of problems, 1 Corinthians requires the interpreter to take careful consideration of the letter's ancient milieu and the circumstances that precipitated its composition. This commentary aims to offer a culturally informed interpretation of the letter in light of a hypothetical reconstruction of the problems that lay behind it. In offering such an interpretation, the commentary offers not a word-by-word analysis but a broad exposition of the text focused on the structure of Paul's argument in each of the letter's main units.

Preliminary to interpretation, it is necessary to consider background issues relating to the historical context in which the letter was written, the identity of the audience and author, and the unique features of the letter as a literary composition.

Ancient Corinth

The city of Corinth sat on the southern side of the roughly five-mile-wide isthmus that separated the Corinthian and Saronic bays and connected mainland Greece with the Greek Peloponnesus. Ensconced there, between the port cities of Lechaeum (to the west) and Cenchreae (to the east), Corinth was situated as a connecting point between west and east, allowing traffic traveling the seas a way across and preventing the need to sail the treacherous seas around Greece.

Corinth was a prosperous city. Due to its happy location, it made profits from trade (Strabo, *Geogr.* 8.6.20), banking (Plutarch, *Vit. aere al.* 7), and travel (Dio Chrysostom, *Cor.* 37.8.36; Philostratus, *Vit. Apoll.* 7.10). It was a notable commercial center, acclaimed especially for its production of bronze (Pliny, *Nat.* 34.1.6-8; *Ep.* 3.6; Josephus, *Vit.* 68). The city's prime location and coveted wares won Corinth renown as one of the wealthiest cities of its time.

Nevertheless, economic stratification was great (Welborn 2016). While Corinth offered extraordinary opportunities for social advancement, it was in many ways a typical city of the ancient Roman Empire. Some people were wealthy, but most were not, and a vast majority of the city sat near or below subsistence level (Brookins 2017b).

The Corinth in which Paul gathered his flock was a young city. Devastated by the Roman army in 146 BC, the Greek city of Corinth was re-founded a century later as a Roman colony (44 BC). In 27 BC, it was honorably named the capital of the Roman province of Achaia, and thus it became the residence of the Roman provincial governor as well as an important node connecting Rome with the eastern provinces. Originally populated by freed slaves, by the mid-first century the population of Roman Corinth had swelled to nearly 30,000 (Millis 2010; Willet 2012).

Culturally, the city bore the marks of its Greek past but also exhibited features inherited from Rome (Friesen, Schowalter, and Walters 2010; Harrison and Welborn 2016). It hosted attractions popular in Rome— hunting shows, gladiatorial contests, circuses, chariot races—though it also played host to the biennial Isthmian games, a Panhellenic event traditionally held in honor of the Greek god Poseidon. The city offered abundant religious options, both Roman and Greek. Temples to the respective gods of various cults surrounded the city—temples to Apollo, Athena, Poseidon, Heracles, Asklepios, Jupiter, and Capitolinus, among others (Pausanias, *Descr.* 2.2–3.1). Although Roman cults dominated (Gill 2017), these were often adaptations of Greek ones, with which they exhibited continuities as well as discontinuities (Økland 2010). Alongside the traditional cults, the city also hosted an imperial cult (Coutsoumpos 2015, 52–56). Greek philosophy found a presence (*IvO* 453), which for many served the function of religion (so Varro; Augustine, *Civ.* 6.5-8). Like many cities of the empire, Corinth was also home to a vibrant Jewish community (Philo, *Legat.* 281; Pliny, *Ep.* 5.8). While the city's layout, administration, architecture, and laws all took their bearings from Rome and official city business was conducted in Latin, Greek (in which Paul wrote his letters to the church) remained the primary spoken language of the population (Millis 2010).

The streets and public spaces of Corinth were crowded with honorific dedications and monuments (*IKorinthKent* 156) honoring the imperial family (*IKorinthKent* 69–118), municipal officers, and private individuals

(*IKorinthKent* 239–77), reflecting well the honorific culture of the first-century empire. This was the world into which the Corinthian church was born.

The Corinthian Church

According to the itinerary recounted in Acts, Paul first came to Corinth during what has been called his "Second Missionary Journey" (Acts 15:36–18:22). Having struck out from his home church in Antioch of Syria, he had wound his way through Asia Minor and Macedonia, establishing churches among the Galatians (16:6-7; cf. 18:23), the Philippians (16:12-40), and the Thessalonians (17:1-9). He then touched in Greece, stopping first in Athens (17:16-34) before settling in Corinth, where he established a fledgling church and stayed for a period of eighteen months (18:1-18). While 1 Corinthians addresses the church as a single entity (1 Cor 1:2), the Corinthian church may have contained several cell groups. These ordinarily met in the homes of private individuals (1 Cor 16:19; Rom 16:5; Col 4:15; Phlm 2) and only occasionally came together as a larger group (1 Cor 11:20; 14:23; Rom 16:23).

This church was essentially a microcosm of the city. Still in its infancy when Paul wrote, the church contained as few as forty or fifty members (Murphy-O'Connor 2002); almost certainly there were no more than one or two hundred (de Vos 1999, 203–205; Hays 1997, 7). While most of these individuals were relatively poor, and some of them likely destitute, a minority in the church seem to have possessed the good fortune of moderate wealth (Theissen 1982b; 2001; 2003; Malherbe 1983; Meeks 1983; Brookins 2014). The resulting social stratification could explain some of the problems addressed in the letter (1 Cor 6:1-11; 11:17-34).

Most of the church's members were Gentiles (1 Cor 8:7; 12:2), of Roman or Greek descent, although Jews also found representation (7:18-19). Many in the church seem to have maintained the connections of their past, still mingling with the chums of their pre-Christian days and participating in the many religious facets of popular civic and domestic life (Barclay 1992). Nonbelievers were welcomed into the church's worship services (14:24); some believers were married to nonbelievers (7:12-16), and some had opportunities to participate in religious meals with unbelieving relations (8:10; 10:14-22).

The Author of 1 Corinthians

The letter's address line names Paul and Sosthenes as the senders. Most of Paul's letters name at least one co-sender: Timothy in 2 Corinthians (1:1),

Philippians (1:1), Colossians (1:1), and Philemon (v. 1); Silvanus and Timothy in 1 Thessalonians (1:1) and 2 Thessalonians (1:1).

Little is known about Sosthenes. Acts identifies a man named Sosthenes as the "ruler of the synagogue" in Corinth (Acts 18:17). This figure falls victim to a beating apparently for his connections with Paul. This is likely the same individual as the one named in 1 Corinthians, for he is described in Acts, as he is here, as both a Corinthian and an associate of Paul, and the name is otherwise unknown in the NT and overall relatively rare in the first century (LGPN).

Despite the presence of Sosthenes in the address line, the first-person singular dominates the letter. Sosthenes possibly comes into view in 1:18-31 and 2:6-16 (Murphy-O'Connor 1993), where Paul uses verbs of speaking in the first-person plural ("we preach," 1:23; "we speak of," 2:6, 7). Otherwise the first-person plural seems to refer to Paul among the apostles (4:9-13).

The Date and Provenance of 1 Corinthians

Paul's eighteen-month stint in Corinth coincided with the year Gallio sat as governor of Achaia (Acts 18:12-18). Since that year can be dated to the twelfth year of the reign of the emperor Claudius (*IG* VII, 1676), it can be determined that Paul's stay in Corinth occurred sometime between early AD 50 and late AD 52. According to Acts, Paul then returned to his home church in Antioch (18:22) before setting out again through Galatia and Phrygia (Acts 18:23) and settling for two and a half years in Ephesus (19:1-41). Most likely it was from here that Paul wrote his "previous letter" to the Corinthians, a letter referenced in 1 Cor 5:9 but now lost. It was from Ephesus also that Paul wrote the present letter, which, although written later than the "previous" letter, is known today as "First" Corinthians (1 Cor 16:8).

In the letter's conclusion, Paul states that he intended to remain in Ephesus "until Pentecost" (16:8). Since Pentecost took place in the spring and delivery of the letter would take several weeks, and since travel would be limited during the winter, it may be supposed that the letter was written and delivered during the fall, prior to the prohibitive months of winter. But of which year? Allowing adequate time between Paul's departure from Corinth for his return to Antioch, for his ministry in Galatia and Phrygia (Acts 18:23), and for the success of his current ministry in Ephesus (1 Cor 16:9), it can be guessed that he wrote 1 Corinthians in the fall of either 53 or 54, but perhaps as late as 55.

The Occasion of 1 Corinthians

First Corinthians presents a prolonged exhortation to unity—a call for the Corinthian believers to stop crowing about their spiritual achievements (1:29-31; 3:1-3; 4:6-7; 13:4), to renounce pursuit of high status (4:8-13), and to pursue the benefit of other people and of the church community as a whole (10:24; 14:3, 5, 12, 26). The appeal came in response to reports from "Chloe's people," mentioned in the letter's opening section, that the church was torn with division (1:10-12). The letter also responds to the contents of a letter apparently sent to Paul directly from the Corinthian church (7:1). Although the symptoms of the church's divisions were many (e.g., people suing each other, 5:1-13; claiming freedom as individuals, 6:12a; 8:9; 10:23a; wielding spiritual gifts as badges of superiority, 12:1-31; 14:1-40; disharmonious observance of the Lord's Supper, 11:17-34; rejection of a bodily resurrection, 15:12-58), the initial chapters of the letter indicate that the underlying problem was tied to some kind of "human wisdom" (1:18–3:23). Some in the church fancied that they alone possessed this wisdom and sat at a higher level of spiritual status than those who lacked this wisdom. These "wise" people upheld a two-tier view of believers: there were the "wise" and there were the "foolish," the "spiritual" and the "unspiritual," the "mature" and the "immature" (cf. 2:15-16; 3:1-3; 4:6-7; 14:20).

It is difficult to say what kind of wisdom this was, for Paul does not offer a detailed account of the Corinthians' views. Nevertheless, it is possible, with caution, to use Paul's responses as a "mirror" for reconstructing their position. Indeed, through his responses it is possible not only to observe *what* the community's problems were but also to identify from these problems recurring patterns in their *behavior*, and indirectly to gather something about their patterns of *thought*. Besides these clues, Paul also quotes the Corinthians on several occasions (6:12a, 13a, 18b; 7:1ab; 8:1a, 4, 5-6, 8), and he frequently appropriates catchwords that were in currency among them (2:6, 14-15; 3:1-3, 18-20; 4:8-10; 6:5; 8:1-2, 9, 10-11; 11:19; 14:37; cf. 13:10; 14:20). While the letter's original Greek included neither punctuation marks nor quotation marks, clues in the text make it possible to identify these places with some confidence (Brookins 2014, 82–103). Together, attention to the church's problems and its language allows one to gather that some in the church were identifying as "wise men" (1:18–3:23), claimed to be "mature" (2:6; 3:1-3; 4:6-7), were obsessed with "freedom" (cf. 2:16; 6:12a; 8:9; 10:23a), and inordinately prioritized the mind over the body and external things (cf. 6:12-20; 8:1; 15:12).

A close look at this evidence suggests that the perspective of the group of Corinthian wisemen was inspired by certain elements of Neo-Stoicism (Brookins 2014), a philosophy that thrived during this period and was well represented by Paul's contemporary Seneca (ca. AD 1–65). Developed in its canonical form in the third century BC, Stoicism claimed to offer to humanity the best form of life, based on the teachings of "Nature." This life was embodied in their picture of the "wise man," who used the divine, and indeed innate, gift of reason to make judgments always in keeping with virtue. Virtue was the only good, vice the only evil. All other things—health and wealth, and their opposites disease and poverty—were "indifferent." Thus, the Stoics described their wise man as "rich" because his virtue was more valuable than all other things. He was "self-sufficient" because the faculties needed to live the good life were available within. He was "king" because he was master over vice, and "free" because he was not a slave to it. Under influence from Platonism, Stoicism over time downgraded the importance of the body and external things, resulting in Paul's day in something close to a mind-body dualism. Evidently certain Corinthians refracted these ideas through the gospel message preached by Paul, resulting in a kind of Christian Stoicism. Thus, they considered themselves "wise men" who were "rich," "kings," and "free"; they believed that, as people equipped with the power to live the perfect life, they were self-sufficient; and they devalued the moral significance of bodily and dietary matters, resulting in many of the problems seen in the letter.

There is reason to believe that those who represented this group were among the wealthier members of the church (see above). While Stoic ideas had entered into popular thinking and could be encountered in some form in Greek and Roman literature, theater, and political discourse, some in the Corinthian church seem to have had adequate enough means to receive some level of formal philosophical education (Brookins 2014, 104–47).

If the culprits had indeed received training in philosophy, then the relevance of the missionary figure of Apollos—whom many interpreters see as the main conduit of the church's "wisdom"—diminishes. While Paul discusses his relationship with Apollos at some length in the first four chapters of the letter (1:12; 3:5–4:6), he never lays blame on Apollos, much less identifies him as the source of the Corinthians' wisdom. On the contrary, he lays the blame directly on the Corinthians.

Themes in 1 Corinthians

Appropriate to its primary theme, 1 Corinthians is rich with metaphors for *unity*. Depicting the Corinthian church as a whole consisting of various parts, Paul compares the church to a building (3:9-17), as well as to the human body (10:17; 12:12-27). He draws heavily from language related to the political sphere (1:10-12; 6:12; 10:23; 12:12-26), likening the church to a city disturbed by division and exhorting them to return to civic harmony. He suggests that the purity of the community depends on the purity of all the parts (3:17; 5:6-13; 15:33). He stresses the oneness of God, the Lord, and the Spirit (12:4-11). And he makes abundant use of kinship metaphors, addressing the Corinthians as "brothers (and sisters)" more than twenty times and describing himself as their "father" (4:15).

Also prominent are the opposing themes of *boasting* and *grace*. While the Corinthians emphasize their own spiritual achievement, Paul emphasizes the *extrinsic* origins of their spiritual status. Some are "puffed up" (4:6, 18, 19; 5:2; cf. 8:1; 13:4). They "boast" as if their spiritual possessions are not gifts from God (4:7). They boast in humanity when they should boast only in the Lord (1:31; 3:21). They fancy themselves "wise men" (3:18-20), advanced in their spiritual achievement (4:7-10; 14:12, 37). Paul responds that God regards not the exalted but the lowly (1:28-31). All that one has comes from God (1:5, 7, 29-31; 2:12; 3:10, 21-23; 4:7). Spiritual manifestations are gifts from the Spirit (12:4-11). Salvation is the result of God's power (1:18-21). By God the church has been washed, sanctified, and redeemed (6:11). People do not reach God, but God has reached out to humanity (8:2; 13:12). The Corinthians belong to Christ (3:23) and exist only "through him" (8:6). Paul credits God for his work in the gospel (3:10; 14:18; 15:10). He uses the language of "riches" to describe the blessings that God has imparted in the gospel (1:5).

Paul's response to the Corinthians is driven fundamentally by his *Christology* and—inseparable from this—his *ecclesiology*. Consistent with his Christology, he promotes a "cruciform," or "cross-shaped," way of life: that way of life, embodied by Christ, that puts others before self. When members of the community practice cruciformity in mutual exchange, the community is built up and strengthened in unity. Those "in Christ" are united not only with God but also with each other; thus ecclesiology flows from Christology.

The Genre and Rhetoric of 1 Corinthians

Although profoundly theological in its content, 1 Corinthians is not a theological treatise. It is a letter, and by ancient standards a long one. The letter could further be categorized either by letter type or by speech type. (1) According to ancient taxonomy, the letter would qualify as a mix of several different letter types, most notably the letter of *admonishment*, the letter of *threat*, and the letter of *advising* (Pseudo-Demetrius). (2) Considered in terms of the ancient taxonomy of speech types, from start to finish the letter fits the description of a *deliberative* speech (M. M. Mitchell 1993). Four notable qualities typify deliberative speech: concern for the future of the audience; appeals to what is advantageous to the audience; proof by example; and a subject appropriate for deliberation (for instance, the subject of factionalism and concord).

Several features of the letter's rhetoric deserve comment. First, reflecting the letter's deliberative purposes, Paul makes frequent appeals to individuals or groups as examples. Deliberative rhetoric overlapped with a kind of rhetoric known as *parenesis*, or "exhortation." Parenetic discourse characteristically appealed to examples, or *exempla*, including both positive and negative ones. Positive exempla were used to spur the audience on to some recommended course of action. Paul appeals to himself as an exemplum with notable frequency in the letter (2:1-5; 3:5–4:5; 4:16; 7:7, 8; 8:13; 9:1-27; 10:33–11:1; 13:11; 14:18-19); he also points to Apollos (3:5–4:5) and Timothy (4:16) as exempla. Negative exempla were used to deter audiences from following a deleterious course of action. In 1 Corinthians Paul uses cautionary exempla with reference to both himself (9:24-27) and ancient Israel (10:1-13).

Second, Paul frequently deploys the conventions of an ancient style of discourse known as *diatribe*. Used as a pedagogical technique in Cynic and Stoic schools of philosophy (Bultmann 1910), the diatribe style relied on short, pithy sentences (15:32-34); abundant rhetorical questions (fourteen times in 9:1-12a; twelve times in 12:1-31); imaginary interlocutors through whom the speaker voiced potential objections to his argument (15:35) and to whom he offered responses (15:36-49); and often abusive replies to the questioner ("Fool!" 15:36).

Finally, throughout the letter Paul interacts allusively with the language of his audience and with the conventional discourses of his culture. Where he borrows language from his audience, he often changes its meaning, using their language against them. Where he draws from the language of his non-Jewish culture, he makes abundant use of themes prevalent in the philosophical culture of his day (6:7; 9:7, 8-10, 18, 24-27; 14:7; 15:33, 39-41), especially Stoicism (3:21; 4:8; 6:19; 7:4, 29-34; 11:14-15; 12:4-6, 12-27; 15:28, 31). His use of the language and tropes of his environment need not mean that he shared exactly the particulars of their meaning. Rather, he used this language—as he used the Corinthians' language—in service of his own purposes, employing language that they understood both to identify with them and to correct them.

Looking Ahead

1 Corinthians 1:1-9

The letter's introduction consists of a greeting (1:1-3) and a thanksgiving (1:4-9). These sections are not only formalities; they also introduce themes that recur throughout the letter. From the start, the letter lacks the formality of letters pertaining to business, administration, or legal matters. This is a personal letter, and it contains a palpable touch of intimacy.

Greeting (1:1-3)

Hellenistic letters typically opened with an address line in the format "X *to* Y" (Klauck 2006, 18). So begins Paul's letter to the Corinthians: "Paul . . . and Sosthenes . . . *to* the church of God that is in Corinth" (vv. 1, 2).

As in nearly all his letters (cf. Phil 1:1; Phlm 1), Paul appends to his name a self-description as an "apostle" (v. 1). While Acts is restrictive in its use of this term, Paul uses the term broadly. He includes as apostles not only the Twelve and himself but also several other individuals (Rom 16:7; 1 Cor 9:5; 12:28; Gal 1:19; Phil 2:25; 1 Thess 2:7) although he does not extend the label to believers at large (12:29). His own apostolic status is due to God's special calling ("*called* to be an apostle by the will of God"; cf. Rom 1:1; Gal 1:15-16), consisting of a specific commissioning to be an emissary to the Gentiles (Rom 11:13). While the self-designation may carry connotations of authority, later sections in the letter show that Paul associated the office inherently with lowly service to others, patterned after the example of Jesus Christ (4:9-13; 9:1-27).

Paul names as his addressees "the church of God that is in Corinth" (v. 2). The Corinthian church probably consisted of multiple house churches, which only occasionally met together as a whole (cf. 11:20; 14:23; Rom 16:23). Paul addresses not one but all of them here. His description of the church as "*sanctified* in Christ Jesus" and as those "called to be *saints*" communicates what they *ought* to be. They are to be "holy" as Israel was to be holy (Lev 19:2), yet the remainder of the letter will depict them as flawed and immature.

A greeting follows (v. 3), as was also customary in Hellenistic letters (Klauck 2006, 18). Paul, however, devises a uniquely Christian variant of the greeting formula. In a play on words, he substitutes for the standard word *chairein* ("greetings") the word *charis* ("grace"). Next he appends the words "and peace," echoing the Jewish idea of *shalom*, a word meaning "completeness," "welfare," or "prosperity." Both "grace" and "peace" are meant in a distinctly Christian sense here, as they allude to blessings received from God in the gospel of Jesus Christ. The full greeting, "Grace to you and peace from God our father and the Lord Jesus Christ" (Rom 1:7; 2 Cor 1:2; Gal 1:3; Eph 1:2; Phil 1:2; Col 1:2; 2 Thess 1:2; Phlm 3), or some variation thereof (1 Thess 1:1), recurs as the standard greeting in Paul's letters.

Thanksgiving (1:4-9)

In Hellenistic letters, a "thanksgiving" conventionally followed the greeting (Klauck 2006, 21–23). The thanksgiving would be directed toward some deity, in gratitude for either one's own or the recipient's well-being. A second-century letter written by a young sailor to his father offers thanks "to the lord Serapis," because when he was endangered at sea, Serapis rescued him promptly (cited by Collins 1999, 55). The thanksgiving might also come in the form of a prayer for the recipient's prosperity. In one surviving letter, a certain Claudius Terentianus opens by saying to his father, "Before all else I pray that you are well and prospering" (cited by Collins 1999, 55).

Most of Paul's letters contain a thanksgiving section (Rom 1:8-15; Phil 1:3-11; Col 1:3-14; 1 Thess 1:2-10; 2 Thess 1:3-12; Phlm 4-7), so its absence would be more significant than its presence (cf. Galatians). Here, Paul addresses his thanks to "my God" (cf. Rom 1:8; 2 Cor 12:21; Phil 1:3; 4:19), noting that he thanks God whenever he prays for the Corinthians.

Paul indicates two main reasons for his gratitude: for the "grace" that God has bestowed upon the Corinthians (vv. 4-7) and for God's faithfulness to preserve them (vv. 8-9).

(1) Verses 4-7 invoke several concepts that turn up later in the letter. While later Paul asks (mockingly) if the Corinthians are "already rich" (4:8), here he emphasizes that they are "rich in him [Christ]" (1:5). While later he chastises those who believe that they "have knowledge" (8:1, 7), here he suggests that they are "rich . . . in all knowledge" (1:5). While later he finds fault with the Corinthians for their self-serving use of spiritual gifts (12:1–14:40), here he says that they are "not lacking in any gift" (1:7). In sum, this section contains already a thinly veiled critique of the Corinthians,

underscoring the fact that while the Corinthians are spiritually blessed, they should not take credit, for the source of every blessing is God.

(2) God has not only blessed the Corinthians but will also preserve them until the "day of our Lord Jesus Christ" (v. 8). In the writings of the OT prophets, the "day of the LORD" referred to the time when God would send judgment (Isa 2:12; Joel 2:31; Amos 5:18-20; cf. 1 En. 54:5-6; 62:1–63:12). Paul adapts this traditional Jewish idea by applying it to the day of Jesus' return. At that time, the final judgment will occur, and those in Christ will receive approval and those not in Christ will receive condemnation. The return of the Lord recurs as an important theme in the letter. In places Paul uses it as a warning of imminent judgment (3:13; 4:5; cf. 5:5), and in places he presents it as a reason for hope (11:26; 16:22). The way it functions for each person will depend on the way one lives (see 3:10-23).

Assuring the Corinthians' preservation is their "communion" (*koinōnia*) with Christ. The idea of *koinōnia* derives from the cultural domain of economics, where it refers to a kind of "partnership" in matters of business; what is good for one partner is good for the other. In Stoic philosophy, the idea of *koinōnia* had a more metaphysical meaning: the parts of the universe are so intimately "associated" that they feel what the others feel (*SVF* 2.532, 546; Hierocles/Stobaeus, *Anth.* 4.84.20; Epictetus, *Diatr.* 1.14.5-6). Philippians 3:10 shows that this approximates Paul's idea of communion with Christ: "I want to know Christ and the power of his resurrection and the *koinōnia* with his sufferings by becoming like him in his death."

Conclusion

Anticipating the remainder of the letter, 1 Cor 1:1-9 puts strong emphasis on God's agency and Jesus' lordship. These verses make reference to "God" six times. God is the agent behind all the actions in the thanksgiving section ("you were enriched," v. 5; "you were confirmed," v. 6; "he will confirm," v. 8; "you were called," v. 9). Reference is made to "Jesus" eight times. Five times Paul refers to him as "Lord Jesus Christ."

Verse 2 contains the first reference in the letter to the expression "in Christ." This expression, which occurs no less than seventy-two times in the Pauline corpus (Campbell 2012), communicates a conviction that is central to Paul's theology. The expression is difficult to define, but it seems best understood in a "locative" sense, i.e., as an expression of believers' situatedness in Christ, where they share in his form of life and in the power that makes such life possible. This idea is closely related with the idea of "communion" with Christ, to which Paul made reference in v. 9.

Also prominent in this section are the associated themes of grace and calling, in conjunction with the theme of election, anticipating themes that will recur throughout the letter and further highlighting the agency of God. "Grace" brackets the letter (1:3; 16:23). Paul wishes the Corinthians "grace" (v. 3). He thanks God for the "grace" given to the Corinthians (v. 4). The Corinthians are "called" to be saints (v. 2). God has "called" them into fellowship with his son (v. 9). While "grace" had multiple facets for Paul (Barclay 2015), his emphasis in the first major unit of the letter (1:1–4:21) is on God's grace as an endowment that empowers the spiritual life of the believer—a point that the Corinthians evidently need to hear.

Division and Unity

1 Corinthians 1:10–4:21

The letter's prescript (1:1-3) and thanksgiving (1:4-9) are more than a formality. They provide a preview of the themes to be treated in the letter's body, now to be introduced.

The first major unit of the letter, comprising 1:10–4:21, bears the hallmarks of a scrupulously designed argument, structured according to the conventions recommended in ancient rhetorical theory (M. M. Mitchell 1993, 184–86). The letter's main purpose is stated in 1:10 (to call for unity and an end to factionalism in the church) and is followed in 1:11-17 with a statement of the facts (summarizing the present situation in the church) and, finally, an appeal in the form of various "proofs" (Paul's recommendations for how to restore concord), of which 1:18–4:21 is the first:

> thesis (*prothesis*), 1:10
> statement of facts (*diēgesis*), 1:11-17
> first proof (*pistis*), 1:18–4:21

The cause of the divisions is difficult to determine. First Corinthians 1:10–4:21 draws together an array of themes, all of which need to be taken into account in reconstructing the situation: unity and diversity, wisdom and the wise, knowledge and understanding, boasting and hubris, judgment and evaluation, spiritual achievement and status, God's grace and power.

Two internally coherent but significantly different readings of the situation require consideration. An *apologetic* reading views these chapters primarily as Paul's defense to the Corinthians of his apostolic authority and as a high-handed attempt to regain his preeminence over the rival missionary Apollos. Alternatively, a *didactic* reading would view these chapters as directed against dissension among the Corinthians, and Paul's discussion of himself and Apollos as serving the function of example for imitation.

The *apologetic* reading can be expanded as follows. After sowing the seeds of the gospel during his initial visit to Corinth, Paul had departed and was succeeded in his ministry upon the arrival of a certain Apollos, with whose learning and eloquence the Corinthians became enamored and whom in hindsight they found vastly more impressive in presence than Paul. Having discovered through reports that he had lost ground to Apollos, Paul aimed to reestablish his preeminence and, by reclaiming the Corinthians under his singular authority, to restore unity in the church.

On this reading, Paul's purposes are double layered. The Corinthians are indeed divided, but as a derivative consequence of the divide that existed between the two "wisdoms" embodied at the level of the church's leadership. Thus, certain members of the church espoused the "wisdom" preached by Apollos; avowed allegiance to Apollos; "boasted" in Apollos; and, after having "evaluated" Paul and Apollos, weighed status in favor of Apollos. Paul responded by arguing that the two men represented two conflicting kinds of wisdom: one a "human" wisdom and the other "God's" wisdom. This "human" wisdom consisted of the "wisdom of eloquence," or the ability to speak impressively and persuasively. Paul's purpose was to set in contrast a wisdom in which persuasion resides in rhetorical skill on the one hand, and a wisdom in which persuasion is wrought by the Spirit on the other (Horsley 1976; Pogoloff 1992; Litfin 1994; Winter 2002; Mihaila 2009; with variations).

A *didactic* reading views Paul's immediate purpose as hortatory and any defensive purpose as secondary at most. According to this reading, the church was mired in dissension, but it was not divided into parties based on leadership; the church was not "boasting" in a particular leader or in any leader's brand of wisdom; nor were they "evaluating" Paul and Apollos. They were evaluating *each other* and, that what they had, they had received *from God*, boasted in *their own* wisdom and spiritual achievement, and by setting themselves above others they embodied a wisdom counter to the cruciform way of self-abnegation for the benefit of others, that is, the "wisdom of the cross." The two clashing wisdoms, then, oppose not the use of rhetoric and reliance on the Spirit as means of persuasion but two distinct accounts of things, two ways of looking at the world: one the *intuitive, status-oriented ethos* of the world and the other the *counterintuitive, status-forsaking ethos* of the cross, the value of which is only understood through an epistemological transformation. Paul invokes Apollos, consequently, not as a perceived rival but in order to set before the Corinthians an exhibit precisely of this wisdom, i.e., a wisdom embodied in service to others and in mutuality of benefit, leading to the unity and edification of the community.

Although both readings appear to be coherent, the latter reading will be followed here, for two main reasons. First, the apologetic reading somewhat awkwardly straddles two levels of controversy at once, and this at points confuses rather than clarifies the text. Second, Paul makes open charges only against one target, and that is against the Corinthians. At no point does he assign blame to Apollos, and at no point does he assign to him the "human" wisdom at issue. On the contrary, he blames the Corinthians for adopting this wisdom, for boasting in their achievements, and for neglecting the enabling role of God's grace.

Dissension in the Assembly (1:10-17)

1:10-12

Having concluded preliminaries, Paul now speaks directly: "I urge you" (cf. Rom 15:30). These words, which Paul repeats in 4:17 to close off the first major unit, set the tone of the letter. It is a letter of "*advice*" (see introduction). The advice is that the Corinthians should be "joined together in the same mind and the same thinking" (v. 10).

The appeal draws noticeably from two distinct realms of discourse, that of *politics* and that of *kinship*. Both the words of the appeal and its theme, concord, evoke the deliberative rhetoric of the day (M. M. Mitchell 1993). Orators used the deliberative style to exhort their audiences, at some critical juncture in time, either to the course of action that most conduced to their benefit or away from the course of action that tended toward their harm. From Classical times and still even under the Roman Empire, public oratory played an influential role in directing politics, shaping social mores, and guiding civic affairs. Since the city figured as the quintessential embodiment of human society, which could tend toward either cooperation or dissension, public speeches in the style of deliberative rhetoric were a common means of healing civic strife.

Deliberative political discourse drew much of its language from Greek and Roman moral philosophy. The philosophers, and the Stoics in particular, had expanded the idea of the local city-state into a cosmic notion of a "world-city" (Seneca, *Marc.* 18.2) in which all peoples were enrolled as co-citizens. At the heart of Stoic philosophy was the idea of an orderly universe, composed of diverse parts that worked together in harmony. The universe, or nature, in turn modeled the normative paradigm for human ethics. Moral philosophers like Seneca (ca. AD 1–65) maintained that the virtues extolled by philosophy were the bond of the cosmic society, the source of mutual benefit and social harmony (see Seneca, *On Benefits*). Paul's language in 1 Cor 1:10 is rich with echoes of political/philosophical discourse: "I urge you," "factions," "say the same thing," "think the same thing" (cf. M. M. Mitchell 1993, 68–70).

Paul also draws from another cultural domain, equally concerned with unity, namely that of kinship (cf. 1:1, 3). His reference to the Corinthians as "brothers" (encompassing both brothers *and* sisters; see BGU II 423) is the first of twenty-one occurrences of this address in the letter and underlines at the outset the intimate ties that the Corinthians shared in Christ; their state of natural spiritual kinship clashes ironically with their dismal state of disunity. Hereafter, kinship language fills the letter. This language establishes in-group and out-group boundaries. Siblings are insiders who share with each other a common status as "saints" in Christ Jesus. Those who do not uphold the standards of the in-group have no right to fellowship in the family (cf. 5:1-8, 11).

How Paul had learned about the church's divisions is disclosed in v. 11: it was from "Chloe's people" (*hypo tōn Chloēs*). This obscure description may refer to slaves or clients employed in Chloe's service. Chloe herself is otherwise unknown in the NT, although she must have been known to the Corinthians and she appears to have been on friendly terms with Paul. Whether she was a Corinthian herself is uncertain, but her connections suggest that she was most likely a Christian. Since Paul writes from Ephesus (16:8), Chloe's people have either come to him on business from their place of residence in Corinth or they have returned from business in Corinth to their residence in Ephesus. That Chloe is not mentioned in Romans 16:3-23 with the other members of the Corinthian church could suggest that she and her people were not from Corinth; yet Stephanus, Crispus, and other Corinthians (1:16; 16:15, 17) are not mentioned there either. The question of her residency therefore remains uncertain.

Based on this report, Paul relates, first, his knowledge that "there are divisions" in the church (v. 11). He follows with the explanatory comment, "Now I mean this, that each of you says, '*I* am of Paul,' and '*I* am of Apollos,' and '*I* am of Cephas,' and '*I* am of Christ'" (v. 12). All four individuals can be identified. The Apollos named is undoubtedly the one whom Acts describes as "a native of Alexandria," a "learned man" who had "a thorough knowledge of the Scriptures" (18:24, NIV). Preaching boldly in the synagogue, Apollos had made a favorable impression on the believers in Ephesus, and from there he had been sent on to minister in Corinth, letters of recommendation in hand (Acts 18:26-28). Apollos would have reached Corinth on the heels of Paul's departure. The one here called Cephas is the apostle "Peter" (or "Rock," which is *Cephas* in Aramaic, *Petros* in Greek), whom Paul almost invariably calls by this appellation (3:22; 9:5; 15:5; Gal 1:18; 2:9, 11, 14).

Of Peter's time in Corinth there is no record, although it can be inferred from his mention that the Corinthians are familiar with him (cf. 3:22; 9:5; 15:5).

There is reason to question whether the four citations reflect verbatim the words of the Corinthians and, relatedly, whether the Corinthians were in fact divided into four distinct parties. Several possibilities present themselves. (1) It is possible that the slogans in 1:12 are verbatim quotations, voicing the cries of those who belonged to four distinct parties. However, (2) the words could represent Pauline constructions designed to conceal some more specific rivalry within a more complex rhetorical situation. This option has several variants: (a) the true rivalry was between a "Paul party" and a "*Christ* party" (Lütgert 1908); (b) the true rivalry was between a "Paul party" and a "*Peter* party" (Schmidt 1801; Baur 1831; revived by Goulder 1991); or (c) the true rivalry was between a "Paul party" and an "*Apollos* party" (Smit 2002). Alternatively, (3) the assertions could be Pauline constructions intended to depict party rivalries as *if* according to leadership but not in fact formed on this basis.

The second option has received wide endorsement among interpreters, particularly in the Paul-Apollos variant. Paul broaches the person of Apollos several times further in the letter (3:4, 5, 6, 22; 4:6; 16:12), once reflecting on their relationship at length (3:4–4:6) and at the conclusion of the letter apprising the Corinthians, with a matter-of-factness that could be interpreted as curt, that Apollos would not be returning to them soon (16:12). While the objection might be raised that Paul does *not* name only himself and Apollos here, it could be surmised that this formulation is strategic on Paul's part: that he has intentionally *concealed* the source of conflict by rhetorically embedding it within a more complex situation, thus only *insinuating* a criticism against the Apollos party (or against Apollos) and avoiding a public, frontal assault so as not to rankle the offending persons (Smit 2002, 248).

Despite the cogency of this reading, there is good justification for preferring the third reading: Paul is not actually quoting the Corinthians and they were not divided into factions according to *leadership*, although he is indeed depicting the Corinthians as factious. While appearing to conflict with a "plain" reading of the text, this reading has much to commend it. First, it deserves attention that the slogans of 1:12 are not presented as the content of Chloe's report but as Paul's own commentary on it ("Now, what I am *saying* is . . ."). Second, there is no evidence at all for the existence of at least two of the named parties, in which case Paul cannot be quoting them. While Apollos reappears in a salient capacity later in the letter (3:4–4:6; 16:12), Cephas virtually disappears (3:4, 22; 9:5), and the Christ-slogan is best understood as a corrective to the factionalism that finds expression in the first three slogans. Indeed, whereas the other expressions recur (3:4, 22), Paul never again names a "Christ" party. Moreover, *all* will have claimed allegiance to Christ, as Paul's immediately subsequent leading question presupposes ("surely Christ hasn't been divided, has he?!"). Third, when Paul later discusses his relationship with Apollos, he concludes by revealing that he has intended to present himself and Apollos as proxies for others, that is, for the Corinthians themselves (see comments on 4:6). Fourth, the non-quotation reading is a natural one when read in light of the conventions of ancient rhetoric (M. M. Mitchell 1993, 83–86). It was conventional in discourses aimed at dissentious audiences to caricature the audience as childish (see Chrysostom, *Or.* 38.21, among other texts). In such instances, the audience need not have used the language cited; rather, speakers *attributed* to them language that *depicted* them as childish due to their inability to get along. Implicitly or explicitly, Paul repeatedly characterizes the Corinthians in this way; Paul describes them as children, for instance, in 3:1-2 (this language recurs 13:11 and 14:20). Fifth, the slogans could be understood as *mimicry* of partisan political discourse, as witnessed when cities were divided by the formation of factions around different political leaders (cf. Welborn 1987, 90–93). Paul's purpose then would not be to describe actual leadership rivalries in the church but to *equate* the Corinthians' divisions to political rivalries of this kind. The Corinthians themselves would have been familiar with such situations and would have understood the comparison.

If, then, the Corinthians did not in fact give voice to such slogans, and Paul was putting his own words to the situation, although factions may have existed in the church there is reason to doubt whether *leader*-oriented parties existed as such. While this might seem to constitute a baseless rejection of the words plainly stated, it should be noted that if a Cephas-party and a Christ-party did not exist, as interpreters agree, then the door to this interpretation has already been opened. What then is Paul doing? He is depicting the Corinthians as childish due to their disunity by speaking *dramatically* in the first person, not quoting them but attributing to them language appropriate to their behavior (what ancient rhetoricians called *sermocinatio*).

1:13-17

The three rhetorical questions that ensue elaborate on Paul's final slogan, i.e., "I am of Christ," countering the Corinthians' dissension by highlighting the unity that believers share in Christ. In effect: "You know that Christ is *not* divided. Christ's crucifixion is the common basis of salvation for *all* of you. You were *all* baptized into Christ Jesus."

The shift to the topic of baptism at this point, on which Paul dwells for the next four verses, may give reason to suspect that baptism was a cause of the church's divisions. If this is so, one is left with a more intricate puzzle in which the church's divisions, baptismal controversy, and wisdom are all somehow related.

Paul's purpose in discussing baptism is less than obvious. (1) One reading has church members falling into factions based on the allegiance of members to the missionary who had baptized them, whether Paul or another (Chester 2003). (2) Another possibility is that the issue was one not of baptism-based allegiance but of conflicting characterizations of Paul and Apollos by the Corinthians: they lauded Apollos as an expert "preacher" but character- ized Paul as a mere "baptizer" ("Christ did *not* send me to *baptize* but to *preach* . . ."; see Pascuzzi 2009). (3) A third reading views Paul's discussion not as a *reflection* of a real dispute over baptism but as an *illustration* of the Corinthians' unity in Christ (M. M. Mitchell 1993, 201n92), invoked to counter their quarrelsome behavior. The third reading is to be preferred. For Paul, the unity of believers in Christ was not a mental construction but a metaphysical reality. The experience of baptism was paradigmatic of unity in Christ, for this experience, which defined entry into the community, was one that all believers shared. Paul's repetition in his letters of what seems to have been a creedal formula connected with baptism (12:13; cf. Rom 6:3; Gal 3:27) suggests that he had indoctrinated his churches with this idea, and his reaffirmation of the idea here suggests that he expected the Corinthians to know and accept it. His subsequent reference to Christ's crucifixion "for you" runs parallel, for baptism and crucifixion converged in Paul's thinking (both represented death to the old self). By invoking baptism and crucifixion, then, Paul's strategy is to call the estranged members of the community back to the place of their initial salvation experience, where they once stood and still stand (metaphysically) united.

Paul's reference to the baptisms of Crispus, Gaius, and Stephanas adds a further element of mystery. Does Paul have strategic reasons for naming names? Is the list of names only selective? Does he only feign forgetfulness of other baptisms? Why does he single out these individuals?

One explanation is that he draws attention to them in order to buttress his authority. Indeed, having been baptized by Paul, *prior* to the arrival of other Christian missionaries like Apollos, Crispus and the others would have been among Corinth's first converts, the "first-fruits" of God's church in that region (see 16:15), and would thus serve as a token reminder that it was *Paul* who had been the community's founder. Indeed, one of those whom he had converted was none other than Stephanas, now one of the

Corinthians' leaders (16:15-16). It is also of interest that these men probably possessed better-than-average means. According to Acts, Crispus was
the *archisynagōgos*, the "head of the synagogue," in Corinth (18:8). Epigraph-
ical evidence frequently attests that those who held this position were public
benefactors (Theissen 2001, 81), suggesting that they were people of at least
moderate wealth. As for Gaius, Paul identifies him not only as his host when
he stayed in Corinth but also as the "host of the *whole church*" (Rom 16:23).
This unusual expression, which is at variance with the more formulaic "the
church in *x*'s house" (Rom 16:5; 1 Cor 16:19; Col 4:15; Phlm 2), suggests
a larger gathering, comprising a number of local cell groups, and hence
implies possession of relatively spacious accommodations (Brookins 2014,
108). Reference to the "household of Stephanas," moreover, indicates that
Stephanas probably owned slaves, for the ancient "household" often included
extended kin as well as slaves and staff. While less than prosperous people
could own a slave or two (Meggitt 1998, 129–32), Stephanas's possession of
a slave would put him, at a minimum, above the lowest social strata. In sum,
one could surmise that Paul mentions Crispus, Gaius, and Stephanas because
they were men of some social distinction. Paul's prestige would then receive
increase by association.

   This reading, however, assumes that Paul is driven largely by apologetic
and polemical purposes. Against this reading is the dissonance it introduces
with Paul's discussion throughout this section. Here, Paul *opposes* the eleva-
tion of oneself as more important than others and *repudiates* the worth of
worldly status symbols like wealth and public honor (esp. 1:25-31).

   The list of names, then, may be intended to highlight not *whom* so
much as *how many* people he had baptized. These people *would* be, of course,
among the church's founding members, for Paul had apparently been the first
missionary on Corinthian soil. The point, however, is that, having baptized
so few, unity in *Christ* stands out all the more clearly. Had *Paul* baptized
more—say, most—of the Corinthians, perhaps then there could be some
question about where their unity lay (it is for this reason that he "thanks
God" that he did not baptize more). But as things stood, the question of
"baptism into Paul" was an absurdity calculated to underscore that on which
they already agreed, namely that they were all united through baptism into
Christ.

   Baptism, then, had nothing to do with the church's divisions. Paul identifies it not as a cause of divisions but as an illustration of unity. As such, his
disclaimer does not reflect a polemic against a real "Paul-party." Instead, it is
a rhetorical construct designed, by its absurdity, to snap his audience's attention back to reality. Paul refers to the experience of baptism as a rhetorical

move for re-centering the Corinthians, pointing them back to an experience that they all shared, namely their initial baptism into Christ.

Verse 17 provides a loose transition from the topic of baptism to that of wisdom, which Paul takes up in the next section (1:18-31). Rather than make a clean start, he sets "baptizing" and "preaching with wisdom" in point-counterpoint position ("not to *baptize*, but to preach, not with word of *wisdom*"), in this way sliding somewhat artlessly from one topic to the other.

The key contrast in v. 17 is between what Paul calls "wisdom of word" and "the cross of Christ," which he sets in direct antithesis throughout 1:18-31; 2:1-5; 2:6-16; and 3:18-20 but which remains implicitly in the background throughout 1:18–4:21 and beyond.

Human Wisdom and God's Wisdom (1:18-31)

Having stated the problem, Paul now launches an attack on its causes. First comes "wisdom" (1:18-31; 2:1-5; 2:6-16; and 3:18-20). Paul announces, in apocalyptic fashion, that there are two kinds of wisdom, the "world's" and "God's." The Corinthians have adopted the former, to their shame.

The precise nature of the Corinthians' wisdom is difficult to ascertain. The rather vague expression in 1:17, "wisdom of words" (NKJV), recurs in other variations in 2:1 ("superiority of speech or of wisdom," NASB), 2:4 ("persuasive words of wisdom," NASB), and 2:13 ("words which man's wisdom teaches," NKJV). The basic interpretive options can be divided in two: it is either a wisdom of *form* (of *how* things are said) or a wisdom of *content* (of *what* is said). These options could be paired, respectively, with a wisdom of *rhetoric* and a wisdom of *philosophy* (Brookins 2010; 2014). Despite the surface potential of the former option to explain certain aspects of the unit, it makes better sense of the evidence overall to view the opposition as one of *content*. In short, Paul opposes two philosophies of life, two worldviews, or, as the next verse suggests, one "account" (*logos*) of life and another.

1:18-25

Having contrasted "wisdom of word" and "the cross of Christ" in v. 17, Paul takes the latter as a point of departure for the verses that follow. He now calls it "the word [*logos*] that is of the cross," implicitly contrasting two kinds of "word," or two "accounts" of reality (Brookins 2020). This transitional sentence offers grounding for the previous statement that the "cross of Christ" should not be "emptied": "*for* [*gar*] it is the power of God for all who are being saved."

Here Paul begins to develop an elaborate contrast between the two wisdoms. Isaiah 44:24-28 stands in the background as Paul emphasizes the irony of reversal in God's plan. The "cross" is viewed from the one perspective as "foolishness" but from another perspective as the "power" of God. The "cross" in this context is a trope, standing not only for the crucifixion of Christ, or "Christ-crucified" (1:23; 2:2), but also for the principle of "cruciformity" (Gorman 2001), the pattern of self-abasement that Christ modeled. That Jesus Christ suffered crucifixion—the "supreme penalty" (Cicero, *Verr.* 2.5.168); "the most wretched of deaths" (Josephus, *J. W.* §203); reserved for insurrectionists, non-citizens, and the lower classes, especially slaves (Livy, *Hist.* 33.36.3; Cicero, *Verr.* 2.5.169)—exposed him as a disgrace not only before humanity but also, from the world's perspective, before God.

For "those who are being saved," however, the cross (or Christ crucified), though a symbol of weakness, is the "power" of God. This is a radically counterintuitive claim, which flips the world's values upside down. Paul finds support for his viewpoint in the Jewish scriptures, including in 1:19 the first (= LXX Isa 29:14) of seventeen scripture citations in the letter. Those who are wise by worldly standards God will bring to naught, for their wisdom is in fact foolishness, and the world's acclamation is God's condemnation.

In v. 20 Paul introduces three figures that represent the world's wisdom, echoing Isa 33:18 but changing the names of the figures themselves: the "wise man," the "scribe," and the "debater." God's rejection of these figures reflects a sweeping condemnation of unbelieving humanity (cf. both "Jews" and "Gentiles" in vv. 23-24)—the "wise man" representing the Gentile philosopher, the "scribe" the Jewish scholar, and the "debater" a general figure covering both categories (Brookins 2014, 160–61). The first figure is foremost thematically, as he shows up first among the three here and is the only one of the three to return later in the letter. Paul names the "wise man" fifteen times in chapters 1–3, and once—if not twice—inserts him into an OT citation in which he is not originally present (3:20//LXX Ps 93:11; cf. 1:20//LXX Isa 33:18). Finally, Paul gives further evidence on two occasions that some of the Corinthians claimed the label for themselves:

"If anyone among you thinks he is a *wise man* . . ." (3:18)
"Isn't there a *wise man* among you who . . . ?" (6:5)

Conceptions of the "wise man" were many, but it was the Stoic philosophers who developed this as a technical category. Others developed their own conceptions next to or against the ideal advertised by the Stoics (Kerferd 1990, esp. 330). Consistent with this, contemporary sources show that in

Paul's day the "wise man" stood as a technical designation for the *philosopher*, just as the "pursuit of wisdom" (cf. 1:22) served as a technical label for *philosophy*. Although some rhetoricians believed that the eloquent speaker should also know philosophy (Litfin 1994), in sources contemporary with the NT the "orator" was not designated by the term "wise man" but by the technical term "eloquent man" (Cicero, *Inv.* 1.1-3; Quintilian, *Inst.* 1.pr.13; Brookins 2014); similarly rhetoric was designated not by the term "wisdom" but by the technical term "eloquence" (Quintilian, *Inst.* 12.2.8; Seneca, *Ep.* 89.4; Cicero, *Off.* 2.5). Often standing in direct juxtaposition to each other, the "wise man" (philosopher) and the "eloquent man" (orator) are consistently distinguished by this terminology in contemporary sources.

For the Stoics, the philosopher–wise man was the human being par excellence, the one who, through proper use of the reasoning faculties, had attained the summit of human perfection. This was a perfection of the mind. External goods, so-called, were a matter of indifference. And so it was said that "the wise man is rich, even in his poverty"; that "the wise man is king, even in slavery"; and that "all things belong to the wise man," since his virtue is his only valuable. Everything of value he possesses. That which he lacks is neutral or indifferent, i.e., neither good nor bad.

Some of the Corinthians seem to have believed that in Christ they had reached an analogous state. Having appropriated a version of the Stoic conception of the wise man, they fixated on their achievement as something that elevated them above others and boasted as if the achievement were their own doing. This outlook, which runs counter to the ethic of the cross, divides in that it discriminates between superior and inferior.

Paul continues to develop the antithesis in vv. 22-24. The dividing line between God's people and the world no longer runs between Jews and Greeks (or Gentiles), but between Christ-believers and nonbelievers, those "being saved" and those "perishing" (cf. 1:18). Although unbelieving Jews and Greeks stand united in their rejection of "Christ crucified," Paul distinguishes Jewish rejection due to "offense" from Greek rejection due to "foolishness." Both sneer at Christ's lowliness. Unbelieving Jews sneer at him because he was not the kind of messiah they expected—a formidable military leader chosen by God to rouse the Jews in rebellion against their Gentile oppressors and, once victorious, to reestablish independence in the land (Luke 24:21; Acts 5:33-39; 21:38; Josephus, *J.W.* 2.261-3; *Ant.* 17.10.5, 6, 7; 20.97-98, 169-72). Unbelieving Greeks sneer at him because it collided with the natural human instinct to pursue not humiliation but honor (Finney 2010). Paul objects to their evaluation of things. The world should not measure Christ by its standards but its standards by Christ. "Christ crucified" is neither an "offense" nor "foolishness" but, paradoxically, God's "power" and God's "wisdom" (vv. 23, 24).

Paul's description of Christ as "power" and "wisdom" echoes contemporary Jewish ideas about divine intermediary figures. Philo spoke of God's "Powers" (*dynameis*) as hypostatized divinities, intermediate agents that represented God's creative and sovereign powers but that were also somehow distinct from him, as shadows are distinct from the solid realities that cast them (*Abr.* 119-121). More widespread was the depiction of Wisdom as a divine intermediary. Drawing inspiration from Proverbs 8, Jesus ben Sirach depicted Wisdom as a "pure emanation of the glory of the Almighty . . . a reflection of eternal light, a spotless mirror of the working of a God, and an image of his goodness" (Sir 7:24-27). Wisdom was the first of God's creations (1:4); it created all things (8:5-6), held all things together (1:7), enveloped the earth (8:1), and was present in all things (12:1), although it made its primary dwelling among Israel (24:8-12). Other writings identified the Law of Moses with divine Wisdom (T. Levi 13:1-9; 4 Ezra 13:56) or at least described the Law analogously. The book of Jubilees depicted the Law as preexistent, recorded on heavenly tablets from all eternity (Jub. 1:29). According to Philo, the written Law was a copy of the eternal law of nature (*Mos.* 2.52; *Abr.* 3), and the lives of the patriarchs was an unwritten embodiment of the same law (*Mos.* 1.162; *Abr.* 4). For Paul Jesus takes over the role played by such entities. Jesus is God's "power" and God's "wisdom."

1:26-31

"For" (NASB) introduces further grounding for the overall point of 1:18-25, i.e., that God's wisdom stands in contrast to that of the world. Paul now describes God's wisdom with sharper focus. It is a wisdom that disregards the world's evaluation of *worth*.

Paul offers as evidence the fact that God did not consider their worth at the time of their calling. Paul recollects, with understatement, that "not many" (i.e., very few) of them were then "wise," "powerful," or "of noble birth." The qualifying phrase "according to the flesh" shows that Paul uses these terms primarily in their socioeconomic sense. While it is possible that the Corinthians ("not many" of them) made boasts in these areas, indications in the letter are that their boasts were more concerned with spiritual qualifications (cf. Welborn 1987, 96). Indeed, they professed to be "spiritual" (chs. 12–14, esp. 14:37) and gave insufficient regard to God's gift as the cause of their status (1:31; 3:21; 4:7). Paul's purpose in alluding to these descriptors is to illustrate, through these outwardly visible social symbols, a larger *theological* principle, namely that God refuses to consider worth in *any* domain that would count from a worldly perspective. Again highlighting the theme of reversal, the words "wise" and "powerful" echo the earlier reference to Christ as "wisdom" and "power" (1:24). The Corinthians could not lay claim to power or wisdom prior to conversion, for these came down as gifts from God. Verses 27-28 drive the point home, emphasizing that human worth is not a condition for God's grace (cf. Barclay 2015). Far from electing the worthy, God elected the "foolish," the "weak," the "low-born," the "nobodies."

The principle of reversal was characteristic of Jewish apocalyptic thinking, and it is affirmed often in Second Temple Jewish texts in contexts of eschatological judgment. In the Wisdom of Solomon 2–6, the wicked, who imagine that they have brought the righteous to an end (3:4-5), receive punishment and become "amazed at the unexpected salvation of the righteous" (5:2; cf. 1 En. 92-105; 2 Bar. 83:8-23). However, in the Wisdom of Solomon God rewards people in accordance with their *worth as righteous people* (Barclay 2015, 194–211). Paul's theology of reversal is virtually unparalleled among Second Temple texts in emphasizing God's gift of grace to the *unworthy* (Barclay 2015, esp. 570).

The principle of "unconditioned grace" (Barclay 2015, 500), as vv. 29-31 affirm in conclusion, rules out the possibility of human boasting. Boasting runs as a major theme through the letter (1:29, 31; 3:21; 4:7; 5:6; 9:15-16; cf. 4:6, 18, 19, 5:2). Despite the honorific focus of Greco-Roman culture, condemnation of boasting was common, but for pragmatic rather than theological reasons (cf. Quintilian, *Inst.* 11.1.16-28; Plutarch, *On Self-Praise*). Paul's point is that human beings have no *theological* grounds for boasting. Salvation is not given as wages but as gift (cf. Rom 4:4-5), being bestowed not upon the worthy but upon the unworthy (cf. Rom 5:6, 8). Here the emphatic "*you*" (v. 30) refers back to the lowly people of vv. 28-29: "And *you* all (examples of the unworthy) are in Christ by God's doing." The Corinthians are what they are only in Christ, who became "wisdom and righteousness and sanctification and redemption" *for* them. In short, salvation was not conditioned by their own worth; it was the choice of God.

Paul's theology of grace stands in sharp contrast with the Stoic doctrine of "self-sufficiency" (*autarkeia*), and it is worth speculating whether the Corinthians might have been influenced by Stoic thinking on this point. It was commonplace of the philosophers that one "should not seek from another what is available from oneself" (Epicurus, *Vat.* 65; Seneca, *Ep.* 80.4-5; Epictetus, *Diatr.* 1.9.32; 1.29.4). The Stoics grounded this axiom in a metaphysic that viewed divinity as a property resident within people *by nature* (Seneca, *Ep.* 41.1-2). Thus, the power of virtue was available within (Seneca,

Polyb. 5.1; 14.4); happiness was available within (Marcus Aurelius, *Med.* 7.59); and happiness could be reached by one's own efforts (Seneca, *Ep.* 31.5; 92.2). Consequently, one could boast in what was "one's own" (Seneca, *Ep.* 41.6-7), and one had oneself to thank for one's possession of virtue (Seneca, *Ep.* 93.8), for it was generated from within. By contrast, Paul viewed righteousness as an "exogenous" effect: it came from without. And so, while Paul affirms that believers are located "in Christ" and "have" the Spirit, he does not collapse his theology into anthropology, or God into humanity, in such a way that would allow believers to boast in *themselves*. Boasting in oneself (v. 29) and boasting in God (v. 31) cannot be reconciled.

First Corinthians 1:26-31 presents a serious obstacle to the view that Paul was responding to a Corinthian preference for Apollos as a superior orator. On that reading (see Winter 2002, 186–94), Paul would be suggesting (1) that God brings low those of high status, i.e., orators, and has *elected* those of low status, i.e., those whom the orators disdain; (2) that faith comes from God and not by means of the contrivances of wise rhetoric; and (3) that because salvation comes by God's initiative there are no grounds for boasting, whether in one's social superiority, i.e., in one's sophistic status, or in one's ability to save through human cleverness (cf. Litfin 1994, 203–204; Winter 2002, 193).

Such a reading poorly fits the context. First, if social status is the main issue, it is not clear why it is relevant that the guilty individuals be identified as orators. Second, the emphasis here is not on God versus rhetoric as the means of salvation; it is on God's sovereign choice versus the worth of the individual as a condition for salvation. The discourse structure in the original Greek points in this direction, in that it fronts not election but lowliness. That is, it is not "God *elected* these people to salvation (i.e., you did not win them over with eloquence)," but "*The lowly people* God elected (i.e., not the worthy)" (*ta agenē tou kosmou ekseleksato o theos . . .*). Third, it must be asked who is "boasting" (1:29, 31) and why. Is the "sophistic" preacher boasting that he has reeled in his listeners with a clever display of rhetoric? Or are the Corinthians boasting in the sophistic preacher, whose rhetoric they have found so delightful? Confusion between the two possibilities enters at this point precisely because the reading is torn in two directions, needing to account for two levels of conflict at once: first and chiefly the putative rivalry between Paul and Apollos, and second the attitude of the Corinthians themselves.

There is a simpler explanation, and one that adheres more closely to the text. If the Corinthians are boasting in themselves, then the supposition that they were boasting in Apollos can be considered an unnecessary, and unnecessarily complicating, addition to the scenario. Paul gives no evidence that he is critiquing anything other than the Corinthians' own boasts in themselves. Supporting this interpretation is the contrast at the opening of v. 27: not many were of high status (v. 26), *but* (*alla*) they were of low status (v. 27). That is, God did not call them because they were of high status *but* because they were of low status. As such, the contrast is not (a) between boasting in the status of others and being elected as a low-status person. That makes little sense and only complicates Paul's point. The contrast, rather, is (b) between being elected as a high-status person and being elected as a low-status person. The result is that there is no room for boasting.

Proclaiming Christ Crucified (2:1-5)

The first person personal pronoun, "I" (*kagō*), marks a change in the topical frame, from the topic of God's wisdom to the topic of Paul as an embodiment of God's wisdom (i.e., "And *as for me*"). In comporting himself with lowliness when he came to the Corinthians ("in weakness and in fear and in much trembling"), he became a living example of God's wisdom.

Here is the first of several instances in the letter where Paul appeals to himself as an example to be followed (see also 3:5–4:5; 4:16; 7:7, 8; 8:13; 9:1-27; 10:33–11:1; 13:11; 14:18-19). Such appeals were often used in parenetic contexts where the speaker aimed to inculcate virtue in their audience. Doctrines (*doctrinae*) could push one only so far. To impress virtue on the soul, one also needed concrete examples to imitate. Such were known as *exempla*. These could be even more effective than "doctrines," for "people put more trust in their eyes than in their ears" (Seneca, *Ep.* 6.5). Seneca recommended that people should fix their eyes on some moral person as a pattern to imitate (*Ep.* 11.10). For Seneca and the Stoics, the original pattern was set by Nature herself, or by the gods (Seneca, *Ep.* 66.39; Epictetus, *Diatr.* 2.14.13), with whom Nature was identical (Seneca, *Ben.* 4.7), and it was replicated in the most virtuous. In Paul's case, his own example replicated the example of Christ (cf. 11:1) and was embodied in the ethic of "Christ crucified" (2:2).

Here again Paul distances himself from that other kind of wisdom (cf. 1:17). His reference to "superiority of word or of wisdom" serves as a hendiadys for "superiority of wise words" (just as "my word and my preaching" = "my proclaimed message" and "Spirit and power" = "the powerful Spirit" in 2:4) and is roughly synonymous with the earlier expression "wisdom of word" (1:17). Thus, Paul refers again to a particular *account* of life, a particular way of seeing the world.

To read this section as a repudiation of rhetoric or sophistical devices misses the point (cf. Winter 2002, 147–61; Litfin 1994, 204–209); hence, Paul's own use of "rhetoric" here need not be viewed as hypocritical. His purpose is not to repudiate persuasive rhetoric as the means of salvation but to underline the way of lowliness, contrary to the world's way of seeing, as the embodiment of the cross. He did *not* preach the world's wisdom (content) but he preached God's wisdom (content), and having preached "Christ crucified" and having come "in weakness and in fear and in much trembling," he both preached and modeled the way of humility. As it happens, the Spirit *is* the mechanism through which one comes to see this as God's way (2:4), but the point is that the ethic of the cross runs counter to the worldly values of strength and status, and in that way it is a "mystery" (2:1; cf. 2:6-7; 4:1) seen only by a transformation of the mind (see 2:6-16).

Spiritual Wisdom (2:6–3:4)

The conjunction (*de* = "Yet," "Now then") marks a transition in the argument. Having denounced human wisdom, Paul now discusses the role of the Spirit as a means of spiritual enlightenment. But again the emphasis is not so much on *how* the truth of God's wisdom is revealed as on how the truth of *that* wisdom—that wisdom of self-lowering that runs counter to basic human instincts—comes to be seen as true.

Paul operates within a traditional Jewish apocalyptic framework, now revised around the Christ event. The old way of seeing is the way of "this age," a time when Sin, Death, and Foolishness reign (1:20; 2:6, 8; 3:18; cf. Rom 12:2; 2 Cor 4:4; Gal 1:4). In "this age," God's wisdom remains a "mystery" (2:7), unfathomable by human thinking and accordingly repudiated by the "rulers of this age," who "crucified the Lord of glory" (2:8). Here Paul, like other apocalyptic texts, links the rulers with demonic power (1 En. 55:4) or with inimical forces in the spiritual realm (Eph 2:2; 3:9-10; Ign. *Eph.* 17.1; 19.1; *Magn.* 1.2; *Trall.* 4.2; *Rom.* 7.1; *Phld.* 6.2; cf. Moses 2014, 84-94), which help keep creation in subjection to Sin (1 Cor 8:5-6; 15:24; Eph 1:20; Phil 2:10-11; Col 1:15-20; 2:10). Although long concealed in mystery, now at the turn of the ages, God's wisdom is revealed *as* wisdom, although he planned this unveiling from ages past, as scripture foretold in Isaiah (2:9 freely adapting Isa 64:3 and 65:16e).

Within this apocalyptic section, Paul mixes language attributable to the Corinthians but borrowed originally from the philosophical realm. Three pairs of terms, indicating discrete levels of spiritual status, appear to have been used by the Corinthians somewhat analogously: wise-foolish (1:18-31; 2:6-16; 3:18-20), spiritual-unspiritual (2:15-16; 15:44, 46), and mature-immature (2:6; 3:3; as a directly contrasting pair in 13:10-11; 14:20). That these were originally the Corinthians' words is evident on two grounds: (1) this vocabulary is uncharacteristic of Paul outside of 1 Corinthians; and (2) differentiation between the spiritual levels of believers is foreign to Paul's thinking (Paul prefers a contrast between believing-unbelieving), while it fits well the mentality of the Corinthians.

With this language the Corinthians again seem to have borrowed from a basically Stoic framework. All three of their antitheses find parallel in Stoic sources. These contrasts start from the fact that the Stoics posed a sharp contrast between the "wise man" and everyone else: beside the "wise man," all others were "fools" (*SVF* 3.668); the wise man alone was "excellent," while all others were "inferior" (*SVF* 3.519); he alone was "perfect/mature," while all others were "immature" (*SVF* 3.519). Whether such a man had ever existed was a question worthy of consideration, and this problem seems to have been a source of some consternation for the philosophers (cf. *SVF* 3.657-70; Cicero, *Luc.* 145; *Tusc. disp.* 2.22.51; *Acad.* 2.145; Epictetus, *Diatr.* 2.19.20-28; Lucian, *Herm.* 76-77). Seneca mused that the wise man was perhaps as rare as the "phoenix," lighting upon the earth only once every five hundred years (*Ep.* 42.1). The Stoics nonetheless maintained that "wise" state was possible to attain (Seneca, *Const.* 6.3-8; 7.1; *Ep.* 64.5; 79.13), and indeed achieving this end was the whole object of the philosophical enterprise (cf. Cicero, *Tusc. disp.* 5.1.2; Musonius Rufus, *Diatr.* 8).

Most of the Corinthians' terminology was common to the broader philosophical tradition. All the philosophical schools had some conception of the "wise man" (Kerferd 1990), and each described him in somewhat similar terms. The idea of the wise man had also worked its way into Hellenistic Judaism (Horsley 1998, 57–63); Philo of Alexandria portrayed Moses in the mold of the philosophical wise man, whose life was in agreement with the Law of Nature (*Alleg.* 3.140). The metaphor of milk as food for the "immature" and solid food as nourishment for the advanced (3:2) was commonplace among the philosophers as well as Hellenistic Jews (Epictetus, *Diatr.* 2.16.39; Seneca, *Ep.* 4.2; Philo *Gr.* 1.46; *Agr.* 1.9; 9.6; *Somn.* 2.10; *Post.* 1.152; *Sobr.* 1.9; Heb 5:11-14).

Yet a Stoic framework offers parallels across the board. With good justification, Stoicism can be considered the most natural context with which to associate the "wise man" language, and Stoicism posed exactly the two-tier contrasts we find used among the Corinthians. Not only did the Stoics maintain that all others apart from the "wise man" were "fools" (*SVF* 3.668); the direct contrast between the "perfect" (*teleios*) and the "immature" (*nēpios*) person is also attested only in the Stoic fragments (*SVF* 3.519). To be sure, the direct contrast between the "spiritual" (*pneumatikos*) and "unspiritual" (*psychikos*) person had no known antecedent. Certainly there are analogous, albeit non-identical, pairs in Hellenistic Jewish texts (Horsley 1976, 280), among other places; however, Stoic physics not only articulated a similar hierarchy but also used precisely the pertinent vocabulary.

According to the Stoics, the Spirit, or breath (*pneuma*), infused all things but at varying levels of "tension" (LS 47M-Q): it bestowed upon inanimate objects the capacity of "coherence" (the *hektikon* kind of breath), upon plants the capacity of "growth" (the *physikon* kind of breath), upon irrational animals the capacity of "perception" (the *psychikon* kind of breath), and upon human beings the capacity of "reason" (the *logikon* kind of breath). Stoic physics became the theoretical basis for the medical philosophy of Athenaeus of Attaleia (mid-first century BC or mid-first century AD), who following the teachings of the canonical Stoic Chrysippus (Galen, *De diff. puls.* 3.641.15–3.642.7) founded a school of physicians known as the "Pneumatists" (*pneumatikoi*). Here, then, we find both an analogous hierarchy of creatures and the very terms that the Corinthians employed. The Corinthians used the pair *pneumatikos-psychikos* to distinguish between, on the one hand, fully rational people, who having reached spiritual perfection styled themselves *pneumatikoi*, and on the other hand, those who fell short of perfection, whom they labeled *psychikoi*, as if to relegate them to the category of "unreasoning animals" (cf. Jude 2:12). While this characterization appears extreme, it manifests a noticeable parity with the Stoic characterization of all but the wise man as "fools" (*SVF* 3.668).

Paul appropriates the Corinthians' language for ad hoc purposes but maps it back onto his two-age apocalyptic framework (see above), with results that must have been unexpected and alarming for the Corinthian wise men. He turns the tables on them by labeling the wise fools and the fools wise, the spiritual unspiritual, and the mature immature. The wise men stand condemned, not because they trust in their eloquence but because they boast in their superior spiritual status and by setting themselves above others *divide* the community into higher and lower tiers. To divide in such a fashion is indeed neither wise nor mature; rather, it exposes the actors as immature, even "fleshly" (3:1-4).

Paul's handling of the issue, as well as his language, should not be understood apart from the context, for his discussion is adapted to the situation and to the language of the Corinthians themselves. Accordingly, his appropriation of the two-tier hierarchy is not a wholesale endorsement of their basic system but a tour de force designed to shake the Corinthian believers back to reality in Christ. All believers are "spiritual," for all have the Spirit; this indeed is the basis of unity (12:4-11). All believers are also "perfect" (Grindheim 2002); they *are no longer* slaves to sin but are slaves to Christ and righteousness (cf. Rom 6:12-23). Paul does not, therefore, cast the Corinthians as "unspiritual," "immature," and "carnal," because (allegedly) immaturity constitutes a stage of belief through which all must progress. Rather, this characterization serves as an *incongruous* counterpoint to the Corinthian believers' *actual* status in Christ, with which they *ought* to act but are not acting in agreement. Paul intends for the sting of his words to wake them from their sleep, to move them from momentary blindness back to sight.

Because it is natural, even "human" (cf. 2:5, 13; 3:4), to measure oneself up against others in this way, Paul suggests that one overcomes conventional wisdom only by an epistemological transformation wrought by the Spirit (2:10-16; cf. 1:21). Paul's condemnation of human wisdom, then, does not amount to a rejection of education, study, or human investigation. Rather, his point is one of perspective: the counterintuitive wisdom of self-sacrifice can be correctly evaluated *as* wisdom only by the intervention of the Spirit (cf. Rom 16:25-26; 2 Cor 3:1-18; 4:3-6; Col 1:26-27). Alluding to Prov 20:27, where the spirit is predicated as the "lamp of the Lord" searching out the deepest parts of the person, Paul suggests that believers possess the Spirit of God, through which they can fathom even the deep things of God, that is, through which they are able to grasp the kind of wisdom that is God's (vv. 10-12).

The place that Paul gives to the Spirit stands in remarkable contrast to the place given by many Jews to the Torah. For many, wisdom was either identified with the Torah (4 Ezra 13:56) or acquired through its study (Sir 38:24-34). It was the absolute standard of righteousness. Josephus presented the Law as a sort of "constitution" (Barclay 2001), a fixed code that defined piety in all matters of life and could neither be changed nor updated (*C. Ap.* 2). Something of the same sort is affirmed by Philo, who said that the Law remained "firm, unshaken, immoveable, stamped, as it were with the seals of nature herself" (*Mos.* 2.14). In a radically revisionist move, Paul replaces the Law as the normative measure of conduct with the Spirit of God. Accordingly, he affirms that he and his associates speak "not with the taught words of human wisdom but with the teachings of the Spirit" (2:13). Only the Spirit can give eyes to see Christ-*crucified* as wisdom (cf. Wis 1:6-8).

It is within this context that Paul's remark about the "mind of Christ" (2:16) is to be understood. Inspired by Isa 40:13, the expression "mind of Christ" bears the same underlying meaning as the opening words of Phil 2:5-10: "Have that *mind* in you that was also in *Christ Jesus.*" In this respect, the "mind of Christ" refers both to the *epistemological orientation* possessed by believers through the Spirit and the *cruciform ethic* of self-abasement for the benefit of others that Christ modeled: with the Spirit one sees the *value* of this kind of life. In sum, the point is not just *how* the truth comes to be accepted but how the truth of God's *counterintuitive* wisdom comes to be accepted.

The reintroduction of Apollos in 3:4 (cf. 1:12) provides a bridge to a new unit in the discourse (3:5–4:5). Paul alludes to the party slogans expressed earlier but now makes no mention of anyone claiming allegiance to "Cephas" or "Christ." This need not suggest that the church was divided only between Paul and Apollos and that Paul's discussion of Apollos indeed functions as a "defense." Rather, as Paul reveals in 4:6, the discussion is intended to offer the *partnership* shared between the two of them as an example for the Corinthians to imitate.

Fellow Workers under God (3:5–4:5)

3:5-9

The initial "then" (3:5) signals a conclusion based on the foregoing discussion, although the logic is somewhat elliptical: "If it is carnal to think more highly of either Paul or Apollos, *then* Paul and Apollos must not be things to be thought highly *of.* We are not superiors but servants! And more than servants, we are co-servants, standing not one above the other but working together. And what we do we do by the grace of God. It is he who causes the growth."

In summary: *believers are (or ought to be) fellow servants united under God.* Packed into this point are three subpoints: (1) believers are to be *servants,* (2) believers stand united *under* God, and (3) credit is owed not to the servants themselves but *to* God. Each of these points serves to erase lines of division. In mutual service to each other, in common subordination to God, and in recognition of God's agency in faith and work, lines of division between superior and inferior dissolve.

As in 2:1-5, Paul is not defending himself but appealing to himself as an example. More precisely, he is presenting himself and Apollos *together* as an example, an embodiment of the kind of harmony he would have the Corinthians emulate. Paul "planted," Apollos "watered," and God "gave the growth" (v. 6). The contrast is not between the higher and lower importance of Paul and Apollos respectively but is about the lower importance of both next to the person of God: "Neither Paul . . . nor Apollos . . . *but God* . . . ." Both Paul and Apollos are "nothing" (v. 7; cf. 10:19; Gal 5:6; 6:3, 15). God is the ultimate agent, the one who "causes the growth" (vv. 6, 7), just as the Lord is the one who "gave" to each of them (v. 5).

The example of Paul and Apollos further undermines the Corinthians' quest for honor. Look at Paul and Apollos: they are nothing but "servants" (*diakonoi*). This designation connotes neither the office of "deacon" (Phil 1:1; 1 Tim 3:8-13; 1 Clem. 44:1-3) nor a position of honor or authority (Pol. *Phil.* 5:3) but instead an informal position of servile ministry. Such characterization may appear to be a conceit, coming from one who had such a high sense of his importance: who indeed advertised himself as an "apostle," called by the "will of God" (Col 1:1); who called himself an "ambassador" (2 Cor 5:20), whose message was backed by the authority of Jesus Christ and God the Father (Gal 1:1); who admonished (1 Cor 4:14) and judged (1 Cor 5:3-5) in the name of the Lord Jesus; whose words were the very words of the Lord (1 Cor 14:37; 1 Thess 4:15), or of God and the Holy Spirit (1 Thess 4:8). Despite the importance he attributed to his call as a herald of the good news, Paul also emphasized his role as an equal and even a servant of his fellow believers. They were to be for each other sources of mutual encouragement (Rom 1:12). Although he was their spiritual father (1 Cor 4:14; 2 Cor 12:14; Phil 2:22; Thess 2:1-12), he was also their brother (1 Cor 1:12, 14; passim). He was a "slave" of Jesus Christ (Rom 1:1; Gal 1:10; Phil 1:1). Those who ministered along with him were his "fellow-workers" (Phil 4:3), "fellow-soldiers" (Phil 2:25), or "fellow-servants" (Col 1:7). As for the office of apostle, Paul defined this by the standard of lowliness (4:8-13; 2 Cor 11:22-33), in keeping with Christ's cruciform example.

Although Paul and Apollos work *together*, Paul affirms that they will be judged *apart* (v. 8). Laying emphasis on their individuality, Paul notes that "each" will be judged for his work. Although in the context he speaks about himself and Apollos, he implies that the prospect of judgment as individuals is applicable to believers generally (see 4:5; 2 Cor 5:10; cf. 3:13, 17). Moreover, since he here offers himself and Apollos as an illustration (4:6), the point serves primarily as a warning to the Corinthians about their own impending judgment, which their choice between the two brands of wisdom will decide (see 3:10-17, 18-20).

Finally (v. 9), Paul pushes himself and Apollos into the background as he foregrounds the Corinthians. At the same time, he changes the scene from that of agriculture to that of architecture. The Corinthians are "God's *field*, God's *building*." Both metaphors issue an oblique warning about conduct: just as the church as God's field must bear fruit, the church must also be wary about the quality of its infrastructure.

3:10-17

The abrupt shift of metaphor from "field" to "building" opens new thematic possibilities, which Paul systematically exploits in this section. The metaphor of the building is carried through in the entailment of both a foundation (vv. 10-11) and building materials (v. 12), and the materials are subject to the possibility of combustion in the eschatological fire (vv. 13-15). Contrary to the metaphor of the field, where the whole landscape could combust, the building metaphor allows Paul to play upon the natural differences in building materials, some being combustible (wood, hay, straw) and others, like the foundation itself, being more durable (gold, silver, precious stones). As Paul sharpens the image further, the church is no longer a generic building but indeed becomes God's *temple*, a holy dwelling place for his Spirit (vv. 16-17; 2 Cor 6:16).

The question in v. 16, "Do you not *know* that you are a temple of God?" mocks the Corinthians' pretenses of "knowledge." The expression "do you not know . . ." occurs ten times in 1 Corinthians, and only once elsewhere in Paul's letters (1 Cor 3:16; 5:6; 6:2, 3, 9, 15, 16, 19; 9:13, 24; Rom 6:16). The reference to "knowing" also echoes the Corinthian slogan cited in 8:1, where the Corinthians claim that they "have knowledge" (cf. 1:5).

The term translated "temple" (*naos*) refers not to a complete temple structure but to the inner sanctuary, the very place of the divine presence. While the term could refer to the temple in Jerusalem (BDAG, 665b; 3 Kgdms 6:5, 17; Josephus, *Ant.* 8.62ff), the same term could denote any structural space set apart for a deity's dwelling, including non-Jewish temples (Diodorus Sicilus, *Bibl. hist.* 5.15.2; Acts 17:24; Justin, *1 Apol.* 9.1). Such temples surrounded the inhabitants of Corinth (Pausanias, *Geogr.* 2.2-3.1) and would have been more familiar to them than the temple in Jerusalem, even to the church's Jewish members.

Metaphorical use of the term "temple" had currency in both Jewish and non-Jewish texts. Reference to the human body as a "temple" was commonplace in philosophical texts (Philo, *Opif.* 136-37). Stoicism affirmed the indwelling of God within a person as connatural; hence Seneca said that God "is within you" and that "a holy spirit dwells within us" (*Ep.* 41.1). Texts found at Qumran describe the Qumran community as a "plantation" and a "house" of God's dwelling (1QS VIII.5; XI.7-8; 1QH XIV.15; XVI.6; cf. 1QS XI.8). Like the Qumran texts, Paul uses the temple metaphor to focus on God's presence within the *collective community*: "*you all* [second person plural] are *a* temple [singular]" (but individuals as temples in Ignatius, *Eph.* 15:3). Herewith Paul builds on and modifies traditional Jewish eschatological expectations. Prophetic and apocalyptic texts forecasted among eschatological occurrences both the glorious restoration of the temple (Ezek 40–48; 1 En. 90.28; 2 Bar. 32.4) and the return of God's presence among the people of Israel (T. Levi 5:2; T. Jud. 22:2; T. Zeb. 9:8; T. Naph. 8:3). Paul brings these two elements together by affirming that *God dwells within the temple of the church body.*

Paul presents this community-temple as a work of God's ministers. Although Paul can boast that he "laid the foundation" (v. 10), this is not an assertion of preeminence over other Christian ministers, for just as he confessed that "*God* gives the growth" (vv. 6, 7), again he lends credit to God: "according to the *grace of God* given to me" (v. 10). This grace is not limited to the grace that God showed in *calling* Paul (cf. Rom 1:5; 12:3; 15:15-16; Gal 1:15-16; 2:9; Phil 1:7) but includes God's sustaining grace. Moreover, the foundation Paul has laid is nothing other than "Christ crucified" (1:23; 2:2), embodied in a message of self-lowering.

Paul relates the remaining discussion about the building to eschatological judgment. The notion of individual post-mortem judgment figures prominently both in Greco-Roman mythical texts and in Second Temple Jewish texts, although the theme is virtually nonexistent in the OT (but see Dan 12:2-3). Paul maintains that "each" person will receive judgment from God for his work (v. 13; cf. 3:17; 2 Cor 5:10). The metaphor of the building is well suited to the eschatological context, for Paul now presents the church as the work, or *product*, of the ministers' labor (cf. Seneca, *Ep.* 34.2) and specifically as a construction made either of combustible (wood, hay, straw) or non-combustible material (gold, silver, precious stones). A traditional eschatological symbol, "fire" functions here not as a symbol of glory (Dan 7:9-10; 2 Thess 1:7, 8), a means of punishment (Amos 7:4; Sir 36:11), a means of exposure (cf. 4 Ezra 7:42), or a means of refinement (Mal 3:2; Sir 2:5; Rev 3:18) but as a means of testing the quality of construction (Zech 13:9; 1 Pet 1:7; Wis 3:6; T. Abr. 12:14). The construction consisting of cheap materials will be consumed, laying bare the vanity of the minister's work (v. 15; cf. v. 17), while the construction consisting of solid materials will stand (cf. T. Abr. 13:12-13), and the minister will receive his reward (v. 14; cf. 3:8). While Jewish eschatological texts traditionally polarized the righteous, whose reward was immortality (2 Macc 7:9; 4 Macc 16:13; 4 Ezra 51:1-9), and the wicked, whose fate was either eternal torment (4 Macc 9:9; 12:12; 1 En. 22:11) or annihilation (Wis 4:16–5:23; LAB 51:5; cf. 2 Bar. 51:6), Paul polarizes the good builder, who receives his "reward" (v. 14), and the bad builder, whose work is lost but who is "saved" nevertheless (v. 15).

The "someone" who builds (v. 12, 14, 15) is at one level of reference the individual minister. Certainly Paul's warning about failure echoes his sentiments stated elsewhere about the efforts of ministers, particularly of himself (9:23, 27; Phil 3:11). Yet Paul continues to use the Paul-Apollos partnership as an object lesson for teaching truths of more general reference. That is, Apollos is not the target of Paul's warnings but is rather, with Paul, a stand-in for the Corinthians. This point will be revealed in 4:6, but it is evinced here by Paul's warning in v. 17: "If anyone *corrupts* the temple of God." This comment stands as a warning to those who "corrupt" the church body (Paul plays here on the semantics of *phtheirō*, "if anyone *corrupts* . . . God will *destroy* . . ."). Paul has made no allegation of corruption against Apollos. Rather, the comment points ahead to the church's transgressions as regards sexual immorality, in connection with which Paul characterizes sexual sin as a contagion that infects the whole body (5:6-8; 6:15-20).

3:18-20

The lack of conjunction (asyndeton) at the opening of v. 18 indicates a syntactical break, but a connection to the immediate context remains. Those who live out worldly wisdom (3:18-20)—*these* are the ones who will receive this judgment (3:10-17). The juxtaposition of these two sections mirrors in condensed form the discursive link shared between 1:10–3:4 and 3:5-17 (the world's wisdom, then judgment on the wise). The point of connection is not the role of Apollos in propagating human wisdom but the presence of human wisdom among those in the Corinthian church and the threat of God's judgment upon such people (so that one need not resort to a fanciful play on *Apollos/apollumi*, as Smit 2002).

Here is the first of four occurrences in the letter of the formula "If anyone thinks that . . ." (3:18; 8:2; 11:16; 14:37). Once again, Paul attributes the problem of wisdom directly to the Corinthians. His phrasing strongly undermines the suggestion even that the Corinthians *looked* to Apollos as their inspiration, for he says not "If anyone thinks that *someone is a wise man*" but "If anyone *among you* thinks that *he himself is a wise man*" (cf. 6:5, "Is there not a *wise man among you* . . . ?"). Apollos, it should be noted, is no longer among them (16:12).

The two OT citations that follow (vv. 19, 20) provide further evidence that "wise man" was a Corinthian self-designation and not simply a Pauline attribution. To LXX Job 5:13, Paul adds the definite article, "*the* wise man," creating for the present situation in Corinth more specific reference to the technical philosophical category of "*the* wise man." In the middle of Ps 93:11, Paul then freely inserts "the wise," in substitution for the more general "people." (For argument that both of these examples are Pauline adaptations, see Stanley 1992, 189–95).

This unit reaffirms Paul's earlier affirmation that the Corinthians' wisdom is foolishness (1:18-31). Now Paul speaks in what seems to be the voice of Socrates. Just as Socrates averred that the beginning of wisdom is the recognition of one's own ignorance (Plato, *Resp.* 354C; *Charm.* 175A-B; *Lys.* 222D-E; *Prot.* 361A-B; Epictetus, *Ench.* 46.2), Paul suggests that the one who fancies himself a wise man remains a fool. In thinking themselves wise while being fools, they foreclose the possibility of breaking free from their foolishness. As before, Paul does not, in denigrating the wisdom of the "world" (1:20, 21; cf. 2:12), eschew philosophical inquiry or humanistic investigation per se, but a wisdom that sets personal interests above the interests of others and that, in exactly that respect, regards the symbol of the cross as foolishness.

3:21-23

Far from being an intrusion into a self-defense against another competition, the reintroduction of wisdom in 3:18-20 recalls the catalyst of the Corinthians' divisions, namely, a worldly wisdom that promotes self-service rather than an ethic of service to others.

Now follows a conclusion: even the self-proclaimed wise are fools; "*therefore* (*ōste*) one should boast only in God" (v. 21). This statement marks off an *inclusio* that opened in 1:31, where Paul had cited the words of Jeremiah: "Let the one who boasts boast in the Lord" (see Jer 9:24). While this statement could be construed as a prohibition against boasting in human leaders, this interpretation probably misidentifies the issue. Rather, Paul is responding to an anthropological perspective that assigned too much credit to humanity and not enough to the agency of God. In this respect the meaning is "Let no *man* boast in *men*" (KJV). By rendering the boasting *subject* also as "man," the KJV rendering evidently intends to highlight "human beings" (*anthrōpoi*) as a qualitative and all-inclusive category, inclusive of the self or boasting subject. The contrast that results is one between boasting in humanity and boasting in God. This framework dovetails well with Paul's constant emphasis on salvation as God's gift, given irrespective of and prior to human worth (1:28-31) and that operates as the efficacious instrument by which one reaches their new status (1:5; 4:7; cf. 3:10; 6:11).

Paul's emphasis on salvation as gift now builds to a climax. God is to be the sole object of boasting because all things come from him. Still mindful of his audience's proclivities, Paul again borrows from the Stoics. The saying "all things are *yours*" echoes a Stoic precept about the wise man: "All things are the *wise man's*" (*SVF* 3.589). Artfully, this precept also echoes the manufactured slogans of 1:12, except that it now *reverses* the roles of the relationship.

It is not "I am *Paul's*," "I am *Apollos's*," "I am *Cephas's* . . . ," but "all things are *yours*, whether Paul or Apollos or Cephas . . . ." The sequence proceeds to a climax by subsuming both the Corinthians and the apostles under Christ ("We are *yours*, but *you* [emphatic plural pronoun] are *Christ's*") and then Christ under God ("and *Christ* is *God's*"). The sequence encapsulates several principles that inform the discussion of the first four chapters. Paul has introduced himself and Apollos as paradigms to emulate: they are *servants*, and being *under* God they stand *united* under God and owe what is theirs *to* God. In this way, Paul grounds unity in a paradigm of mutual service. This mutuality in turn is a manifestation of an ontological unity shared in Christ and enabled by God's grace.

In sum, from 3:5-9 to 3:10-17, 3:18-20, and 3:21-23 a coherent course of thought can be identified:

A *3:5-9*. Paul and Apollos together stand as an example of harmonious service to God.

B *3:10-17*. The contribution of any and every person to God's work will be determined at final judgment.

B' *3:18-20*. Those living out wisdom other than the wisdom of Christ crucified will receive unfavorable judgment.

A' *3:21-23*. Strife dissolves when believers live out God's wisdom, relating toward each other as fellow servants under God.

4:1-5

The initial adverb (*houtōs*) connects what follows with 3:22. "Things being as they are (= we being *yours*), consider us as attendants (*hypēretas*) and stewards (*oikonomous*)" (cf. Acts 26:16 for Paul as *hypēretēs*). While these could be viewed as positions of relative authority, several pieces of evidence suggest rather that Paul viewed these as positions of servility. First, Paul has had as his focus the virtue of self-abasement (Christ-crucified) throughout the first three chapters of the letter, and he has already presented himself and Apollos as examples of this and indeed as "ministers" (3:5-7, esp. 3:5). Second, Paul does not here present himself and Apollos as authoritative ambassadors of the sovereign "Lord" (*Kyrios*) but as underlings of the redeemer, "Christ" (*Christos*). Third, both terms denote lower-level officials who in many cases held the rank of slave. While *hypēretēs* had a wide range of reference, as an "assistant" position it indicated in all cases a person of subordinate status. *Oikonomos* likewise had a range of meanings, but here it denotes the "private" steward, a servile subordinate of either freed-person or slave status who bore the responsibility of managing the financial affairs of his master and who oversaw the staff of his master's estate (Goodrich 2012).

Paul relates their performance as stewards to the issues of "evaluation" (*anakrinein*) and final "judgment" (*krinein*), topics earlier discussed separately (2:14-15; 3:10-17). In contrast to the philosophers, who advocated constant self-judgment (Seneca, *Ep.* 28.10), Paul here rejects self-judgment. Moreover, he looks scornfully upon any human attempt to size him up (*anakrinein*), advising postponement of any assessment until the final judgment (*krinein*). This comment need not represent a real defense but serves only to make a point about the inappropriateness of evaluating others. Judgment will occur when Christ returns and God brings to light all the secrets of the heart (v. 5). Those who have lived (presumably) by God's wisdom will at that time receive praise from God, thus completing a pattern of movement from lowliness to exaltation, in imitation of Christ (cf. Phil 2:5-11).

Again the supposition that Paul's purposes are primarily apologetic is open to question. Had the Corinthians weighed the two men and given Apollos a more favorable evaluation (Litfin 1994, 229–33)? Possible as this may be, on second look this interpretation transgresses the letter of the text. Even now, Paul is not comparing himself against Apollos but is pairing himself and Apollos as two of a kind. Hence, the discussion continues to serve not an *apologetic* purpose in advocacy of Paul but an *illustrative* purpose for the benefit of the Corinthians. Just as Paul refrains from evaluating himself (v. 3) on grounds that God alone is in a position to issue a final judgment, so the Corinthians should leave off evaluating themselves so highly (cf. 4:7-8) and evaluating others in the church as inferior (see discussion on 2:6–3:4).

4:6-13

If any question remained about Paul's reasons for discussing Apollos, the reason is now revealed: "so that . . . ." Specifically, his purpose was not to defend himself but, through the two of them ("in us"), to teach the Corinthians a lesson ("so that they might learn . . .") about their own conduct ("that one not be puffed up . . .").

Paul's opening reference to "these things" (v. 6) refers to the discussion contained in 3:5–4:5, where he and Apollos figured as the primary topic. How one understands the purpose of this discussion depends largely on the meaning of the word rendered in many translations as "applied" (ESV, NAB, NIV, NRSV), *metaschēmatisa*. Although the meaning of this word is difficult to determine, a thorough lexicographical survey reveals that the word almost invariably referred to an "alteration of appearance," where something that appeared in one form appears now in some new or different form (Mihaila

2009, 200–12). Thus, Paul means that, while his discussion has referred outwardly to himself and Apollos, in application it is meant with reference to the Corinthians. Put differently, he has "changed" (or switched) the individuals described in relationship with each other from the Corinthians to himself and Apollos. The latter then serve as a model for the Corinthians to emulate.

This interpretation does not rule out the possibility that a conflict was "real" on both levels—that the Corinthians viewed Paul and Apollos in competitive terms *and* that the Corinthians fought among themselves based on these allegiances. The context, however, does not (*pace* Mihaila 2009, 211) require this dual-level interpretation. Everything that Paul has said about himself and Apollos since 3:5 can be satisfactorily accounted for on the premise that his biographical references are *illustrative*, in keeping with the deliberative style of rhetoric (M. M. Mitchell 1993). That he declines to speak directly, speaking instead allusively, even covertly, about the perpetrators is a testament to his rhetorical awareness. Such sensitive situations were no time for "frank speech" (Sampley 2004). By concealing the identity of the culprits, he avoided publicly shaming them and thus minimized the risk of alienating them, helping to facilitate his goal of restoring the church to unity (John Chrysostom, *Hom. 1 Cor.* 3:1; Fiore 1985).

Paul says that the purpose of his device was to prevent the Corinthians from going beyond "what is written." It is unclear whether this refers to what is written (1) in the OT or (2) in his citations of the OT, to (3) what he has written previously in this letter, or to (4) something else altogether (see Oropeza 2017, 55–58), but Paul relates the maxim immediately to the issue of self-assessment. Here we find for the first time in the letter Paul's allegation that the Corinthians are "puffed up," a criticism that he will return to repeatedly (4:7, 18, 19; 5:2; cf. 8:1; 13:4). That the issue is not the Corinthians' boasting in their leaders but their boasting in themselves and others in their community is clarified later, where Paul notes that the Corinthians are puffed up with pride in their "knowledge" (cf. 8:1; 13:4; cf. 4:7-8). While Paul notes here that they are "puffed up one *on behalf of another*," this likely alludes to the issue treated in the chapter that follows (see below on 5:1-13). Moreover, Paul immediately shifts the focus to their own conceitedness: "What do you have that you did not *receive*? And if you did *receive* it, why do you boast as if you did not *receive* it?" Paul uses the language of benefaction, depicting God as a gift-giver to whom recognition and thanks are owed (cf. Epictetus, *Diatr.* 1.7.41), though he refers not to material or social gifts but to spiritual gifts. The Corinthians somehow accredit their spiritual status to themselves. They fancy themselves "wise" (3:18), "perfect" (2:6), and "spiritual" (2:15), possessed of laudable "spiritual powers" (12:1ff), heedless that all these things come from God (1:5, 7, 29-31; 3:21-23); they have accepted the gift but refuse to credit the giver.

In crediting themselves, and by boasting in their qualities, the Corinthians may again have been inspired largely by Stoic ideas. Divinity, for the Stoics, dwelled in human beings by nature. This, then, being a peculiar property of the human being, divinity was something in which the human had every right to boast. As Seneca said,

> No one ought to glory except in that which is one's own. . . . The virtue that is a peculiar property of the vine is its fertility; in a human being, as well, this thing should be praised that is its own. . . . Praise the quality in a person that cannot be given or snatched away, that which is the peculiar property of a human being. And what is this? The soul and reason made perfect in the soul. (*Ep.* 41.7-8)

Although the Corinthians probably viewed their heavenly endowment as something received not at birth but at the moment of conversion, they seem to have shared the Stoics' perspective that their higher faculties were now *proper* to their new human nature and gave them grounds for boasting.

This interpretation receives immediate support in v. 8, where Paul paints the Corinthians in the colors of the Stoic wise man. The exclamation "Already you are rich! Already you are kings!" finds exact parallel in the Stoic maxim, "Only the wise man is . . . *rich* and *king*" (*SVF* 3.655). By calling the Corinthians' perspective into question, Paul sets two worldviews against each other: on the one hand that of philosophy, which viewed perfection as a quality possible to acquire now, in this life, and which held little or no expectation of a life beyond the grave, and, on the other hand, a two-age, Christ-centered apocalyptic schema, which viewed life here and now as subject still to the downward drag of the present evil age. The Corinthians, then, did not have an "over-realized" eschatological perspective but rather a *lack* of eschatological perspective (Doughty 1975; Kuck 1992, 16–25, 216–19): they viewed the consummation of the blessings available to human beings as a reality possible to achieve here and now.

The sequence of thought in vv. 6, 7, and 8 is not easily understood under the supposition that Paul is dealing with leadership rivalries. Specifically, a jump from pride in particular church leaders (v. 6) to the Corinthians' failure to recognize their own (spiritual) possessions as a gift from God (v. 7) and their pretensions of high spiritual achievement (vv. 8-10) is difficult to make sense of. That is, if the issue in the first part of the chapter is pride in particular church leaders, it is unclear what the Corinthians' self-evaluation might have to do with it (*pace* Still 2004, 30). The verses read more smoothly if one supposes that the Corinthians boast in themselves and in those within their circle who share their anthropological perspective (see 5:1-13).

Paul's mocking presentation of the self-satisfied Corinthians sets off a lengthy antithesis between the Corinthians and the apostles, in which Paul again sets in contrast the world's lust for honor and the gospel ethic of lowliness (vv. 10-12). As Paul describes them, the Corinthians exhibit a high estimation of their status and in this way take a stance antithetical to the paradigm symbolized by the cross. Again appealing to the apostles as examples, Paul characterizes the apostles as embodiments of cruciformity, wherein they appear foolish, weak, and dishonored; they go hungry, naked, and homeless; they labor with their hands; they bless when they are reviled and in persecution forebear (perhaps alluding to Matt 5:44//Luke 6:27-28). Paul's reference to laboring "with the hands" alludes to his choice to support himself with manual labor rather than charitable donations (cf. 1 Thess 2:9; 2 Cor 11:7, 9; 12:13). In choosing this route he voluntarily lowered himself on the social scale, for manual labor was denigrated among elites as inferior to the more honorable work of intellectual pursuit.

As a whole, Paul's list of hardships follows the form of the conventional "*peristasis* catalog" (Fitzgerald 1988). Such catalogues appear often in ancient literature in connection with the philosophical sage, who suffered hardships and reviling insults but who endured through them, demonstrating his resignation in circumstances outside his control. While Paul seems to utilize this form here (also in 2 Cor 4:8-9; 11:23-29; 12:10), his own experience under hardship is used to prove quite a different point, i.e., that godliness consists in lowly service of others (see Tabb 2017). From the world's perspective the apostles are the "scum" of the earth (v. 13), but from a gospel perspective they are imitators of Christ.

This section epitomizes the meaning, or rather the meanings, of the concept of "cross" in Paul's apocalyptic imagination. The cross serves as a multilayered symbol, connoting on one level a *life of lowly service* of others, on another level *persecution and even physical death* in a world that regards the cruciform way as foolishness, and on still another level *an epoch* in which spiritual blessings have not reached their consummation. Paul's presentation of the problem indicates that the Corinthian troublemakers are living other than a life of lowly service, and by eschewing self-sacrifice they evade the trying external circumstances that such a life invites and embody an inadequately "eschatological" perspective of God's blessings.

Fatherly Admonition and Warning (4:14-21)

Asyndeton marks a break in thought as Paul moves to conclude the first part of his letter. The repetition of "I urge you" in v. 16 (*parakalō hymas*) echoes the letter's introduction proper in 1:10 (*parakalō . . . hymas*) and thus signals that the conclusion applies to all that has intervened. Hence, the reference to "these things" points to 1:10–4:13.

Despite Paul's shift to the topic of travel plans, one need not assume that this section marks the conclusion to what was originally a separate letter. This section instead serves as an intermediate checkpoint in Paul's larger rhetorical strategy of moving the Corinthians to unity, where references now to visits from Timothy and himself serve as warnings of future accountability as he moves ahead to further stages in his argument (M. M. Mitchell 1993, 222–25).

Paul's words draw abundantly from the cultural domains of the household and education (White 2017), as Paul presents himself as a "father" (2 Cor 12:14; Phil 2:22; Thess 2:1-12) in contrast to a "pedagogue" (v. 15). While elsewhere Paul regards fellow believers as his "brothers" (1:12, 14; passim) or "sisters" (cf. 7:15; 9:5; Rom 16:1, 15; Phlm 2), this horizontal dimension is conspicuously absent here. It is noteworthy that while Paul otherwise invariably conjoins the meta-comment "I urge you" with "brothers" (1:10; 16:15; Rom 12:1; 15:30; 16:17), he omits the vocative here. Its omission seems deliberate and likely reveals an intention to hide filial equality and to highlight his patriarchal authority. Paul's words would have evoked the idea of the *paterfamilias*, or paternal head of the household, who in Roman culture wielded authority over all household entities, including servants, children, and spouse. This figure stood high above the figure of the "pedagogue." The pedagogue was an elementary teacher responsible for overseeing the education of children in the household but who had limited teaching responsibilities and was usually of slave status (Plato, *Lysis* 208C; Euripides, *Ion* 725; *Elec.* 287; Lysias, *Diog.* 32.28). Paul offsets his hyperbolic assertion that the Corinthians had "ten thousand pedagogues" in Christ with the intentional understatement that they had "not many" fathers (but rather one).

Despite his tone of authority, Paul's reference to himself as a father also has another purpose: as his children in Christ, the Corinthians should also be his *imitators* (v. 16). In what way? In his embodiment of God's wisdom, the way of Christ crucified (2:1-5). It is "for this reason" that he sent Timothy to them (v. 17; cf. 16:10). Timothy had been a missionary companion of Paul for some time and shared an especially intimate relationship with him (here, "beloved"; cf. Phil 2:20-22). He had also been with Paul during his founding visit in Corinth (Acts 16:2-3; 18:5; cf. 2 Cor 1:19). Paul exhibits high confidence that Timothy will be a fitting surrogate in his absence, embodying in concrete form both the way of life that Paul lived and the way that he would have the Corinthians emulate. Thus, Paul sees imitation proceeding in a series—from Christ, to Paul, to Timothy, to the Corinthians—like the emanations of a mirror reflected and then reflected again and again (cf. 11:1).

The rhetorical question in v. 21 continues to reflect the domain of education ("Should I come with a *rod* or with a spirit of love and gentleness?"). Corporal punishment was widely, although not universally (Quintilian, *Inst.* 1.3.14-15), accepted as a tool of correction for students who misbehaved or performed poorly, as both Jewish and Greco-Roman texts attest (Dutch 2005, 263–68). While the question here appears to voice a threat, pragmatically it has a different function. The course of action that the question projects represents the *alternative* to the way of relating that Paul has been proposing, i.e., it reflects the way of domination rather than the way of love and service. Since domination cannot be what they want (nor what he wants), the question further undermines their fundamental orientation.

Again it is said that the Corinthians are "puffed up" (cf. 4:7); and again there is no indication that their inflated state connects with their allegiance to specific leaders. Nor need it be supposed that Paul's reference to an impending visit indicates that he is responding to reports that the Corinthians disbelieved in his return. Rather, his purpose is to sound a warning: he will come to them (v. 18), and when he does he will deflate their swollen egos.

In vv. 18-20, Paul plays on the words "speech" (*logos*) and "power" (*dynamis*). Both words echo discussion from chapters 1 and 2. The former term echoes Paul's presentation of two different "accounts" of reality—"wisdom of word" and the "word of the cross" (cf. 1:17, 18). The latter term echoes the paradoxical presentation of Christ crucified as the "*power* of God" (1:24; cf. "Spirit of *power*," 2:4). This discussion resonates in the background as Paul now redeploys this pair to indicate a contrast between "theory" (*logos*) and "praxis" (*dynamis*). It was a commonplace belief of the philosophers that these two things ought to be in agreement (Epictetus, *Diatr.* 49; Musonius Rufus, *Diatr.* 1; 8), for indeed philosophy was not merely theoretical; it was fundamentally the "art of right living" (Cicero, *Tusc. disp.* 4.3.5; cf. *Nat. d.* 1.7; Musonius Rufus, *Diatr.* 5; Marcus Aurelius, *Med.* 10.16; 11.29). Paul would agree (Rom 15:18), but his point is that the proof of a doctrine's legitimacy is in its effects: the legitimacy of the Corinthians' doctrine will be exposed in the practical results that arise from it. Does their wisdom strengthen the community, or does it produce division?

Summary (1:10–4:21)

The first unit of the letter depicts a church in a state of disarray. Paul had left his children home alone, and in his absence they lacked the maturity to keep the house in order. They were infants after all, still in need of milk. Instead of bending down to nurture each other, they had raised themselves above each other in a spirit of competition. Some boasted in their wisdom, disparaging others as fools, imperfect, and unspiritual. Like the Stoic wise man, they themselves were "rich," "kings," "perfect," "prudent," and much more. They were self-sufficient, licensed by their possession of the Spirit to boast in those higher faculties they believed they could call their own. In Christ they had climbed to new heights.

Paul's response is that the Corinthian wise men had lost their bearings. Having climbed to the summit, they only stood further from the goal. In a reversal of literally apocalyptic proportions, Paul hurled them down from their lofty summit. Yet their fall was not to be for their destruction but for their salvation, for the way of Christ was the way down. By lowering himself, Christ lifted up others. This is the wisdom of Christ crucified, a counterintuitive wisdom that collides directly with the world's wisdom of self-aggrandizement and that comes to be accepted only by a Spirit-wrought transformation of the mind, which comes by God's gracious initiative, leaving no grounds for boasting.

In the course of his exposition, Paul repeatedly points to himself as an example to the Corinthians. While he could be seen as reasserting supremacy over Apollos, Paul's autobiographical remarks, including those about himself and Apollos in partnership, can be fully accounted for in terms of the rhetoric of exemplarity. By contrast, to read these chapters as a response to both the wisdom of the Corinthians *and* the wisdom of Apollos confuses two levels of reference. Did the Corinthians consider Apollos a "wise man," or did they use this designation of themselves? Were they attributing lofty spiritual qualities to Apollos or to themselves? Were they boasting in Apollos or in themselves? Were the Corinthians disregarding God's initiative of grace in the life of Apollos or in their own? An alternative reading has been proposed here. The church seems to have been divided not between specific leaders but primarily between the self-proclaimed wise and everyone else in the church. Although explicit mention of wisdom fades into the background in the letter's ensuing sections (cf. "wise man" in 6:5; "wisdom" in 12:8), the influence of the Corinthians' wisdom evidently stands behind several other problems soon to be treated. There, too, the influence of Stoicism will be evident.

Scandal, Litigation, and the Body

1 Corinthians 5:1–6:20

All that Paul has said so far is preparatory. The gospel of Christ crucified, presented in the first four chapters, forms the foundation on which he now attempts to rebuild the broken community. While he has criticized the church's childishness in general terms, in chapters 5 and beyond he runs through a long list of specific behavioral problems.

Having received information about these problems from at least two different sources (1:11; 7:1), he has arranged his treatment of the issues according to a strategic rhetorical pattern. Between 5:1 and 16:24, the topics cohere into several discrete units, each held together by verbal and thematic ties.

Chapters 5 and 6 form the first unit. Here three issues are treated: the case of an adulterous man (5:1-13), a case of intra-community litigation (6:1-11), and the Corinthians' illicit use of their bodies (6:12-20). Tying these sections together are the topics of sexual immorality (5:1; 6:9, 18), boundaries between insiders and outsiders (5:2, 9-13; 6:1-6), and judgment within the community (5:2-5, 12-13, 6:1-5).

Although Paul jumps abruptly in 5:1 from his discussion of wisdom (1:18–3:20) to a discussion of the church's specific behavioral problems, chapters 5 and 6 reveal an appreciable cluster of verbal ties with 1:10–4:21. Shared between these sections are the terms "puffed up," "boasting," "the name," "power," "the day," and "judgment"; and while wisdom fades into the background, again there is reference to the "wise man" (6:5).

Scandal (5:1-13)

5:1-8

Paul's opening remark echoes—in shocking contrast—his earlier remarks about the community: while he had said, "the *Spirit of God* dwells among you" (3:17), he now observes that "there is *sexual immorality* among you" (Sampley 2015, 726). A "certain" unidentified man (*tis*) is in a sexual relationship with a woman ("has," *echein*) whom Paul describes as "his father's wife" (*gynaika tou patros*). Solicitous about the community's purity and zealous for the man's restoration, Paul declares *in absentia* a sentence of excommunication.

Paul's condemnation of the man and disregard for the woman indicates that the man was a believer while the woman was not. From a traditional Jewish perspective, the man's sin was indeed grievous. While the woman was not the man's biological mother (Paul would then have said "his own mother"), his having a sexual relationship even with his stepmother or civil relation of his father qualified under Jewish Law as incest. The Law prohibited various forms of incest (Lev 18:6-18), including incest with one's stepmother (Lev 18:8; 20:11; Deut 27:20), in which case both parties received the penalty of death (20:11). Paul's reviling description of the sin as being of a sort "not even found among the Gentiles" carries him to the point of exaggeration (while incest of this kind did happen, Gentiles often condemned it; so Talbert 2002, 26–27), although among Jews the association of Gentiles with rampant sexual immorality was indeed commonplace (Lev 18:3, 27; Wis 14:22-27; T. Jos. 4.5-6; Rom 1:14-27).

Why the community looked the other way Paul does not say. In the context of a patron-client culture, and in view of evidence for some relatively well-to-do individuals in the Corinthian church (see introduction), it makes some sense to imagine a situation in which the man held a distinguished position as a benefactor in the community and the church was loath to bite the hand that fed it (Chow 1992; Clarke 1993; Winter 2001, 44–57). Moreover, it could be that the man had married the woman not out of perverse desire but so as to preserve his father's inheritance, which after his father's death (if that had not happened already) would otherwise fall to his father's new wife (Clarke 1993). Motives are complex, and social and economic factors cannot be discounted. However, the Corinthian slogans cited in the next chapter (6:12a, 13a, 18b)—which assert freedom in matters related to sex and diet—together with further references to the Corinthians' claim to freedom (8:1-13, esp. "that freedom of yours" in 8:9) and attention to Paul's persistent efforts to curb their enthusiasm on this point (8:13; 9:1-27), suggest that their motives may well have stemmed from their brand of wisdom. As will become apparent, they consigned bodily matters to the realm of indifference (Pascuzzi 1997) and regarded "sin" as error related strictly to the mind (6:18). Thus, they apparently exempted sex from the realm of moral concern (see 6:12-20). In this light it is possible to venture an explanation for why the wise Corinthians not only refused to "grieve" over the situation but were also positively "puffed up" (v. 2): because the man's behavior in their minds reflected an enlightened "knowledge" of the freedom obtained by virtue of their new status in Christ.

Far from supporting their position, Paul declares that the man's actions call for excommunication. Paul's pronouncement in v. 13, "Drive out the evildoer from your midst" (cf. v. 2), recites a refrain repeated throughout Deuteronomy (17:7b; cf. 19:19; 21:21; 22:24; 24:7), where Moses calls upon the community to excommunicate law-breakers. In this way Paul treats the assembly of Christ-believers as an analog of ancient Israel (note also that he speaks in v. 1 of "the Gentiles," as if the Corinthian believers are not themselves Gentiles; cf. "our fathers" in 10:1). The extreme measure of excommunication was common in Paul's day. Sectarian communities, like that at Qumran, practiced it for violation of community rules (1QS 7.16-19). The practice of exile was routine in Greek and Roman cities. Common in political discourse was a comparison of the city to a body and of its wicked citizens to a disease or gangrene that, unless eradicated or cut out, could contaminate the whole body (Lee 2006, 40–41).

Grounding such practices was a deep sense of community solidarity and a strong commitment to community boundaries. Using a Passover metaphor, Paul likens the sinful man to "leaven," which unless expurgated would infect the whole "lump" (v. 6). During Passover Jews ate only unleavened bread—bread that did not need time to rise—in order to symbolize the haste with which their ancestors had fled Egypt (Exod 12:15-20). Because the stipulation required that the house be swept clean of yeast entirely (Exod 12:15; *Pesaḥ* 1.1; *'Or* 11, 12), in time yeast arose as a figure for impurity or vice (Matt 8:15; 16:6, 11; Luke 12:1; Gal 5:9; Philo, *Spec.* 1.293). And so, just as the Law stipulated that those who were unclean of yeast be "cut off" from the community, Paul demanded that the church excommunicate the offending man. Yet, with a unique development of the Passover metaphor, Paul grounds his demand for purity in the death of "our Passover lamb," whom he here calls "Christ," highlighting his role as redeemer (v. 7).

Paul's concern was not only for the community as a whole but also for the spiritual well-being of the sinful man. In a long, cumbersome, and enigmatic sentence (see 5:3-5 in KJV), Paul declares *in absentia*, on the authority of the "Lord" and in solidarity with the whole community, a resolution to hand the man over to "Satan" for the "destruction of the flesh." Here Paul's purpose is not to curse the man's health or to declare a sentence of death. Rather his purpose is to leverage excommunication as a means of shaming and thereby restoring the man (2 Thess 3:14-15; cf. 2 Cor 2:6-7; Gal 6:1; 1 Tim 1:20; Matt 18:21-35; Jas 5:16, 20). The community represented an eschatological beachhead, claimed by Christ as the firstfruits of new creation.

Cast out into the domain of "Satan" (a metonym for the "domain that lies under Satan's dominion), this man would be deprived of God's benefits and driven to remorse. The man having repented, the Spirit would be "preserved" in him (LSJ I.2). The distinction between the "flesh" and the "s/Spirit," then, recalls not the language of Platonic dualism but a distinction between flesh as a figure for the man's "sinful desires" (cf. Rom 6:19; 7:25; 8; 13; Gal 5:13, 24) and the Spirit as an indwelling reality without which the man has no part with God (Rom 8:9). In short, excommunication puts to death *sinful desire*, and in this way the man remains *in the Spirit*.

5:9-13

Paul suspects that the Corinthians' neglectful response to the situation was shaped by their misunderstanding of a "previous letter" he had sent (which has not survived). In that letter he had apparently forbidden social interaction with various types of immoral people, which he here groups into three categories: fornicators, coveters and swindlers, and idolaters (v. 10). That he names "fornicators" first shows that discussion of the sexually immoral man remains in view.

Paul now clarifies that his instructions in the previous letter were intended to prohibit social interaction, not with *nonbelievers* but with immoral *believers*. In a climactic pronouncement, he commands that with such people believers are "not even to eat" (v. 11). By forbidding commensality, he was effectively cutting the offenders off from one of the primary contexts of fellowship: the meal.

Paul's pronouncement evinces a grave concern for community boundaries but, at the same time, a less than intuitive policy for their enforcement. Indeed, while he distinguishes clearly between "insiders" and "outsiders" (vv. 12-13), he repudiates the idea (probably for missional reasons) that the former should *avoid* the latter, since then one would need to go "out of the world" (v. 10). Rather, insiders should avoid those who allege themselves to be insiders (i.e., are "called brothers or sisters") but *live* like they are outsiders.

Paul's emphasis in this paragraph is puzzling when considered in connection with 5:1-8. If Paul's purpose is to call for the excommunication of an *insider* (or one who purports to be), does he now stray from his purpose? Certainly his explicit reference to the judgment of insiders (vv. 11, 13b) continues in the trajectory of the preceding section (vv. 1-8), but otherwise the paragraph focuses on details apparently extraneous to this purpose by centering on the injunction *not to avoid outsiders* (v. 10) and rather to leave their judgment to God (vv. 12-13; see also 1QS IX, 16-17; X, 16-20). Paul's emphasis is best accounted for under the supposition that the Corinthians had in fact shunned the wrong party. That is, the church had avoided contact not with the believing man, who in their minds had been "purified" in Christ, but with his "father's wife," an outsider. They had misidentified the threat. Contamination did not come from the outside; it was already festering within. Paul repeats, "Drive out the evildoer from your midst" (v. 13; cf. v. 2).

Litigation (6:1-11)

6:1-8

Paul shifts topics with startling abruptness, setting a wrathful tone from the start: "*Dare* any of you . . . ?" Someone—a believer—has dared to file a legal allegation against another believer in the community and, doubly outrageous, has brought them before the secular courts rather than settling matters in-house. Despite the break from the preceding section, major thematic links hold chapters 5 and 6 together, particularly the issues of intra-community judgment and concern with boundaries between insiders and outsiders.

It is possible that the case of litigation relates closely with the issue that precedes. If the adulterous man was motivated by ambition to procure his father's inheritance, the case could consist of charges of fraud (Richardson 1983; Derrett 1991; Clarke 1993, 59–71). Fictional legal cases from antiquity preserved as rhetorical school exercises frequently describe cases of fraud in inheritance disputes between biological "brothers" (Peppard 2016), suggesting that such situations must have been especially common. That the matter here was related to fraud is indeed not improbable (see the language of "defrauding" in v. 7). Still, the possibility that the matter was related specifically to that of the adulterous man remains no more than speculation.

Other possibilities are worth considering. To be sure, possible philosophical motivations for the plaintiff's action are hardly salient, and practical and especially socioeconomic payoff could be sufficient to account for the action. Still, given the Stoic proclivities of the Corinthians evident elsewhere, the possibility that the plaintiff found at least ex post facto justification for his action in philosophical teaching seems feasible. While according to the Stoics the wise man could not be wronged (evil consisting only in vice, it was something one could inflict but not receive), Stoic texts insisted with curious frequency that assailants should nevertheless receive punishment according to the law. They reconciled the apparent discrepancy by playing on a distinction between the technical/Stoic and the public/conventional meaning of the term "injury" (Seneca, *Ben.* 2.35.2; Clem. 2.7.1-4; also Cleanthes, *On Litigation*; cited in Diogenes Laertius, *Vit.* 7.175; see also *Vit.* 7.123 and Arius

Didymus, *Epit.* 11d/*SVF* 3.640): in the Stoic sense, one could not receive injury; in the public sense, one could.

The likelihood that this interpretation is correct is made less remote by several features of this section. (1) Paul six times repeats the refrain "Do you not *know* . . . ?" in this chapter (6:2, 3, 9, 15, 16, 19; outside 1 Corinthians, only in Rom 6:16). Imbued with sarcasm, this question alludes almost certainly to the Corinthians' pretensions of "wisdom" (1:18–3:23) and "knowledge" (8:1-13). (2) Paul surprisingly reintroduces the "wise man" into the discussion (6:5)—the only other place where the wise man appears in the letter outside chapters 1–4. Here, Paul evokes the classic depiction of the wise man as a philosopher-king or a just judge moved by the virtue of prudence (Plato, *Prot.* 343a). (3) Paul also cites a recognizable commonplace of the philosophers: "Why not rather be wronged [*adikeisthe*]? Why not rather be defrauded?" (6:7). While the allusion ideologically parallels certain sayings of Jesus (Matt 5:38-42; cf. Rom 12:17, 19; 1 Cor 4:12-13; 1 Pet 2:23), in form it tallies more exactly with a maxim of the philosophers about the wise man, touted from the days of Plato's Socrates onward (*Gorg.* 469C; 408B; 509C; Aristotle, *Eth. nic.* 5.11.7-8; *Rhet.* 1.7.22; Philo, *Jos.* 20; Seneca, *Ep.* 95.52; cf. *SVF* 3.567-81). An almost exact parallel occurs in the discourses of Paul's contemporary Musonius Rufus, who said that the wise man ought to be disposed "to look upon doing a wrong [*adikein*] as worse than suffering one [*adikeisthai*] . . . and to regard being worsted as better than gaining an unjust advantage" (*Diatr.* 3 [Lutz 41]; cf. *Diatr.* 10).

Whatever the plaintiff's motivation, his use of the secular courts may suggest that he was of some means and perhaps wished to take advantage of a defendant whose resources were limited (A. Mitchell 1993). The costs of litigation were high, owing to both the legal fees and the authorities' not uncommon expectation of bribery (although Tsai 2016 has shown that previous estimates of the costs are exaggerated). The socioeconomic advantage of the wealthier party would virtually assure their victory (Theissen 1982, 97).

Although Paul refers to the litigant in the singular (*tis*), he addresses the audience throughout this section in the second person plural, extending the blame for "wronging" and "defrauding" apparently to the community (6:7) but especially to the group of self-professing wise men (cf. 6:5). Paul undercuts the wise here with the same kind of ironic reversal as appeared in 1:18–3:23. Asking mockingly if there is not a "wise man" among them to act as judge, and why they do not play the part and take a wrong rather than giving one, Paul sets them in direct antithesis with the true wise man, with an emphatic "but *you* (*hymeis*) both wrong and defraud!" Those who profess to be wise again prove themselves to be fools. In their place Paul would seat "the despised" (6:4), the very people whom God—who has shamed the wise—has "elected" (1:28)!

Quite evidently Paul is concerned for the reconciliation of individuals within a crumbling community, where "brother goes to law against brother" (6:6). However, he is also concerned with the way in which the situation reflects disregard of community boundaries and abdication of the believing community in its responsibility in the unfolding eschatological drama. He introduces the unbelieving judges as the "unrighteous" (v. 1), i.e., those not justified in Christ. His point is less to underline the corruption of the Roman legal system (although there may be semantic resonance with the notion of "injustice") than to highlight the irony of abdicating responsibility of judgment to the unbelieving—in "mundane" matters of all things (v. 3)—given that believers will judge not only the "world" (v. 2) but even "angels" (v. 3)! While absent from the Torah and prophetic writings, the tradition that God's people would serve a role in eschatological judgment was widespread in Second Temple literature (that they would judge the nations: Dan 7:22-23; Wis 3:7-8; Sir 4:15; Jub. 24:29; 1 QpHab 5:4-5; 1 En. 95:3; that they would judge the angels: 1 En. 13:1-10; 1QM XIII.2). Speaking as though the Corinthians are already familiar with the idea ("do you not know . . . ?"), Paul transfers this responsibility to the church.

6:9-11
Verses 9-11 play a strategic role in tying together 5:1-13; 6:1-8; and 6:12-20. References to greed and robbery (6:8, 10) tie 6:9-11 together with 6:1-8, and references to sexual immorality (6:9) and the Spirit (6:11) tie 6:9-11 together with both 5:1-13 and what follows in 6:12-20.

Here the irony continues as Paul accuses the litigious Corinthians of playing exactly the part of the "unrighteous" secular judges. Using the same semantic root, Paul refers to the secular judges as "the unrighteous" (*adikoi*; v. 1) and accuses the Corinthians of "committing injustice" (*adikeite*; v. 8). The Corinthians act as if unaware that the "unrighteous" (*adikoi*) will not inherit the kingdom of God (v. 9).

The ensuing admonition, "Do not be deceived" (e.g., Epictetus, *Diatr.* 4.6.23), employs the rhetorical style of diatribe, a style of speech frequently used by the popular philosophers in instructing their pupils (see introduction). Paul's admonition calls the listeners to full attention as he warns them that they are courting disaster: "Fornicators, idolaters, adulterers, male prostitutes, sodomites [so NRSV], thieves, the greedy, drunkards, revilers, robbers—none of these will inherit the kingdom of God" (vv. 9-10).

Lists like these, cataloguing classes of offenders or their corresponding vices, occurred commonly in both wisdom literature (Wis 12:2-6; 14:22-26) and the discourse of moral philosophy (Philo, *Post.* 52), as they do in the Pauline epistles (5:9-10; Rom 1:24, 26, 27, 29-31; 13:13; 2 Cor 12:20-21; Gal 5:19-21; Eph 4:31; 5:3-5; Col 3:5-8). Such lists were often generic. The references here to the *malakoi* and the *arsēnokoitai* have no apparent connection to the situation. The first term referred to men regarded as either "morally soft" ("lacking in self-control"; Plato, *Rep.* 556c; Aristotle, *Eth. nic.* 1150a33) or "effeminate" (Philo, *Somn.* 1.123) and by extension could designate the passive partner in homosexual intercourse (Philo, *Spec.* 3.37-42). While the second term had no known antecedent and may have been a Pauline neologism, it alludes rather straightforwardly to texts in Leviticus that, using the same two roots (*arsēn* + *koimasthai*), prohibited "male" (*arsēn*) from "lying" (*koimasthai*) with "male" (Lev 18:22; 20:13)—against the more restrictive translation "sodomites" seen in the NRSV. The terms "thieves" (*kleptai*), "coveters" (*pleonektai*), and "swindlers" (*harpagēs*) could connect with the issue discussed in 6:1-8, if that was a matter of fraud, though that is not clearly indicated. Nowhere else in the letter does the word "revilers" (*loidoroi*) appear, and concern with fornication and idolatry (both traditional Jewish concerns) are ubiquitous in Paul's letters (e.g., outside of 1 Corinthians, idolatry in Rom 2:22; Gal 4:8-9; 5:20; Col 3:5; 1 Thess 1:9; fornication in Gal 5:19; Col 3:5; 1 Thess 4:4-7). Even so, the list seems to be at least partly tailored to the situation in Corinth (Oropeza 2017, 70). Apart from their prevalence in Paul's letters, the topics of fornication and idolatry are demonstrably germane to the issues treated in chapters 5–6 (5:1, 9; 6:13-18) and in other places in 1 Corinthians (chs. 8–10). Moreover, Paul says in 11:21 that when the church meets together some of them have been getting drunk (cf. "drunkards"). Perhaps, then, some of the other items relate to the situation in Corinth as well.

Paul's characterization of the Corinthians as "unrighteous" people in danger of forfeiting inheritance of the kingdom is highly rhetorical, being designed to highlight the incompatibility of their behavior with their status in Christ. Although Paul considers them "saints" (1:2), "enriched in every way in him" (1:5), still they reveal themselves to be "unrighteous" (6:1), just as they reveal themselves to be "immature" and "carnal" (3:2-3). Thus, in the first six chapters of the letter, Paul has presented to them, as it were, a mirror revealing an unflattering image of unrighteousness. Now he conjures up before them again a forgotten picture of their image at the moment of conversion, when they "*were* washed, *were* sanctified, *were* justified" (6:11). Unrighteous they are not. They must come back to themselves.

The Body (6:12-20)

A new section reintroduces the topic of sexual immorality (5:1-13) but now under the wider heading of the physical human body and its moral relevance. The Corinthians have justified both intercourse with prostitutes and certain unspecified dietary habits (cf. chs. 8–10) by appealing to a principle of "freedom" and by relegating the body and its functions to the level of moral irrelevance. Paul counters that the body belongs to the Lord and therefore must be used as honors him.

This section contains two parallel units, with vv. 12-18a paralleling vv. 18b-20 part by part (Naselli 2017, 984):

vv. 13ab	v. 18b
vv. 13c-14	v. 18c
vv. 15-18a	vv. 19-20

The section as a whole contains several Corinthian quotations, followed by Paul's own refutations, often in the form of rhetorical questions. Thus, the section exhibits numerous features characteristic of the diatribe style (see introduction).

Paul opens by citing two Corinthian slogans (so a majority of commentators and English Bible translations; see Brookins 2014, 92, Tables 4-5): "All things are permissible for me . . . . All things are permissible for me" (6:12a, c) and "Food is for the belly and the belly for food, and God will destroy both the one and the other" (6:13a, b). Paul cites the first slogan twice (v. 12a, c), following each time with a strong adversative conjunction (*all*) and a rebuttal (v. 12b, d). The second slogan consists of two parts (v. 13a, b) and receives a two-part rebuttal (vv. 13c, 14). While Paul does not explicitly attribute this material to the Corinthians, his antithetical responses and several pieces of evidence garnered from the letter suggest that the words indeed were their own. Most notably, Paul will later refer to "that freedom *of yours*," using the same root (*exousia*) here translated "are permissible" (*exestin*), and he will later dwell on the topic of "freedom" (*eleutheria*) at length in response to those who claimed freedom in the matter of eating "meat sacrificed to idols" (8:1–11:1).

The slogans have the quality of "maxims," pithy sayings that encapsulate conventional wisdom but that could mean different things to different people (Aristotle, *Rhet.* 2.21; Quintilian, *Inst.* 5.11.41; Dio, *Or.* 7.98; Seneca, *Ep.* 8.8; 12.11; 29.10-11; etc.). If these slogans originated with Paul (Hurd 1965), he makes evident here that the Corinthian wise men have misapprehended his meaning and extended the principle of freedom into areas that he would not.

The first slogan contains unmistakable echoes of Stoicism: "all things are *permissible* (*exestin*)." It was one of the "paradoxes" ("astonishing sayings") of the Stoics that "only the wise man is *free*" (Cicero, *Par. St.* 33-41; Diogenes Laertius, *Vit. phil.* 7.121-2; though Stoicism introduced this idea also into Hellenistic Jewish thinking: e.g., Philo, *Prob.* 59). In an almost exact parallel with 1 Cor 6:12ac, Diogenes Laertius records the Stoic view that all things belong to the wise, since "the law has given to them *all-complete authority* (*pantel exousian*)" (*Vit. phil.* 7.125; cf. Dio Chrysostom, *Or.* 14.18). This principle represented an internalization of a political idea, formulated as a solution to the problem of political and social constraints on freedom. In its Stoic formulation, the question whether one had freedom was relative to one's perspective on the relevance of outward circumstances. For the Stoics, physical and external circumstances such as health, wealth, and pleasure, and their opposites death, poverty, and pain, were neither "good" nor "evil." Standing, as it were, between good and evil, these things were morally indifferent—hence their technical designation "indifferents." Good and evil consisted, respectively, only in virtue and vice, and virtue and vice were strictly matters of *intellectual* discretion (*SVF* 3.70). If true freedom consisted in free moral choice, which the body and other external circumstances could not impact, there would remain no limits to freedom. The tyrant could threaten to imprison, maim, or kill you, and yet he did not have the power to overcome your sovereignty of moral *judgment* (Epictetus, *Diatr.* 1.29.9-10; see also 2.1.23).

While appropriating these ideas into a Pauline framework, the Corinthian wise men shed some of the nuances of the Stoic doctrines, but they did so with the grain of other emerging tendencies in Stoicism. In orthodox Stoicism, the wise man's freedom was about the freedom to *choose virtue*; and virtue could involve judgments about use of the body. On the other hand, under the influence of Platonism, Stoicism had grown increasingly attracted to anthropological dualism, precisely in order to preserve the mind's freedom, unfettered by the circumstances of the body (Long 1982). In a unique configuration of these ideas, the Corinthians mapped an anthropological dualism onto the doctrine of indifference to create an extreme position in which the body became morally irrelevant (cf. Epictetus, *Diatr.* 1.14.5-7, 11-14; 2.8.9-23).

Knowing his audience, Paul quips with a Stoic argument of his own: "but not all things are *beneficial* (*sympherei*)." Although common in political discourse concerned with the unity of the city (M. M. Mitchell 1993,

33–35), this language derives from Stoicism, in which the importance of the "common benefit" (*koinon sympheron*) followed from the notion that the universe was a single *body* of which all particular things were *parts* (cf. 12:12-28); hence, this language appears frequently in political treatises explicitly shaped by Stoicism (Cicero, *Off.* 1.23-26; 1.85; *Fin.* 3.64; cf. Sir 37:28). That Paul selected his words with special awareness of his audience's proclivities is indicated by the extreme rarity of this language in his letters (the related substantive adjective, *symphoron*, appears only in 1 Cor 7:35 and 10:33 in the NT; the neuter participle, *sympheron*, occurs only in 1 Cor 12:7; 2 Cor 12:1; Heb 12:10 in the NT).

The second part of Paul's response emphasizes the necessity of moral self-mastery. Although the semantic similarity is difficult to bring out in English, Paul's answer plays on the Corinthians' language of freedom:

Corinthians: "All things are *permissible* (*exestin*) for me" (v. 12a).

Paul: "But I will not be *under the power* (*exousiasthēsomai*) of anything" (v. 12c).

The second Corinthian slogan reflects a similar indifference toward bodily matters, except that it relates indifference to the matter of diet: "Food is for the belly and the belly for food, and God will destroy both the one and the other." While the Corinthians may have known Jesus' teaching that all foods are clean (Mark 7:15-19), the thinking reflected here is related to a different philosophical framework. Here the letter gives its first hint that the Corinthians denied the survival of the physical body into the afterlife. The body is impermanent (it will be destroyed). The Corinthians then used this idea to ground a position of indifference on matters of diet (see 8:1–10:33). If the body is impermanent, why should one's diet be restricted? Philosophically, this perspective dovetails with several tenets of Stoicism: the body is impermanent; it is not an essential part of one's identity; and since physical objects, including foods, are neither good nor bad in themselves, one has freedom in matters of diet.

To the Corinthians' two-part slogan, Paul again issues a two-part response. In the first part (paralleling v. 13a), he responds that the body is not meant for fornication but for the Lord (v. 13c). In the second part (paralleling v. 13b), he emphasizes that the body is morally relevant indeed, and grounds his argument in the resurrection: just as God raised Christ from the dead, so he will also raise the bodies of those who are in Christ (v. 14).

Paul draws a direct line from the Corinthians' philosophy of freedom to sexual intercourse with prostitutes (v. 15). While Greek and Roman culture generally condoned prostitution (Athenaeus, *Deipn.* 13.571ff), the Jewish scriptures frequently condemned it (see a lengthy condemnation in Prov 5), and in a figurative extension of this stance presented Israel's waywardness from God as a kind of harlotry (Hos 2). Whether the Corinthians were in fact engaging in intercourse with prostitutes or Paul is only speaking hypothetically, he evidently understood their position to be one that downgraded the moral relevance of the body. (Note that he speaks here to *men*.) Following are two metaphors that highlight the importance of sexual purity. First, using the metaphor of the human body (cf. 12:12-28; Rom 12:4-5), Paul suggests that the "body" of each believer ("your *bodies*") is a "member" on Christ's "body" and should therefore not be applied to impure purposes. Next, he uses the metaphor of marriage (cf. 2 Cor 11:32; Eph 5:22-32), invoking the marriage formula of Gen 2:24: "The two shall become one flesh." Both metaphors serve to illustrate the turpitude of fornication with prostitutes.

With these metaphors Paul illustrates his deeply ingrained thinking about the "participation" of believers "in Christ" (cf. Campbell 2012) and the incompatibility of a believer's union with anything outside the boundaries of Christ's influence (see 10:16). While the point that believers are united with the Lord "in *Spirit*" is maintained, the relevance of this unity to the *physical* body is also evident from Paul's prohibition of physical intercourse itself.

Verse 18 contains three parts. The first part (v. 18a) rounds out what precedes with a succinct conclusion: "Flee fornication." The second part (v. 18b), consisting of another Corinthian slogan, introduces a new paragraph: "Every sin that a person commits is outside the body." While only a minority of commentators and modern translations recognize this as a Corinthian quotation (among translations, only the HCSB [but not the revised CSB 2017], and the BJ [which includes also v. 18c in the quotation]), the evidence strongly suggests that these words belonged to the Corinthians (Murphy-O'Connor 1978; 2009, 30–31; Smith 2008; 2010; Naselli 2017). Hence, Paul is not suggesting that sexual immorality stands in a category of its own (where some translations have "Every [*other*] sin…"; cf. Rom 6). Rather the *Corinthians* have suggested that one commits sin with the mind but not with the body. This reading of v. 18b coheres well with other evidence in the letter. The wise regard physical matters as morally irrelevant; on this basis they regard both sex and diet as matters of indifference (5:1-13; 6:12-20; 8:1–11:1), and, as shall be seen, they deny a bodily resurrection (15:12-58).

The final part of the verse (v. 18c) follows up the Corinthian slogan with a characteristic Pauline rebuttal: "But the one who commits fornication sins against his own body." To hammer his point home, Paul adds two further arguments: the body "is a temple of the holy Spirit" (v. 19) and "you are not your own, for you were bought with a price" (v. 20). Both arguments work within metaphorical systems prevalent in Paul's letters. The first, employing a metaphor of sacred space, echoes Paul's earlier reference to the community as a temple and the locus of God's indwelling presence (3:16). The second draws on the language of slavery and redemption, depicting believers as slaves rightfully purchased by God (cf. 7:23), a new and benevolent master. "You are not your own" again parallels a Stoic mantra, but now with a total reversal of its meaning. The Stoic mantra was that the *body* was "not your own," the person being defined by the rational faculty alone and the body being consigned to the realm of external things and therefore to the realm of indifference (Epictetus, *Diatr.* 4.1.66, 78, 87, 158; 4.7.17, 31-32; Seneca, *Ep.* 42.8; 120.18-19). Quite the reverse, Paul's argument is that because the believer is "not their own," what they do with the body really matters!

Debate surrounds the question whether "body" refers to that of the individual or that of the church. These seem to be false alternatives (Gupta 2010). Paul is concerned both for the well-being of the community and for the individuals who comprise it (as is evident also in the case of the adulterous man; 5:3-5). On the one hand, Paul expresses concern for one's use of their own body ("your *bodies* are members," v. 15; "*the one* who joins himself with a prostitute," v. 16). Even his reference to "the body of you all"—where he refers to a singular *body* but qualifies this with a *plural* personal pronoun (*to sōma hymōn*)—points inconclusively to a corporate referent, for use of the "distributive singular" was common in the NT, including Paul's letters ("their conscience," 8:12; "in your [pl.] heart," Eph 2:7; "your [pl.] spirit," Gal 6:18; Phil 4:20; the "redemption of our body," Rom 8:23; "their own belly," Rom 16:18; and see BDF, §140). On the other hand, the bodies of individuals are constitutive of the larger body of Christ (see 12:12-28) and could be agents of contamination to the body as a whole (cf. 5:6-7). In this regard, Paul's final references to the body in vv. 18 and 19 ("sins against his own body . . . your body is a temple of the holy Spirit") may refer to the body of the individual but, by way of double entendre, *also* to the body of the church.

Just as the preceding paragraph concluded with a sharp summary ("Flee sexual immorality"), so Paul concludes this paragraph: "So then glorify God in your body!"

Social Status at the Present Time

1 Corinthians 7:1-40

In response to those who claim that "all things are permissible," Paul has just established that no principle of freedom exists that would justify intercourse with prostitutes (6:12-20). Now he turns to face those who take a different position: that "it is well for a man not to touch a woman" (7:1b). This opens up a fairly lengthy inquiry into the value of marriage (7:1-40). The question of community boundaries remains in view (7:13-16; cf. 5:1-13; 6:1-11).

The chapter divides into three main sections. The first covers a variety of marital questions, relating respectively to different marital status groups (7:1-16). The second takes a brief excursus into social roles parallel to those of married/unmarried and through these examples highlights the central principle that drives Paul's advice as regards marriage (7:17-24). The final unit returns to the issue of marriage, exploring several further issues before offering a final recapitulative summary of Paul's personal conviction about the general impracticality of marriage (7:25-40).

Instructions about Marriage (7:1-16)

The opening of chapter 7 brings to life the nature of Paul's letters as *correspondences*, for here he takes as his point of departure a citation from a letter that the church had sent to him. The opening formula, "Now concerning" (*peri de*), marks a transition to a new topic (M. M. Mitchell 1989). The succeeding words identify what follows as a Corinthian quotation: ". . . the things about which *you wrote*: 'It is well for a man not to touch a woman.'"

The quotation sets off a discussion of the general topic of marriage. The first unit (7:1-16) breaks down into several subsections. The first addresses the value of sexual intercourse and hence indirectly the general question of whether one should marry (vv. 1-7). Paul then offers instructions to several different marital status groups: the unmarried/widowers and widows (vv. 8-9), the married (vv. 10-11), and the "rest," i.e., believers married to nonbelievers (vv. 12-16).

7:1-7

The chapter begins with a Corinthian slogan: "It is well for a man not to touch a woman." The thrust of the slogan is that one should abstain from sexual intercourse ("touch" being a euphemism for sexual intercourse; see Fee 1980 for references). This sentiment flies directly in the face of the cry of "freedom" proclaimed by others in the church (6:12a, c). This datum suggests that the slogan in 7:1b represented an alternative position in the Corinthian church, brought forth perhaps in response to the wise men who touted sexual freedom and now presented to Paul in appeal for sanction. In response, Paul presents marriage as a context for mutual satisfaction of sexual desires and as a preventative measure against "sexual immorality" (already a problem in the community: 5:1-13; 6:12-20). It is not altogether implausible that the dissenting party consisted of certain "charismatic women" who believed that by virtue of their new status in Christ they had transcended social hierarchies and declared themselves liberated from subjection to their husbands, now claiming "authority" (*exousia*) over their own bodies (Wire 1990). Yet Paul assigns instructions evenhandedly throughout the discourse, not singling out women as particularly more ascetic than men but enjoining mutual obligations upon both (7:2, 3, 4, 12, 13-14, 16).

Paul's presentation of the bilateral obligations of husbands and wives, set in parallel syntax, stands out against his predominantly patriarchal, even misogynistic, culture and is redolent of the more egalitarian sentiments of some ancient philosophers. Both Greek and Jewish texts often presented women as naturally inferior, whether in their reasoning faculties (Let. Aris. 250), in their character (Sir 25:19; 42:14; T. Reu. 5:1; 6:3; Josephus, *J.W.* 2.121; Philo, *Opif.* 151, 165; Vergil, *Aen.* 4.93-94, 561-3, 569-70), or in their overall nature (Plato, *Tim.* 42A; *Resp.* 453b-456A; *Tim.* 90E; Aristotle, *Rhet.* 1.9.22; *Pol.* 1252b; *G.A.* 737A28). Moreover, it was a typical expectation in Greco-Roman culture that women should submit unilaterally to their husbands. The moral philosophers of the Hellenistic era, however, tended in a countercultural direction. In Paul's declaration that spouses do not have "authority over their own bodies" (v. 4) there are clear echoes of Stoic moral philosophy. Indeed, Hierocles the Stoic said much the same thing, maintaining that husband and wife should set "everything in common up to their very bodies, or rather up to their very own souls" (Hierocles//Stobaeus, *Anth.* 4.67.23 [Ramelli 2009, 77]). Similarly, the Stoic philosopher Musonius Rufus said that husband and wife should hold "nothing peculiar or private to one or the other, not even their own bodies" (*Diatr.* 13a [Lutz 1947, 58]; cf. *Diatr.* 14). A similar sentiment appears in some Jewish works but not in the same terms (Jos. Asen. 20:4; see also Ruth 1:16-17; T. Jos. 17:7). For both Paul and the Stoic moralists, the mutual ownership of the body was seen as a corollary of a deep metaphysical unity or "fellowship (*koinōnia*)" shared between husband and wife (cf. 2 Cor 13:13; Phil 2:1-2; Hierocles/ Stobaeus, *Anth.* 4.67.24), such that physical exploitation would be self-defeating. This unity was of the same kind as that shared between the parts of the body, where the honor or suffering of one part is also transferred to the others (see 12:12-28). Paul, then, sets limits around both a "freedom" that indulges sexual desire to the point of profligacy (6:12-20) *and* a "freedom" that by denying sex disregards the needs of others (7:1-4).

While Paul encourages mutual recognition of each other's sexual needs, he does not prohibit short stints of abstinence, if and when it is initiated by mutual consent and for purposes of devotion to prayer (v. 5). This divergence of instructions—between marrying so as to channel sexual desire on the one hand and abstaining from sex for a short period of time on the other—creates a major crux in the interpretation of v. 6: "*This* (*touto*) I mean by way of *concession* (*suggnōmēn*), not of command." Whether "this" refers to the *taking* of a spouse together with the sexual obligations entailed (vv. 2-4) or to temporary agreed *abstinence* (v. 5) is unclear. The former interpretation, however, seems preferable for at least two reasons. First, it better accounts for the logical progression signaled by the conjunctions in vv. 6 and 7, where the alternative interpretation leaves the conjunction introducing v. 7 without satisfactory explanation. The following paraphrase adequately captures the drift:

> Each person may take a spouse, and should render to them the necessary obligations . . . . **6** Now (*de*), I mean this in the spirit of permission rather than as a command; one does not *have* to take a spouse. **7** Moreover (*de*), I would prefer that you be *single*, as I am. But of course (*all*), each one has his or her own gift.

Second, the view that Paul's concession refers to "taking a spouse" dovetails better with his emphasis across the chapter that, while marriage is "good," celibacy is "better" (vv. 8, 38).

Paul was not alone in questioning the fittingness of marriage. Jesus' teaching that there would be no marriage in heaven (Matt 22:30//Mark 12:25//Luke 20:34-35) must have inspired some to transfer the eschatological future into the present (cf. Gal 3:28; Neutel 2015, 184–233). Indeed, asceticism grounded in an "over-realized eschatology" became common among certain Christian groups (as witnessed in 1 Tim 4:3; cf. 2 Tim 2:18). In the context of Greco-Roman education, practice speeches in schools of rhetoric took up the question "whether one should marry" as one of the more common "theses" of debate (Aphthonius, *Prog.* 13; Libanius, [Foerster 8:550–61]; Quintilian, *Inst.* 2.4.24-25). Yet, in his preference for celibacy, Paul departed both from the norm established in the Jewish scriptures and from customary practice in the contemporary culture. The Jewish scriptures promulgated marriage as an ordinance of nature (Gen 2:18, 24). Jesus reaffirmed this pronouncement (Matt 19:4-6, 10-12). Procreation, which was most often linked with marriage, was of highest importance and one of the fundamental ways in which humanity fulfilled its status as God's image-bearers (Gen 1:28; cf. Gen 30:23; Judg 11:37-40; 1 Sam 1:3-9; Isa 4:1). Cases of celibates like Jeremiah were exceptional (16:1-4). In Paul's time marriage was the universal expectation for Jews except among reportedly celibate groups, like the Therapeutae (Philo, *Contempl. Life* 13-16; 68; 70; *Prob.* 79) and perhaps some Essene communities (Josephus, *J.W.* 1.119-22; 2.121; Philo, *Hyp.* 14-15, 17; *Contempl. Life*).

Apart from rare exceptions, Greco-Roman culture viewed marriage as a crucial institution for maintenance of societal stability. Marriage established legal sureties for the transference of property and other rights of inheritance. It also encouraged procreation in the context of a stable household. For this reason, the emperor Augustus issued marriage laws (in 18 BC, and a revision in AD 9) penalizing the unmarried and rewarding those who married as well as those who produced children (Dio Cassius, *Hist.* 54.16.1; 56.1-10). Many viewed procreation as the primary purpose of marriage and moreover as essential, since the population constituted the strength of the city (Cicero, *Fin.* 4.17; Hierocles/Stobaeus, *Anth.* 4.75.14; Musonius Rufus, *Diatr.* 15; Epictetus, *Diatr.* 2.23.38; 3.7.19; 3.21.5-6). A preference or demand for abstinence was exceptional. Abstinence was restricted primarily to certain cultic groups, where devotees committed themselves exclusively to the deity of worship (Apuleius, *Metam.* 11), and to certain philosophical groups who viewed sexual activity either as surrender to the vice of *erōs* (Stobaeus, *Ecl.* 2.90,19-91.9//*SVF* 3.394) or as a distraction from the philosophical life (Seneca, *Ep.* 116.5; Epictetus, *Diatr.* 3.22.68-70; the Cynics in Diogenes Laertius, *Vit. phil.* 6.54; and Epicurus in Diogenes Laertius, *Vit. phil.* 10.118-19).

Paul's deliberation on the fittingness of marriage seems to mirror an ongoing debate within Stoicism about the value of marriage (Deming 2004). Whereas the Stoics' Cynic cousins rejected marriage as a sociological construction, i.e., as something invented by humans and not rooted in nature, Stoics adopted either of two alternative viewpoints: either that marriage was a natural "good" and valuable to society or that, although marriage was sometimes beneficial, in certain circumstances it should be avoided. Paul adopted the latter position, conceding to the benefit of marriage for some but considering it a hindrance for others—perhaps even for the majority.

7:8-16

A transitional conjunction (*de*) and a change in topic marks the opening of a new paragraph. Paul now shifts from discussing marriage as a general preventative measure against *porneia* (sexual immorality) to investigate the value of marriage for three specific marital status groups.

(1) The category "unmarried and widows" (vv. 8-9) probably encompasses bachelors, widows, and widowers (for which Greek did not have a special word); young maidens are excluded as they are singled out later (vv. 25-38). To these groups Paul reiterates the advantage of celibacy over commitment to marriage ("remain as I am"; cf. vv. 7, 8) but again acknowledges the benefit of marriage as a solution to sexual desire (for "burning" as a trope for strong passion, see 2 Macc 4:38; 10:35; 3 Macc 4:2; 2 Cor 11:29).

(2) Paul then addresses "the married" (vv. 10-11), passing on instructions apparently rooted in a mandate from "the Lord." The source of the mandate is not special revelation but—as is found somewhat rarely in Paul's letters—the teachings of the historical Jesus. As in Mark's Gospel, where Jesus addresses both men and women (Mark 10:11-12; cf. Matt 5:32; 19:9), Paul commands (*paraggellō*; cf. 11:17; 1 Thess 4:11) both wives not to divorce their husbands and husbands not to divorce their wives (*chōristhēnai* and *aphienai* are virtually synonymous; otherwise v. 11c is superfluous). In forbidding divorce, Jesus' teaching controverted what was sanctioned for men by the Jewish Law (Deut 24:1-4). While divorce initiated by the wife was not sanctioned in the Law, evidence survives that women did initiate divorce (Talbert 2002, 61). Divorce was legal for women under Roman law and thus in the Roman colony of Corinth.

(3) Paul's instructions to the "rest" apply to a special subset within the category of "the married" consisting of believers married to nonbelievers (vv. 12-16). Paul now clarifies that the instructions are his own, for no relevant tradition has come down to him from the historical Jesus (v. 12). Still formulating his instructions in even, reciprocal fashion, Paul enjoins those whose unbelieving spouses "consent" to live with them not to leave (vv. 12-13). Having previously issued instructions first to the woman and then to the man, he now reverses the order, perhaps for the sake of balance. These mixed marriages offer the first instance discussed in the chapter of social situations in which Paul advises maintaining the status quo.

Incidences of believers terminating marriages with nonbelievers may well have occurred in the Corinthian church. The Corinthians' misapprehension of Paul's instructions given in the previous letter (cf. 5:9-10), such that they shunned social interaction with nonbelievers rather than with sinners who went by the name of "brother," could have manifested itself in this way (cf. 10:27-29). Paul opposes such a practice. He grounds his instructions in a principle of sanctification: the believing spouse sanctifies the unbelieving one (just as believing Israel sanctifies unbelieving Israel; Rom 11:16). Though in the case of the adulterous man (5:1-13) and in the case of intercourse with prostitutes (6:12-20) Paul suggested that impurity contaminated believers, he now suggests that a reverse process takes place and that a believer's holiness overcomes the nonbeliever's impurity. He appends an argument that seems less than intuitive but that he must have considered a shared premise: the children of mixed marriages *are* holy, and how could this be unless the parents too (both of them) are holy?

Despite Paul's support for commitment in marriage, like Matthew's Jesus (Matt 19:9) he also permits divorce in certain circumstances. Whereas Jesus permitted divorce in cases of *porneia* (probably meaning "sexual immorality"), Paul concedes permission to divorce in cases of mixed marriages where there is no hope of maintaining peace. Despite attempts to read vv. 15-16 as a call to reconciliation, the evidence does not support this reading. In v. 15d Paul poses a contrast (*de*) not between divorce and peace in *reconciliation* but between slavery to marriage and peace in *separation*; he then concludes, *pessimistically*, by asking believers to be realistic about the prospects of "saving" their spouses (v. 16). Several items support this reading: (a) the parallel sentence structure of the original Greek ("*Not enslaved* is the brother or the sister in such circumstances, but *in peace* God called you"); (b) the fact that the conjunction at the opening of v. 16 (*gar*) connects more naturally with the final portion of v. 15; (c) the fact that Paul elsewhere compares marriage to slavery (Rom 7:1-6); and (d) the fact that "slavery" and "peace" were a commonplace antithetical pair in Greco-Roman discourse (Plutarch, *Luc.* 20.2; Cicero, *Phil.* 8.12; 13.2; Livy, *Hist.* 36.7.12; Tacitus, *Hist.* 4.17.2; Augustus, *Res gest. divi aug.* 1; cf. Gal 5:13). In short Paul says that, in mixed marriages as well as in some other circumstances, peace may prevail only in separation.

The Christian Calling and Social Status (7:17-24)

Paul momentarily breaks away from discussing married/unmarried status to explore two other social polarities: circumcised/uncircumcised (vv. 18-19) and slave/free (vv. 21-22). This section highlights the central principle that drives Paul's advice on marriage, repeating three times—once at the outset (v. 17), once after the first example (v. 20), and once at the conclusion of the section (v. 24)—the refrain that one should remain in God's "calling." The refrain echoes Paul's earlier affirmation that each one has "his own gift from God" (v. 7).

Taking its cues from Reformation and post-Reformation conceptions of "vocation," traditional Protestant scholarship has viewed Paul's reference to "calling" in sociological terms, such that Paul advises remaining in the *social condition* to which one was "called." This reading misrepresents Paul's language of "calling" and "apportionment" (v. 17), as it flies in the face of every other reference to "calling" found in Paul's letters, which invariably refers to God's calling of believers *to the gospel* (perhaps besides Paul's language of "calling" to the role of apostle, on the OT model of the commissioning of a prophet, though, not without justification, this calling could be considered a conversion to a new worldview/philosophy/theology). Paul, then, does not suggest that one's calling *consists in* one or another of these social roles but that these *social roles* should be relegated to a position subordinate to one's *calling*. Here, as in Paul's discussion of marriage, his point is to prioritize one's calling in the gospel over and above social status and to commend a lifestyle in which this calling moderates social contingencies.

Although Paul associates the "calling" with "apportionment" or "gift" from God, he does not mean to suggest that God ordains social positions (cf. Epictetus, *Diatr.* 2.10.7-12; 3.22.7-8; *Ench.* 17); Paul rather refers to God's apportionment of *spiritual* gifts (see Rom 12:3-8, which uses *merid-zein* in the context of *charismata*), faculties conferred upon believers by the infusing of the Spirit (cf. 12:4-11). In this regard, believers ought to remain devoted to what is of chief importance, i.e., their calling to Christ, but they should do so in a way that is fitting to their gifts. Because gifting varies, what is fitting for one person may not be fitting for another.

Paul's orientation toward social status reflects a close parallel with the Stoic orientation toward "indifferents" (Deming 2003). With the Stoics, Paul supposes that, while some things are neither good nor evil in themselves, they may be either preferred or non-preferred, depending on the situation.

Paul illustrates with two examples. (1) The example of circumcision presents ethnic status as a matter of indifference. There is no reason why the circumcised should seek to reverse their circumcision, nor the uncircumcised seek to be circumcised. For the Corinthians, the example of circumcision was probably more illustrative than cautionary, for 1 Corinthians reveals no evidence of a dispute over the value of circumcision in the Corinthian church (cf. Galatians). Yet the possibility of reversing one's circumcision was real:

epispāsthai = literally, "to draw the skin [back] over." Several Jewish texts make reference to a reversal procedure in connection with Jews eager to participate in gymnasium activities (performed naked) without risking derision (1 Macc 1:14-15; Josephus, *Ant.* 12.241; cf. Josephus, *Ag. Ap.* 2.137; Philo, *Spec.* 1.2). In such cases, *epispasm* took place for social rather than for theological reasons. Paul's point is theological. Circumcision in itself is not a bad thing, and indeed (he says in Rom 2:25; 3:1-2), it could even be "profitable"; but above and beyond this the chief thing is that one should keep "God's commandments" (v. 19; Gal 5:6; Rom 10:12). By "commandments" Paul refers not to "all the prescriptions of the Law" (for circumcision itself was among the Law's prescriptions) but to what he elsewhere calls "the Law of Christ" or "the Law of the Spirit" (see discussion at 9:21). In short, one's status in Christ is more important than one's ethnic status.

Again echoing Stoic language, Paul concludes that circumcision and uncircumcision are—in a word—"nothing" (v. 19; cf. Epictetus, *Diatr.* 1.9.13; 3.16.15), i.e., are things of no inherent *value* (cf. "nothing" in 8:4; "not anything" in Gal 5:6; 6:15). The point is not that one should remain as they were—circumcised or uncircumcised—when they were called, but that one's status either way is a thing of lesser importance than one's calling. What *matters*, that in which they should *remain*, is their calling to the *gospel*. To paraphrase: "Do not elevate the importance of circumcision or uncircumcision, but of your calling. In *this* you should remain."

(2) Next Paul presents slave/free status as a matter of indifference (vv. 21-22). But is one state *preferable* to the other? The crucial sentence is elliptical (v. 21), resulting in some ambiguity. Paul says, "if you are able to become free, rather use (*mallon chrēsai*)," omitting the desired direct object. The implied object is either "your slave status" or "the opportunity for freedom" ("your calling" can be ruled out since calling is not a matter of social status). The evidence points compellingly in favor of "freedom." (a) The idea of freedom is more proximate in the context (*eleutheros*). (b) Use of the aorist infinitive grammaticalizes undefined aspect (making use of an *opportunity* for freedom) rather than continuous aspect (continually making the best of one's slave status). (c) Diachronic evidence suggests that the combination *ei kai* more often meant "if also" than "even if" (Caragounis 2006, 294–95). (d) The logical progression of the discourse requires that the conjunction "but" (*all*) be understood as posing a contrast between "not worrying" about being a slave on the one hand and the preferable state of becoming free on the other: "You were called as a *slave*: *do not worry* about it. *But* if you are indeed able to become *free*, become *free*." In other words, the contrast is between finding resignation in one's slave status and embracing

the preferred status of freedom. (e) Paul's use of modal language indicates an unmistakable bias toward freedom. "If you are *able* to become free" implies preference, not willy-nilly occurrence. (f) Contemporary literature attests to a universal preference for freedom. Although it was true that slavery could in cases be an opportunity for social advancement (Martin 1995), and by contrast that manumission could introduce new burdens (Epictetus, *Diatr.* 4.1.36-37), sources repeatedly present the notion that freedom was better than slavery as not just as the perspective of elites but a universal assumption ("freedom is the greatest of blessings, while slavery is the most shameful and wretched of states"; Dio Chrysostom, *Or.* 14.1; "no slave can be truly happy" and slavery is "the greatest of evils"; Philo, *Prob.* 41, 57). Considering also the perspective of slaves themselves, a comprehensive look at available evidence reveals ancient slavery to have been every bit as woeful as the sources suggest (Bradley 1984; 1994; 2011).

Paul drives home his point about status in society by reconfiguring social roles in relation to Christ (vv. 22-23): a believer in the role of slave in society is a "freed-person" of the Lord, and the believer of free status in society is a "slave" of Christ. The metaphorical use of slave language was common in the ancient world (see Philo, *Prob.* 18). While Paul's use of the metaphor may have originated from the OT idea of Israel as slaves of Yahweh, who had liberated them from slavery in Egypt (Ps 123:2; 143:12; Byron 2003), here he works within a Roman framework. In the Roman system of orders, one was born into "free" (*eleutheros*) status, but a "freed-person" (*apeleutheros*) was one who had once been a slave. The names of freed-persons were legally changed, so that the name of the redeemer appeared in the genitive case after the nomen—e.g., Marcus Ulpius *Augusti libertus* Erastus = Marcus Ulpius Erastus, *a freedman of Augustus.* In keeping with this convention, Paul identifies the believer as a "freed-person *of the Lord* (*Kyriou*)." While he here transfers slaves to the rank of freed-persons and the free to the rank of slaves, he does not mean to reverse the social hierarchy, putting slaves now *above* the free (*pace* Martin 1990, 66). His intention rather is to *relativize* social distinctions by showing that in Christ they come to nothing. Moreover, the freed-person/slave roles of believers together represent the two sides of a basic Pauline paradox, as both characterize all believers at the same time: Christ redeems believers *from* sin (*apeleutheros*) and thus they become his slaves (*douloi*).

Echoing an affirmation made earlier (6:19-20), Paul completes the slave metaphor by affirming that Christ has "purchased" those who believe. Ownership is exclusive. Having been rightfully "purchased" by Christ, believers ought not to be "slaves of humans." In this way, the slave metaphor comes to apply in both a vertical and a horizontal sense. In the vertical sense, it means that believers have been freed from someone or something to serve their new master Christ (in Rom 6:6-22, they have been liberated from sin, death, and the flesh to serve Christ and righteousness; see also Rom 8:2; Gal 4:3, 8). In the horizontal sense, it means that believers should not be slaves to the *values* of humanity, that is, the values of the *world.* Specifically, they should set value not on their social status but on their status in Christ. Thus, standing implicitly in the background is Paul's earlier discussion of the wisdom of "humans" in contrast to the wisdom of God (Fee 1987, 320): they should not be a slave to "human values," or "human wisdom."

The example of slave/free status, then, makes the same point as the example from circumcision/uncircumcision, with the difference that Paul now presents one state as being preferable to the other, namely the state of freedom. Together these two examples illustrate that social status is a matter of secondary importance to one's calling, even when one state is preferable to another.

Further Instructions about Marriage (7:25-40)

Paul returns now to the basic issue about which the Corinthians had queried (see 7:1). Verses 25-40 comprise a contained unit, opening and closing with the affirmation that it is better not to marry and that Paul's opinion on the matter is trustworthy (vv. 25-26, 40). Within are five subsections: the first discusses "virgins" (vv. 25-28), the second the necessity of disinvestment in worldly affairs during the present age (vv. 29-31), the third the distractions of marriage (vv. 32-35), the fourth the taking of "virgins" in marriage (vv. 36-38), and the fifth the remarriage of widows (v. 39), to which is appended a recapitulation of the chapter's main point (vv. 40).

7:25-28

The "now concerning" (*peri de*) formula recurs (cf. 7:1). It signals a change in topic (M. M. Mitchell 1989) but need not imply that the Corinthians had asked about "the virgins" specifically (v. 25). Here, as before (cf. 7:10), Paul states that he has not been the recipient of any "command" (*epitagē*) from the historical Jesus. While he characterizes his remarks instead as his "inclination" or "opinion" (*gnōmē*), the added qualification that he has been "shown mercy by the Lord" alludes to his commissioning as an apostle and thus bolsters his remarks with some authority (Rom 12:3; 15:15; 1 Cor 3:10; 15:10; Gal 2:9; Eph 3:2, 7, 8; Col 1:25; 1 Thess 2:4).

The "virgins" (*parthenoi*) to whom Paul refers are young women. While the same term is used in Rev 14:4 with reference to men, the Greek of Revelation is unidiomatic, and the term appears several times here with the feminine article (vv. 28, 34, 36, 37, 38), never with the masculine. The content of Paul's pronouncement shifts to a more neutral term further down: "I think . . . that it is good for a *person* (*anthrōpos*) to be thus" (v. 26). However, the shift to *anthrōpos* does not equate the *parthenos* with the *anthrōpos*, but reflects an a posteriori argument that establishes a general principle, applicable to any "person," starting from the *example* of the "virgins." In this regard, the adverb *houtōs* serves an anaphoric purpose, pointing back to "the virgins." Consequently, "it is good for a person to be *thus*" = "it is good for a person to be *like the virgins.*" In other words, just as the virgins should remain thus (i.e., abstinent), so people in general should remain thus. In v. 27 Paul extends this advice specifically to unmarried men, but with the necessary proviso that men already married should not seek a divorce.

As before, Paul qualifies his instructions. Although marriage is less than ideal, it is (usually) better to remain married than to divorce (v. 27; cf. 7:15-16), and although it is "good for a person" to remain like the virgins, it is not sinful to marry (v. 28).

Here Paul begins to offer justification for his preference of celibacy (vv. 7, 8). Celibacy is better (1) because of the present "crisis" (*enestōsan anagkēn*) and (2) because those who marry will suffer "distress" in the flesh (*thlipsin . . . tēi sarki*). Both the "crisis" and the "distress" could be understood in relation to the so-called "eschatological woes" described in the Gospels (cf. Mark 13:20; Luke 21:3). However, Paul refers here not to the "*coming* crisis" but to the "*present* crisis" (so always, *enistēmi* in Paul: Rom 8:38; 1 Cor 3:22; Gal 1:4; 2 Thess 2:2; so also Heb 9:9; 3 Macc 1:16; 2 Tim 3:1), and "crisis" (*anagkē*) refers specifically to eschatological pressure only in Luke 21:3, against the broader meaning attested in multiple texts (Rom 13:5; 1 Cor 7:37; 9:16; 2 Cor 6:4; 9:7; 12:10; 1 Thess 3:7). Moreover, while "distress" (*thlipsis*) is eschatological in Rev 7:14 (cf. 4 Ezra 5:1-13; 6:13-24; 9:1-23; 2 Bar. 25:1-4; 27:1-15; 67:1-9; Jub. 23:22-32), Jewish texts often maintain that God would *protect* the righteous in the time of affliction (Sib. Or. 3.702-7; cf. 2 Bar. 6:25; 7:27; 13:24-26; 29:2; 40:1-4; 71:1), and Paul himself elsewhere refers to general rather than specifically eschatological "distress" (1 Thess 3:7; 2 Cor 6:4).

On the other hand, present troubles cannot be neatly separated from eschatological ones. The ages overlap. The "present form of this world is passing away" (v. 31). While still feeling the effects of "this age" (1:20; 2:6, 8; 3:18), believers are already living in the last days (v. 29).

What, then, is the "present crisis" and "distress"? It is one's living in the "present evil age" (Gal 1:4), a time in which humanity lives vulnerable to disease, pain, and death. In this context it is wisest to reduce human vulnerability as much as possible. The fittingness of marriage is impugned since marriage contributes further to human vulnerability by introducing additional, and unnecessary, perils: "those that threaten one's spouse, and those entailed in childbirth (with its enormous rate of mortality), and in the care of highly vulnerable children" (Barclay 2016, 264). Of such afflictions Paul wishes to "spare" his audience.

7:29-31

A new paragraph expounds on the preceding remarks (vv. 25-28): "Now, I am saying *this* (*touto*)." Specifically, these remarks expound not on the present "crisis" or "distress" but on Paul's justification for his advice to remain unmarried.

It is good not to marry because "the time is short (*ho kairos sunestalmenos estin*)." While this affirmation could allude to Jesus' saying that the period of eschatological woes would be curtailed (Mark 13:20, using *kolobaō*), it more likely refers to the shortness of time remaining for the "present shape of the world" (v. 31)—a common theme in Jewish apocalyptic literature (LAB 19:13; 2 Bar. 67:1-9; 4 Ezra 4:26-28; 14:11-12). It is not, then, that judgment looms large, but that time is a limited commodity. In this brief period, believers must invest their time selectively, pursuing the things that matter most. One is not to invest in things that are transient. Buying and selling are temporary investments. Pleasure is fleeting. Marriages, too, will end shortly.

Paul grounds his advice in the portentous declaration that the "present shape of the world is passing away" (v. 31). This declaration finds loose parallel in both Jewish and non-Jewish literature. Isaiah foretold the coming of a "new heaven and new earth," together with a "new Jerusalem" (65:17-25). Later Jewish texts follow in this trajectory (1 En. 91:16; LAB 3:10; 16:3; Jub. 1:29; 4:26; 4 Ezra 7:112-115; 44:11-12; 74:1-4), many of them adding that the present world would be destroyed (1 En. 91:16; Sib. Or. 3.53-54, 80-89; 2 Bar. 44:9; 85:10; cf. 4 Ezra 40:1-4; 44:9-12). The Testament of Job, similar to Paul, emphasizes that one's mind should be focused on the "upper world" (33:3) since the present world is "passing away" (33:4).

Belief that the world would come to an end was not universal in the Greco-Roman world. Among the philosophical schools, some believed that the world was uncreated and indestructible (Aristotle), others that it was created but indestructible (Plato), and others that it was both created and destructible (the Stoics and the Epicureans). Philo, a Hellenistic Jew, adopted Plato's view that the world indeed would have no end (Philo, *On the Eternity of the World*). Among those who foresaw an end to the world, the Stoics posited that its destruction would come through a great conflagration (Seneca, *Marc.* 21.2; 26.6-7; *Ep.* 71.13), a view shared in some Jewish and Christian texts (Sib. Or. 3.80-89; 2 Pet 3:7-12; cf. 1QH[a] XI.26-36). Destruction would follow with cosmic regeneration, and so the cycle would recur throughout all eternity (Marcus Aurelius, *Med.* 9.28).

Paul's perspective most resembles that of Jewish apocalyptic texts in the mold of 4 Ezra, 2 Baruch, and 1 Enoch. The present world would come to an end and creation would be renewed (Rom 8:19-23). Paul gives no indication that the world would end by fire, and no indication that a cycle of cosmic destruction and regeneration would repeat itself. He does not address the world's passing away with philosophical precision either here or elsewhere. However, he seems to have conceived of its passing as having both a sociopolitical and an anthropological-cosmic dimension. In its sociopolitical dimension, the world's passing entailed the triumph of Christ over all other powers and the reestablishment of God's single and sovereign lordship over creation. In its anthropological-cosmic dimension, it entailed the transformation of the corruptible body into an incorruptible one and the profusion of God into all of creation. On these things Paul will elaborate later (15:20-49).

7:32-35

Time is short. Believers ought to maximize attention to things of ultimate significance. Marriage does not rank among these things. The married are distracted by matters pertaining to their spouse. Unmarried people are free to devote themselves to matters pertaining to the Lord.

With the Greek philosophers, Paul recognized that life confronted people with competing goods, which needed to be ordered appropriately. The Stoics provide a close (but not exact) parallel to Paul's perspective. For the Stoics, one's highest duty was to God, followed by either duty to country or duty to parents (Epictetus, *Diatr.* 3.24.60; Hierocles/Stobaeus, *Anth.* 2.9.7; 3.39.34; cf. Epictetus, *Diatr.* 4.1.159). In all things virtue was the highest and, indeed, the only good. This was the Stoic solution to the knot of competing goods. Once one recognized the supreme good, all other goods (so-called) became infinitely puny in comparison and could be regarded with a sense of detachment.

Seneca applied this framework to the observation that time was "short." On the scale of infinite time, all events lost their individual significance, being but a flash in comparison with eternity and mundane in their similarity to countless similar occurrences. Across time, Fortune has brought each and every thing to an end, and will continue to do so:

> A rich city has been laid in ashes, the jewel of the provinces, counted as one of them and yet not included with them; rich though it was, nevertheless it was set upon a single hill, and that not very large in extent. But of all those cities, of whose magnificence and grandeur you hear to-day, the very traces will be blotted out by time. (Seneca, *Ep.* 91.10; cf. Marcus Aurelius, *Med.* 7.48-49)

This was the Stoics' cosmic basis for the ethical principle of indifference toward external "goods." All but the highest reality, the rational principle/the Logos/God/etc. will perish. All other things are ephemeral. And yet people invest their time in paltry pursuits, and between these things their attention is divided. Seneca observes, "[E]verybody agrees that no one pursuit can be successfully followed by a man who is busied with many things . . . since the mind, when its interests are divided, takes in nothing very deeply but rejects everything that is, as it were, crammed into it" (*Brev.* 7.3; cf. *Brev.* 10.6). Out of this framework came the Stoic debate about the fittingness of marriage. Some Stoics recognized marriage as beneficial for some people, but many regarded it as a source of "anxiety" and "distraction" from the pursuit of philosophy (Balch 1983).

Paul's advice on life in the interim is analogous to the Stoic view in several respects: in his ordering of higher and lower priorities, in his recognition of the "shortness of time" during which these goods compete for attention, and in his recognition that marriage itself could be a source of anxiety and distraction, "dividing" one's attention (vv. 32-34). On the other hand, Paul refrains from advising Stoic *detachment*. Rather, he advises selective "*investment*" of attention (Barclay 2016). Ordinary activities continue, but one's investment in them should diminish. Although he can still acknowledge marriage as "good" (see 7:37, 38), Paul singles out marriage specifically as something that adds unnecessarily to the afflictions of the present age, at a time when a new age, of higher importance, has already dawned.

7:36-38

Paul returns to the person of the "virgin (*parthenos*)" (cf. vv. 25-28), but this time he takes interest in "someone (*tis*)" other than the virgin herself. Although this "someone" could be the virgin's father, weighing his decision to marry her off (KJV, NASB), the passage as a whole makes better sense if this "someone" is the virgin's betrothed, faced with the decision to take her in marriage or to leave her a virgin; i.e., the betrothed is faced with the decision whether to marry.

Paul treats the issue with the same flexibility with which he treated the other marital issues. In certain instances, marriage may be the most appropriate option (v. 36). If the man thinks that he is "acting disgracefully" (*aschēmonein*) toward his betrothed in the event that he is feeling "sexually charged" (*hyperakmos*), and thus marriage seems the best option, he should marry, and he does not compromise morality in doing so. The situation resembles that seen in v. 9: marriage may be the optimal solution to uncontrollable passion. On the other hand, if a man is *free* of "sexual impulses (*anagkēn*)" (for this sense of *anagkē*, see Winter 1998, 85n.62) and is able to make his resolution on the basis of the free conviction of his heart (v. 37), a man does well in refraining from marriage (vv. 37-38).

Verse 38 aptly summarizes the chapter. Here Paul reaffirms the higher advantage of celibacy: in this case, "The one who does not marry will do *better*." Yet he diminishes the evaluative contrast between marriage and celibacy by avoiding an adversative conjunction (*alla, de*) and using instead a coordinate construction that sets the two contingencies in simple juxtaposition: "[It is true] both (*kai*) that the one who marries his virgin does well (*kalōs*) and (*kai*) that the one who does not marry does better (*kreisson*)." In this way, Paul at last acknowledges marriage as a "good" thing (*kalōs*) but remains firm in his conviction that it is usually not preferred.

7:39-40

The final verses of the chapter follow somewhat disjointedly from what precedes. Addressing the obligations of "a woman" as a representative of a class, Paul presents marriage as an indissoluble bond, to be broken only by death (cf. Rom 7:1-6). Despite the abruptness of the transition, this section fits intelligibly as a complement to vv. 36-38, in which Paul addressed men, thus completing again the reciprocal pattern of instruction that has characterized the chapter (7:2, 3, 4, 12, 13-14, 16, 32, 34).

Here Paul reaffirms a strong stance against divorce, underlining again that the married person should not divorce (cf. vv. 10-11); but here he also fills in areas previously left unaddressed. First, while divorce is prohibited or should be mended by reconciliation (vv. 10, 11), a woman's remarriage is permissible if her husband passes away. Second, although the desire of the "virgin" appeared to play no role in the event of marriage in vv. 36-38, here the woman presumably possesses freedom ("she is free") to make a decision about *re*marriage. Third, while believers are permitted to continue in marriage with nonbelievers (vv. 12-16), a widowed woman, should she decide to remarry, ought to marry a believer (i.e., one "in the Lord").

Despite its application specifically to women considering remarriage, v. 40 provides a fitting conclusion to the chapter, driving home the point that celibacy is preferable to marriage: "But in my judgment she is more blessed if she remains as she is [And I think that celibacy is better!]. And I think that I too have the Spirit of God." Although Paul characterizes his advice only as a personal "judgment/opinion" (*gnōmē*), he adds that it is also the opinion of one who has the Holy Spirit. With this remark he not only reinforces his instructions with stronger backing but obliquely resumes his attack on the self-ascribed "spiritual" people, who allege themselves to be spiritually exceptional.

Conclusion

Paul's answer to the Corinthians' query about marriage suggests that the issue was too complex to be settled in the form of a slogan (7:1b). Qualifying the ascetics' position, Paul articulates a flexible position in which celibacy is declared to be preferable to marriage (vv. 7, 8, 26, 38, 40), but marriage remains acceptable nonetheless (vv. 2, 3-5, 9, 36); divorce is forbidden in general (vv. 10-11) but is in some cases an admissible option (vv. 15-16); and remarriage is not preferred (v. 11), but one is free to pursue it should one desire (v. 39). With similar balance, Paul affirms that his instructions are nonbinding (vv. 10-12, 25-26, 40) while also carrying the weight of authority (vv. 25, 40).

Paul's handling of the marriage question reveals that he viewed marital status as a matter of indifference analogous to circumcised/uncircumcised or slave/free status. While he had his preferences, he refused to lay down inflexible prescriptions on such matters. Instead, he offered the Corinthians a theological framework that on the one hand allowed freedom to the individual to decide as seemed best suited to their gifting and on the other hand promoted the preferableness of certain kinds of social status. Despite his flexibility, Paul also underscored both the need to reduce challenges that made one's commitment to the gospel more difficult and the shortness of time remaining before Christ's return, and thus urged believers in the interim to prioritize their calling to Christ over social commitments.

God and Idols

1 Corinthians 8:1–11:1

Forming a discrete unit within the letter, 1 Cor 8:1–11:1 consists of a prolonged discussion about the ethical implications of eating "idol-meat" (*eidōlothūta*). While this unit echoes several of the themes discussed earlier (freedom, food, unity, imitation), its principal theme reprises the earlier theme of "wisdom" now under the name of "knowledge."

Opening with the theme of idol-meat in 8:1-13, the unit then carries into a brief interruption presenting relevant examples for the Corinthians (9:1-23, 24-27; 10:1-13), before resuming discussion of eating in 10:14–11:1. Thus the discussion falls into a concentric pattern (Talbert 2002, 73; citing Collins 1963, 582):

A Eating meat sacrificed to idols (8:1-13)
  B The example of Paul (9:1-23)
  B' The examples of Paul and Israel on self-control (9:24-27; 10:1-13)
A' Eating meat sacrificed to idols (10:14–11:1)

Interpretation of this section is fraught with difficulties. First, it is unclear whether and at what points in 8:1-13 Paul could be quoting Corinthian slogans. Second, Paul addresses more than one set of circumstances surrounding the eating of idol-meat in 8:1-13 and 10:14–11:1—eating at the "table of demons" (10:14-22; cf. "reclining in an idol's temple," 8:10), eating idol-meat sold in the marketplace (10:25), and eating idol-meat served at private dinners (10:27-30)—and it is not clear how they all relate. Third, Paul appears to express conflicting views on the permissibility of eating idol-meat (esp. 8:9-13; 10:14-22; 10:23–11:1).

Believers and Food Dedicated to Idols (8:1-13)

The *peri de* ("now concerning") formula again signals a change in topic (cf. 7:1; 7:25): "Now concerning *the things sacrificed to idols* (= idol-meat)."

This introduces the general topic of discussion treated front and center in 8:1-13 and 10:14–11:1 and indirectly in 9:1–10:13.

Chapter 8 may contain as many as five Corinthian slogans: 8:1b; 8:4; 8:5a, 6; 8:8a-b. The slogans reveal that some of the Corinthians claim to have a kind of "knowledge" that justifies eating idol-meat; those who abstain they denigrate as "weak" in mind (cf. Rom 14:1-12, where Paul discusses the "strong" and the "weak"). Those responsible for the slogans not only regard the eating of idol-meat as a matter of indifference but heedlessly flout the principles of those whose scruples counsel avoidance of such things. Paul responds that in this way such people elevate pretensions of knowledge above the principles of love and unity.

8:1-6

The issue of idol-meat could have been among the subjects broached in the Corinthians' letter to Paul ("now concerning *the* idol-meat" = ". . . the idol-meat [that you spoke of?]"). The word "idol-meat" (*eidōlothūta*) occurs nowhere in the sources prior to 1 Corinthians, but it betrays a distinctly Jewish and Christian perspective (4 Macc 5:2; Sib. Or. 2.96; Acts 15:29; 21:25; Rev 2:14, 20). From the perspective of the "knowledgeable," such meat was innocuous, since idols were indeed "nothing" (8:4) and there was no God but "one" (8:6).

Paul unfolds the Corinthian perspective and his own response in a series of quotations and rebuttals. The first slogan comes in 8:1b: "We know that we all have knowledge." While Paul does not explicitly attribute the words to the Corinthians, the emphasis here on knowledge (cf. wisdom in 1:18–3:23), the tacit two-tier perspective on spiritual status (cf. 2:6–3:3), and Paul's swift rebuttal (vv. 2-3, 7) reveal that they were indeed the source. Paul responds immediately by contrasting knowledge with love (8:1c), though it is not "knowledge" itself that he opposes (cf. Rom 15:14; 1 Cor 1:5; 12:8; 14:6; Phil 3:8) but its particular expression among those who claimed it in Corinth. Their "knowledge" was self-serving, enlarging the self; love serves others, building up (or enlarging) the community (v. 1cd).

Verses 2 and 3 stand structurally parallel, further elaborating the antithesis. Echoing Socrates' maxim that the beginning of wisdom is in knowing that you know nothing (Plato, *Resp.* 354C; *Charm.* 175A-B; *Lys.* 222D-E; *Prot.* 361A-B; Epictetus, *Ench.* 46.2) and his own earlier comment that "if anyone thinks that he is a wise man, he must become a fool in order that he may become wise" (3:18), Paul now suggests that "if anyone thinks that he *knows* something, he does not yet know as he *ought* to know" (v. 2). Despite the UBS[5]/NA[28] reading of v. 3, there are strong intrinsic and transcriptional grounds for preferring the reading of 𝔓⁴⁶ (see Letteney 2016): "If anyone loves, this person is known." The meaning is, "if anyone loves (people), this person is known (by God)" (cf. 13:12; Gal 4:9). That this is about love for other people is suggested both by the context (esp. vv. 7-13) and by the fact that Paul rarely talks about humanity's love for God (Rom 8:28 may be the only exception). The condition is of the evidence-inference type: a person can be identified as one known by God if that person loves. The shift from the human to God as the knowing agent slightly disrupts the symmetry, but it throws into relief Paul's relentless emphasis in this letter on divine initiative (1:5, 7, 28-31; 3:10, 21-23; 4:7). Taken together, vv. 2-3 continue the antithesis between knowing and loving, thus complementing v. 1cd.

> If anyone thinks that he *knows*, he does not yet know as he ought to know (v. 2).
> If anyone *loves* (people), this person is known (by God) (v. 3).

It is not, then, a matter of either knowing or loving, but of knowing truly (or of belonging to God) only when one loves (cf. 13:2).

Verse 4 resumes the position set forth in v. 1 (cf. Fotopoulos 2005, 624–25):

> We know that we all have knowledge. . . [v. 1]
> Concerning the food of idol-sacrifices, therefore (*oun*), we know that . . . [v. 4].

And what the knowledgeable claim to know is that
> "an idol in the world is nothing"
> "there is no God except one"

Verses 5 and 6 continue the quotation and elaborate on the singular existence of God and God's responsibility for all that is. Verse 5 refers rather dismissively to other "gods," of which popular thinking recognized a great many. The reference to gods "in heaven and on earth" may intend to distinguish between the gods of the celestial sphere on the one hand and deified humans on the other. Representations of these gods and monuments in their honor were ubiquitous in the environment. Archaeological evidence has survived of more than two dozen temples, altars, and shrines in Corinth dated to the Roman era (see *IKorinthKent* 50-68 for the Latin inscriptions; cf. Pausanias, *Descr.* 2.2-3.1). Inscriptions dedicated to the "divine" emperors (gods "on earth") were to be found in cities all over the empire, including

Roman Corinth (e.g., "to the divine Julius Caesar," *IKorinthKent* 50; "to the divine Augustus," *IKorinthKent* 51).

Verse 6 bears the stamp of an early Christian creed (cf. Eph 4:6). In form, it resembles the so-called "prepositional formulas" used to describe God in Greek philosophical texts (Marcus Aurelius, *Med.* 4.23; cf. Rom 11:36; 1 Cor 11:12; McFarland 2017). Nonetheless, the formula has a distinctly Christian character, expressing in parallel form the common responsibility of "one God the Father" and "one Lord Jesus Christ" for the protological origins of the cosmos ("from . . . through") and for the power that sustains existence ("in . . . through"). Conceptually, the formula evokes contemporary Jewish traditions that attributed creative power to God's "Wisdom," "Word," or "Powers" (see 1:18-25); thus Paul elevates Jesus to the level of divinity but without losing a distinction between Jesus and God "the Father" (Kugler 2020).

The quotations of vv. 5-6 articulate views that Paul cannot have disagreed with outright, and it is not inconceivable that he was their original source. Derision of idols as inert matter created by human hands was common-place in Jewish tradition (Isa 44:9-20; Jer 10; Hab 2:18-19; Wis 13:10–14:1; the Epistle of Jeremiah; Bel and the Dragon; Let. Aris. 135–138; Apoc. Ab. 3:8–4:6). Moreover, it was one of the fundamental creeds of Jewish tradition that there was "one" God (drawn from Deut 6:4-6), and this affirmation appears in Paul's earliest letters to have comprised one of the rudimentary elements of his teaching to Gentiles (1 Thess 1:9-10; Gal 3:20; cf. Rom 3:30). Even if the creedal material in v. 6 did not originate with Paul, it was almost certainly from him that the Corinthians received it.

Yet the Corinthians appear to have drawn inferences from these doctrines to which Paul took exception. As he continues, he suggests (1) that "knowledge" about what an idol really is does not in itself legitimate eating idol-meat and (2) that the Corinthians have been too quick to dismiss the existence of other "gods." Indeed, parts *a* and *b* of v. 5 stand in some tension, and the latter may represent Paul's own insertion, introduced into the quotation as a parenthetical aside and caveat:

> for if indeed there are entities called gods in heaven and on earth (v. 5a)
> (as indeed *many* gods and *many* lords there *are*). (v. 5b)

Many Jews were amenable to the designation "gods" in reference to other spiritual powers (Philo, *Somn.* 1.229; *Opif.* 27; *Spec.* 1.13ff; Ps.-Phoc. §70-75), although in using the term they meant it in a qualitatively distinct way from its normative usage in Judaism. Paul himself acknowledged the existence of a whole host of evil powers ("Satan," "Beliar," "elements," "principalities") and could even refer to Satan as the "*god* of this age" (2 Cor 4:4). Shortly, he will also acknowledge the existence of "demons" (1 Cor 10:20-21).

8:7-13

The self-congratulatory discourse of the enlightened Corinthians crashes to an abrupt end as Paul drops in the way a strong adversative (*all'*): "But *not all* have this knowledge" (v. 7a). Paul now distinguishes between two kinds of people, "you who have knowledge" (v. 10) and the "weak" (vv. 7, 9, 10, 11, 12). Again the distinction probably originated with the Corinthians, as it seems to be analogous to the distinctions posed earlier between the "wise" and the "foolish" (esp. 3:18), the "perfect" and the "immature" (cf. 2:6; 3:1), and the "spiritual" and the "unspiritual" (2:15-16). While it seems possible to take the language of "weakness" in a socioeconomic sense (Theissen 1975; Thiselton 2000, 644), both the present context and the nature of the analogous pairs reveal that this language is primarily noetic. The knowledgeable proclaim license to eat idol-meat, understanding that "an idol is nothing." The "weak," the knowledgeable believe, lack this knowledge and thus full understanding of the freedom that they have in Christ.

The most likely background for these views is found in Stoicism. For the Stoics, ignorance was the result of "weakness" of mind (*SVF* 3.177, 473, 548). "Weakness" constituted a lapse in the reasoning faculties, i.e., capitulation to irrational impulses called "passions." Among the passions, "fear" was defined as "an irrational shrinking [aversion] or avoidance of an expected danger" (LS 65B [Long and Sedley 1987, 412]). This is precisely the problem that the "knowledgeable" see in the others. Some, in their scruples to avoid that which they perceive to be pernicious, have given in to "weakness" of mind, succumbing to the passion of "fear" and thus failing to open their eyes to the enlightened position demanded by reason, namely that an idol is "nothing."

That the knowledgeable viewed idol-meat with indifference is demonstrated by yet another Corinthian slogan, cited in v. 8: "Food will not bring us close to God. We are no worse off if we do not eat, and no better off if we do." Presentation "to God" refers to the event of final judgment. The second part of the slogan is more puzzling, because it reverses the situation present in the church (the knowledgeable *do* eat but do not think that in this way they are *worse off*; cf. Murphy-O'Connor 1979). Yet the same underlying principle applies: diet will make no difference before God's judgment seat.

It is possible that the slogan originated with Paul, for it exhibits a close parallel to Paul's view on circumcision: if one does *not* circumcise he is no worse off, and if one circumcises he fares no better (cf. 7:19; Gal 5:6; 6:15).

Yet Paul's immediate caveat again suggests that the Corinthians have veered off track: "*But* (*de*) beware lest that freedom of yours become a stumbling block to the weak" (v. 9). The words "that freedom *of yours*" suggest that the knowledgeable themselves appealed to "freedom" (*exousia*) in the matter. The word *exousia* evokes the language of the slogan cited earlier, "all things are permissible (*exestin*) for me" (6:12a, c), which Paul had cited in association with another slogan that expressed indifference toward food (6:13a, b).

The Corinthians' failure as Paul saw it was that they had set their personal "rights" above the well-being of others. In focusing on the individual they neglected the needs of the community. The irony is that the very thing they treated with indifference became the occasion of another person's destruction (v. 11; cf. Rom 14:15). In their effort to "build up" the weak (to see it their way), they actually tore them down. How so? By eating idol-meat they induced those who refused to do so to follow them. But to follow them was to act against conscience and, in that way, *intentionally* to fall back into idolatry by eating idol-meat *as* idol-meat (cf. v. 7). The consequence was not only their moral collapse but their fatal ruin (cf. 10:9-10; 15:18; Rom 14:20-21). Paul underscores the tragic irony of the situation by referring to the weak victim as a "brother" (v. 11) and the enormity of the crime by equating the act with sin "against *Christ*" (v. 12), so closely were believers identified with him. Such were the consequences, all in the interest of their "knowledge."

Having clarified the stakes, Paul concludes by advocating an extreme level of accommodation to the weak: "If meat is a cause of their falling, I will never eat meat until all eternity, so that I may not cause one of them to fall" (v. 13). Paul's proposal is laced with hyperbole (not just "idol-meat" but "meat" generally; not just in certain settings but "never" and into perpetuity), so as to underscore the seriousness of the matter. Although Paul lays these restrictions particularly upon himself, in doing so he offers himself as an example, thus reprising a theme encountered repeatedly in 1 Corinthians and providing a transition into the extended discussion of his personal example in the chapter that follows.

Paul's Use of Freedom (9:1-23)

With the final verse of the previous chapter as his point of departure (8:13), Paul launches into a prolonged exposition of his personal example. Appeal to "examples" (*paradeigmata/exempla*) was a subtler approach to parenesis than the so-called "bold speech" (*parrhēsia/licentia*). Bold speech confronted the audience head-on, calling them to correction through censure (Pseudo-Cicero, *Rhet. her.* 4.48; Quintilian, *Inst.* 9.2.27). Examples offered a more indirect approach to confrontation, correcting the audience by presenting a model to which they do not conform.

Here Paul depicts himself as one who has freedom—in fact more freedom than others—but who uses that freedom to serve others. This section divides into five paragraphs:

9:1-3. Paul establishes his freedom as an apostle.

9:4-12a. Paul cites three areas in which he has freedom as an apostle.

9:12b-14. Paul establishes and waives his apostolic rights.

9:15-18. Paul again waives his apostolic rights.

9:19-23. Paul expresses his freedom as slavery.

This section does not function as a real "defense," for Paul and the Corinthians presumably agree on the main point (that ministers have a right to receive pay). Rather, Paul's purpose is to offer himself as an example for *imitation*, where his example is applicable especially to the question of eating idol-meat and the principle of accommodation to the "weak" (8:1-13). In this sense, the unit may be regarded as a contrivance, or "mock defense" (Willis 1985). If Paul has selected an area of real concern as the focus of his illustration (his freedom to receive pay), that purpose is ancillary to the purpose of the chapter as it relates to the surrounding discussion.

9:1-3

Paul begins with a series of four rhetorical questions, each expecting the answer Yes (v. 1). The first question indicates that Paul, too, has freedom. The second grounds Paul's freedom in the fact that he is an apostle. The third and fourth questions are restatements of the second, defining apostleship in terms of (a) Paul's having seen the Lord and (b) his activity as a founder of believing communities. Verse 2 continues in the vein of the final question, highlighting the very existence of the Corinthian community as proof of Paul's apostleship. In affirming his apostleship, Paul's purpose is less to respond to specific doubts about his credentials (where "If I am not an apostle *to others*" means "Others doubt my apostleship") than to emphasize his unique *relationship* with the Corinthians as constitutive of his status as an apostle ("I am *to you*" = "I was *sent out* [*apostolos*] to *you*, not to others. *You* are the *seal* [proof] of my apostleship").

Despite the segmentation decision of the UBS[5]/NA[28], v. 3 ("This is my defense to those who would examine me," NRSV) belongs not as the first sentence of the next paragraph but as the conclusion to this one. Hence, the "defense" points not ahead to vv. 4 and following but back to what immediately precedes: the proof of his apostleship is the very existence of the

Corinthian church. Several items support this conclusion. First, vv. 4-12a in no way constitute a "defense" of Paul's practices. Paul argues not *for* the right but *from* the right—which the Corinthians apparently already agree is legitimate—to a particular use of rights. Conversely, it makes good sense to understand Paul's "defense" with reference to what precedes: to any who evaluate him negatively he can point to the concrete existence of the Corinthian church as evidence of his apostolic validity. Second, use of the emphatic pronoun in v. 3 (*eme*) is best explained as a signal back to the pronoun in v. 2 (*mou*): "For it is you who are the seal of *my* (*mou*) apostleship. *This* is (or *you* are) my defense to those who judge *me* (*eme*)." Third, a paragraph break between vv. 3 and 4 creates better symmetry between the adjacent units, so that v. 1 opens a paragraph with three rhetorical questions introduced by *ouk/ouchi*, and vv. 4-5 open a paragraph with three rhetorical questions introduced by *mē*.

9:4-12a

The question whether Paul is defending himself against real charges has to take this into account: that he alludes to *three* areas in which he has freedom, not one, and that there seems to have been no controversy about the first two of them: (1) He is free "to eat and drink" (v. 4). (2) He is free to take a wife along with him (v. 5). (3) He is free to take pay for his ministry (vv. 6-18).

The first question alludes to the immediately relevant issue of eating idol-meat (8:1-13). The second alludes to Paul's *free* choice of celibacy (cf. 7:7, 8), his freedom being shown by the fact that others, including the "rest of the apostles and the brothers of Jesus and Cephas," took wives along with them (the "rest of the apostles" probably refers to a group including but not limited to the Twelve; cf. 1 Thess 2:7; Phil 2:25; Rom 16:7; 1 Cor 15:5, 7).

The third question shares no obvious ties with the rest of the letter. While all three questions are spoken in the first person plural ("do *we* not have . . . do *we* not have . . . do *we* not have . . ."), only in the third question does Paul specify his company: " . . . or do only *I and Barnabas . . . .*" Paul and Barnabas worked together closely in their missionary endeavors, having been commissioned together by the church at Antioch to travel west (Acts 13:1–14:28). Apparently they shared the same policy about work: they would not take pay for their ministry.

Yet, Paul insists, they possessed the right to do so. Here follows a battery of "proofs." First, Paul asks a series of leading rhetorical questions, centering on examples from everyday life: doesn't the soldier have a right to wages for his services, the planter a right to his produce, and the shepherd a right to the milk of his flock (v. 7; cf. Seneca, *Ep.* 109.8)? Second, Paul appeals to the Law, construed in its allegorical sense. Citing Deut 25:4, "You shall not muzzle an ox while it is treading out the grain," Paul denies the text's literal meaning ("Surely God doesn't care about oxen?!") and muses that the text actually speaks "*entirely* for *our* sake" (*pantōs di' hēmas*). That is, God provides primarily with humanity in mind, not beasts (Cicero, *Nat. d.* 2.156; Philo, *Spec.* 260). Here, as throughout the paragraph (esp. vv. 4-6, 11), the first person plural refers to the apostles, but especially to Paul and Barnabas. As laborers they ("we"), like oxen, should expect ("hope for") a share of the harvest. Verse 11 then comes not as a new argument but as an elaboration of the allegorical interpretation just proposed: the one who has sown the gospel ("spiritual things") has a right to harvest pay ("material things") from his work (cf. Rom 15:27).

The final sentence of the paragraph (v. 12a) presents several interpretive challenges. Who are the "others" (*alloi*)? What does Paul mean by "right" (*exousia*)? And whose "right" is it? To take "others" as an implicit reference specifically to Apollos is unwarranted. In context, the reference is much wider: it is *all* missionaries. Despite the rendering of most modern translations, the meaning is not that others share a "right *over*" them (NKJV; NASB; cf. "rightful claim on," ESV), for the Greek word order rules this out (*tēs hymōn exousias*, whereas the genitive of subordination never precedes but always follows the head noun in the NT). Rather, the "right" belongs to the Corinthians themselves, *along with* those who "share" in it; in other words, "You have 'right.' Others share that thing you call 'right.'" In sum, "If others share that thing you call 'right,' do I and Barnabas not, in this matter, have still greater 'right,' that is, a right to take pay for our ministry?"

9:12b-14

After reviewing the arguments that substantiate pay (to which the Corinthians already assent), Paul now takes an unexpected turn. Referring back to his initial visit to Corinth, he states, "But (*all'*) we did not make *use* of this right." Why? Because the appearance that he was engaging in mercenary practice would pose a hindrance to the advancement of the "gospel of Christ" (cf. Rom 15:19; 2 Cor 9:13; 1 Thess 3:2).

The content of vv. 13-18 mirrors that of vv. 7-12c: the earlier analogies of the soldier, the farmer, and the shepherd are now paralleled in the analogy of temple servants (Num 18:8ff; Deut 18:1-5), and the authority of the Law is now paralleled with the teaching of the historical Jesus. It is a sign of great resolve that, even though Jesus himself instructed missionaries to take provisions from those to whom they ministered (Matt 10:10//Luke 10:4-8; cf. *Did.* 13:1-2), Paul did not exploit his right to support. That he instead supported himself through manual labor is attested by the witness of both Acts and his own letters (Acts 8:3; 1 Thess 2:9; cf. 2 Cor 11:7, 9; 12:13; 2 Thess 3:8; but see the exception in Phil 4:15-19). While his decision was motivated partly by a desire not to "burden" anyone (2 Cor 11:9; 12:13-16; 1 Thess 2:9), it was also intended to preclude any perception that he peddled his message for personal gain ("so as not to impose any obstacle to the gospel of Christ," v. 12d; cf. 1 Thess 2:5-6).

Among ancient philosophers, the question whether teachers ought to take pay for their instruction was a topic of enduring debate. While some argued that this was a legitimate means of livelihood (said of Socrates, Zeno, Cleanthes, and Chrysippus in Quintilian, *Inst.* 12.7.9; of Epicurus in Diogenes Laertius, *Vit. phil.* 10.120), others considered this to be the very definition of sophistry (cf. Aristotle, *Eth. nic.* 9.1.7; Philo, *Mos.* 1.24; Diogenes Laertius, *Vit. phil.* 7.188; Arius Didymus, *Epit.* 11m). Paul's choice to support himself through manual labor was exceptional, though among the philosophers this practice was not unparalleled (Musonius Rufus, *Diatr.* 11). By contrast, traveling orators and street-corner philosophers who pocketed rewards for their speeches or advice were familiar characters throughout the empire, and such figures were often chastised as hucksters greedy for gain (see, e.g., Lucian, *Peregr.* 15-16). Paul, as an itinerant preacher of what many probably perceived to be a "philosophy" (see Acts 17:16-21), recognized the potential for others to fit him into the same category, and he was apparently intent on avoiding the comparison.

9:15-18

Paul now retraces his earlier remarks. Verse 15a repeats the assertion of v. 12b, but now using the perfect tense: "As I *did not* exploit this right (when I was among you) . . . , I (still) *have not* exploited this right." Paul proceeds to cast himself in the role of the Stoic wise man (Malherbe 1994). Just as the wise man yielded willingly to circumstances assigned to him by God and externally outside his control, so Paul submitted willingly to his commissioning to preach the gospel (cf. Gal 1:15). He again describes his apostleship in terms of household management (cf. 4:2): he is a "steward," charged with a specific task by his Lord. In serving his charge, he is owed nothing. Payment is the reward of those who work (cf. Rom 4:4), not of those who fulfill necessary obligations.

Yet, while he *preaches* by divine necessity, Paul preaches *without reward* by his own free choice. Still echoing the philosophers, Paul insists that, while a compulsory action is not worthy of praise, a willing action is (Seneca, *Ep.* 66.16; 82.17). And so, while he has condemned boasting throughout the letter (1:31; 4:6-7; 13:4; cf. 4:18, 19, 5:2; 8:1), he now lays claim to a boast of this own: that he preaches the gospel *"free of charge"* (v. 18). Boasting was frowned upon in antiquity, but many people recognized that, under certain circumstances, it could be justified. Plutarch found boasting inoffensive when it was used in answering allegations (*Mor.* 540C-E; 541E); when one mixed in with it self-effacing remarks (544B); and when its purpose was to incite others to follow one's example (544D-E). Moreover, Paul's boast runs paradoxically counter to the honorific culture of the day, since it is again predicated upon the ethic of Christ crucified: while the Corinthians boast in their excellence, Paul boasts in his service.

9:19-23

Paul's policy about money has been illustrative of a broader principle, which he now succinctly states: his *freedom* he uses to *enslave* himself, that is, to the lifestyle choices of others, so as not to offend and turn them away from the gospel. Paradoxically, this is not a freedom to do something but a freedom *not* to do it. Such freedom is a form of slavery.

Paul's policy of adaptability could be understood against a wide range of cultural backdrops (summarized in M. M. Mitchell 2001, 198): the wiles of Odysseus, the distinction between friendship and servile flattery, Cynic-Stoic arguments about inner freedom, the Proteus legends, the concept of the enslaved leader, political discourse about the factionalist versus the nonpartisan, philosophical psychagogic techniques, or the theological concept of divine condescension. Whether Paul had in mind any of these traditions in particular, the similarity between his policy and these comparanda reveals that in his flexibility toward his audiences he was very much at home in his culture.

Apart from these parallels, Paul's language of slavery in particular picks up a theme evoked frequently in his letters, namely, that of believers as "slaves" to each other (see 3:5-9). Yet an interesting modification of the slave/free theme occurs here. Frequently Paul describes freedom as a freedom *from* something; e.g., in Galatians freedom is a freedom from the *law* (2:4; 4:21–5:1; 5:13; cf. Rom 7:3). If Paul had taught something like this to the Corinthians, this could easily have given rise to a conception of freedom as license. It seems not unlikely that Paul's teaching on freedom had itself induced the Corinthians to construe freedom in this way, so that they now exercised their license to the detriment of their fellow believers. While Paul's discussion of freedom from the law in Galatians was not detached from the basic principle underlying his discussion here—that freedom from the law goes hand in hand with service of others (cf. Gal 5:13)—here he underlines the point in a more emphatic way, precluding the possibility of misinterpretation by defining freedom *as* slavery.

While Paul claimed freedom to adapt to the lifestyles of others, he did not apply this freedom in matters of moral concern. He applied this freedom, rather, in areas that he considered to be morally indifferent. In such areas, he could act differently among different groups. He mentions three groups in four parallel clauses: first, Jews, referred to as "the Jews" and as "those under the law" (although the second label could also encompass "Judaizers"; see Gal 3:23; 4:4, 5, 21; 5:18); second, Gentiles, called "those not under law"; and third, the "weak."

Evidently, Paul did not view observance of the law as an obligation, although in some sense he also did not regard law-observance in itself as blameworthy. He pursued whichever route best served those with whom he interacted in his respective contexts. Since "circumcision is nothing, and uncircumcision is nothing" (7:19), one was—he was—free to observe or not to observe the law on this point, without risking moral compromise. What, then, does he mean by the "law" here? He poses a contrast that illustrates a kind of equivocal orientation toward this entity: he is *not* "under the law of God," yet he *is* "in the law of Christ." Evidently, this distinction plays upon two meanings of the word "law" (*nomos*). The "law" that he is *not* under is that which he elsewhere calls the "law of sin," the "law of works," the "law of sin and death," the "oldness of the letter," the "written code," etc. The "law of Christ," in distinction, expresses a concept that he elsewhere calls the "law written on the heart" (Rom 2:15), the "law of faith" (Rom 3:27), the "law of God" (Rom 7:22, 23; 8:7), the "law of my mind" (Rom 7:23, 25), the "righteous requirement of the law" (Rom 8:4), the "law of the Spirit of life" (Rom 8:2), the "newness of the Spirit" (Rom 7:6), or even, simply, the "Spirit" (2 Cor 3:6). While law as conceived in the first sense, i.e., as a code the observance of which is a condition for justification, is at cross purposes with the gospel (esp. Gal 3:7-20), the "law of Christ" is not optional but the defining reality of new creation existence, the outward expression of the power of the Spirit.

Paul, however, also introduces a third sense of the word "law," saying that he becomes "to the Jews as a Jew" and "to those under the law as under the law." Law here serves as a morally *neutral* category of cultural identity (something that marks him out as culturally Jewish but that he does not see as a condition for his election), which Paul observes so as to remove barriers to one's receptivity to the gospel. In that sense its observance is not obligatory but voluntary.

Paul's reference to the "weak" brings the discussion full circle, making evident the direct relation between his discussion of freedom and his discussion of idol-meat, to which he will return shortly; in sum, one's freedom should not be used to the detriment of others but for their benefit. The final verse of the paragraph provides a transition from Paul's discussion of his use of freedom to two cautionary examples to the Corinthians that emphasize the danger of final "disqualification" (9:24-27; 10:1-13).

Two Cautionary Examples (9:24–10:13)

In two moves, Paul transitions artfully from his personal example back to the Corinthians. First, he suggests that despite his positive personal example (9:1-23), without maintaining self-control he himself stands in danger of eschatological disqualification (9:24-27). Following, he offers the cautionary example of Israel, who despite their salvation privileges came to destruction in the wilderness. By appealing to Israel as a negative moral example, Paul echoes other Jewish contemporaries (Philo, *Spec.* 2.170). Yet the wilderness generation, he muses, is a paradigm of the Corinthians themselves (10:1-13). These two examples—that of Paul and that of Israel—sound a warning to the Corinthians against overconfidence. The latter example begins to close the circle after Paul's detour on freedom by reintroducing the issue of idolatry, to which he will directly relate the issue of idol-meat in the sections that follow (10:14-22; 10:23–11:1).

9:24-27

Paul depicts the life of the believer as an athletic contest. Although athletic metaphors run all throughout Paul's letters (see Phil 1:30; 3:13-14; 4:1; Col 1:29; 2:1, 19; 4:12), his use of an extended athletic metaphor here targets the unique cultural experience of the Corinthians. They were surrounded by athletic images. Corinth hosted the Isthmian games, the largest of the ancient athletic competitions, held every two years (Pausanias, *Descr.* 2.2.2; Dio Chrysostom, *Or.* 8.5-10; Aelius Aristides, *Or.* 46.23). One of the most distinguished municipal offices in Roman Corinth was that of "president of the games" (see the inscriptions in *IKorinthKent* VIII 208-30). Archaeological evidence reveals that there was a gymnasium, or center for athletic training, in Corinth dating to the 50s AD (Wiseman 1972).

Paul's metaphor evokes a philosophical trope in which athletic contests served as a metaphor for the pursuit of virtue. Moral philosophers chastised the population for praising the assiduousness of athletes in their training for physical mastery while neglecting the more crucial matter of mastery over vice (Dio Chrysostom, *Or.* 8). Seneca appeals to the example of athletes in a passage that closely resembles Paul's statements here:

> What *blows* do athletes receive on their faces and *all over their bodies*! Nevertheless, through their desire for fame they *endure* every torture . . . . So let us also *win the way to victory* in all our *struggles*—for their *reward is not a garland or a palm* or a trumpeter who calls for silence at the proclamation of our names, but rather virtue, steadfastness of soul, and a peace that is *won for all time*. (*Ep.* 78.16)

Fourth Maccabees and other Jewish works make similar use of the athletic metaphor (Wis 4:2; Philo, *Spec.* 2.183; T. Job 3:10-11; 27:3-5). Fourth Maccabees depicts the martyr Eleazar as a "noble athlete" (6:10) and his trial as a "divine contest" that has as its prize "immortality in eternal life" (6:12). Paul appeals in particular to the Corinthians' predilection for honor, but he attempts to redirect their zeal from earthly victory (a "corruptible crown") to spiritual victory (an "incorruptible crown"). With Paul's example of self-enslavement to others still in view, ironically the spiritual victory is shown to be equivalent to forfeiture of personal interest.

Having applied the athletic image to believers in general (v. 24), Paul finishes by applying it specifically to himself (vv. 25-27). He continues with the metaphor of a race but then moves summarily to boxing, stating that he treats his body severely, "bruising" and "enslaving" it. This language is not an endorsement of self-mortification, although it does emphasize, hyperbolically, the relevance of the body in spiritual training (cf. 5:1-13; 6:12-20; 8:7-13). The consequences are of gravest seriousness: failure to maintain sufficient discipline results in disqualification. The reference is to e*schatological* disqualification (see also 2 Clem. 7:4-6; Ignatius, *Trall.* 12:3), a failure to receive the blessings stored up for believers after judgment. As the next example shows, the consequences of failure may indeed be fatal.

10:1-5

A new paragraph begins with a meta-comment, but Paul now departs from the earlier refrain "do you not know," using instead the more cynical "I do not want you to be ignorant" (also in 12:1; Rom 1:13; 11:25), reinforced by the solemn vocative "brothers (and sisters)." The conjunction "for" (*gar*) loosely grounds Paul's immediately preceding remarks about the importance of self-mastery (9:24-27) as he now moves on to say that failure to practice self-mastery can be fatal (10:1-13).

Together this paragraph (10:1-5) and the next (10:6-13) narrate the story of the wilderness generation in summary, drawing especially from Exodus (portions of Exodus 12–17), Numbers (portions of Numbers 11–25), and perhaps Psalms (LXX Psalm 105), but not in any definite order, and changing many of the details by imposing the experience of Christ-believers as the governing framework. This form of re-narration, which finds extensive expression in the "rewritten scripture" tradition of the Second Temple period (see, e.g., *Jubilees* and Pseudo-Philo's *Biblical Antiquities*), exhibits little concern with the literal meaning of the original narrative and is governed more by interpretive questions that press on the contemporary audience.

Paul aligns the experience of believers with that of "our fathers" in a series of four parallel clauses each introduced by "all" (*pantes*): "*all* passed through the sea . . . were baptized into Moses . . . ate the same spiritual food . . . and drank the same spiritual drink." By referring to the Israelites as "our fathers," Paul creates a tight continuity of identity between ethnic Israel and Jewish and *Gentile* Christ-believers. The proposed correspondences between the wilderness generation and the church are numerous. Passage through the "cloud" (Exod 13:21-22) and the "sea" (Exod 14:22) represent Israel's equivalent of baptism. Baptism into Christ (Rom 6:3; Gal 3:27) is equated retrospectively with "baptism into Moses." The eating of the Eucharistic bread and the drinking of the Eucharistic cup are retrospectively equated with the manna from heaven (Exod 16:4-5) and the water from the rock (Exod 17:1-6; Num 20:2-13).

Paul's description of the rock as "following" deviates noticeably from the accounts presented in Exodus and Numbers, where by all appearances the boulder remains stationary. This added detail, however, comes by extrapolation from the circumstances of the wilderness era: if Israel wandered the wilderness for forty years, they would need water more than once. Several texts of the Second Temple period, sharing this observation, resolve the conundrum by making the rock mobile (Wis 11:4; LAB 10:7, 11:15; cf. Philo, *All.* 2.86; *Tg. Onq.* Num 21:16-20). Paul inherited this tradition but, in a distinctively Christian adaptation, rebranded the "rock" as none other than "the Christ" (Philo, *All.* 2.86; identifies the rock as "Wisdom").

In sum, vv. 1-4 describe a scenario of great privilege and spiritual provision. Israel underwent a "baptism" of its own; had its own recurrence of "Eucharistic" nourishment; and the rock that traveled with them, to top all, "*was the Christ*." And yet the story took a dramatic turn: "But" (*all'*). But from their high position, God brought them low. This tragedy, which describes the fall of people so unsettlingly similar to the Corinthians, sounds a clear note of warning to the church. The waters of baptism do not make them invulnerable, as Paul will show presently, to the dangers of idolatry.

10:6-13

Paul spells out the lesson: "These events happened as paradigms of us (*typoi hymōn*)," i.e., they typify a repeatable pattern. Enlarging the warning implicit in the previous verse, Paul proceeds with another series of parallel sentences, this time issuing five prohibitions, each followed by "as they/some of them did" (vv. 6, 7, 8, 9, 10). The prohibitions highlight five different sins committed by the Israelites: (1) they *coveted* after meat (LXX Num 11:4, 34-35); (2) they committed *idolatry* in worshiping the golden calf (Exod 32:6b); (3) they committed *fornication* with the Moabite women (Num 25:1-9); (4) they *tested* God/Christ (Num 21:4-9); and (5) they *grumbled* incessantly (Exod 16:7; 17:3; Num 11:1; 14:27, 29; 16:11-35; 17:5). In the third, fourth, and fifth instances, destruction ensued: destruction by the judges of Israel (Num 25:9), destruction by snakes (Num 21:6), and destruction by "the destroyer" (Exod 12:23).

The examples do not follow the canonical order, and examples (3), (4), and (5) involve a few noticeable differences from the accounts given in the OT. In example (3), there is discrepancy in the number of casualties that followed Israel's fornication with Moabite women: Paul records 23,000 but Numbers 24,000 (25:9). In example (4), with the second instance of "testing" (*epeirāsan*), Paul omits a direct object (which in LXX Ps 105:14b is "God," *ton theon*). Ellipsis of the direct object in a repeat instance of the verb usually implies repetition of the same object. This would mean that the Israelites tested "the Christ," thus implying his preexistence. Alternatively, it is possible that Paul omits the direct object precisely in order not to suggest (unequivocally?) that the object of testing was Christ. And in example (5), grumbling in Numbers 16 led finally to destruction, which first took Kore and his household (LXX Num 16:23-35) and then 14,700 more (LXX Num 16:41-49). Yet, while the agent of ruination in that case was said to be the "Lord" (Num 16:30, 46), Paul names the agent as "the Destroyer," a reference that he has apparently imported from Exod 12:23 (cf. Wis 18:25; Heb 11:28).

While all five examples sound a warning, the second and third examples tie in most directly with the context. In example (2), the allusions to idolatry and eating in the citation from Exod 32:6b parallel Corinthian engagements in banquets in pagan temples (cf. 8:10; 10:14-22), and in (3), the narrative of Numbers recounts that fornication with the Moabite women resulted in idolatry.

In his admonition against idolatry, Paul exhibits a typically Jewish attitude. He describes Gentile conversion as a turn from worship of idols to worship of the living and true God several times in his letters (1 Cor 12:2; Gal 4:8-9; 1 Thess 1:9), and he condemns idolatry as much as any other vice (Rom 2:22; 1 Cor 5:10, 11; 6:10; 10:14; Gal 5:20; Col 3:5). Although he has not yet characterized the eating of idol-meat plainly as idolatry, it is becoming increasingly clear that he could move in that direction.

In v. 11, Paul repeats his observation that Israel's experiences occurred "in paradigmatic fashion" (cf. v. 6). In fact, the accounts about Israel speak directly to the church, i.e., "these things were written so as to admonish us" (cf. 9:10; Rom 15:4). In these last days ("at the juncture of the ages"; cf. 7:25-35), circumspection is imperative. Neither baptism nor spiritual food and drink offer unassailable protection against the noxious effects of idolatry. The unwary, like the Israelites, can be seduced into downfall (v. 12). As "standing" refers to life lived in Christian faith (15:1; 2 Cor 1:24; Rom 11:20; Gal 5:1), "falling" refers to fatal lapse of faith (Gal 5:4).

The final warning is given a positive spin. The wary can escape disaster. Every temptation faced, humans have faced before. One can endure every temptation unharmed. Lest the Corinthians imagine that they do so by their own spiritual prowess, Paul states that the means to endure will be provided by God, who is faithful (cf. 1:5). This is "the way out": not escape *from* the temptation but the ability to *bear* it. Paul, then, emphasizes not human invulnerability to temptation but divine empowerment under it.

Partners with God or Partners with Idols (10:14-22)

The conjunction marks a conclusion to 10:1-13 and, indirectly, to 8:1-13: "*Therefore (dioper)*, flee from the idolatry." The definite article ("the," not represented in modern translations) is anaphoric, and perhaps suggests "your (unwitting) idolatry." The reference to idolatry puts the issue of idol-meat back at the fore after the prolonged presentation of both positive (9:1-27) and negative examples (9:24-27; 10:1-13).

Paul now addresses the eating of idol-meat within unambiguously religious contexts, where the meat is constitutive of a meal dedicated to a pagan god. Participation in such meals, Paul suggests, *is* idolatry. He roots his argument in two analogies: the first compares sacrificial banquets with the Lord's Supper (vv. 16-17); the second compares sacrificial banquets with the sacrifices of Israel's cult.

Here is the earliest Christian attestation of the Lord's Supper tradition (later, in Matt 26:26-29; Mark 14:22-25; Luke 22:14-20; Did. 9:1-2), and the earliest attestation of the Supper as a Christian ritual. Paul reverses the order of elements given in other texts (except for Did. 9:1-2), putting the cup first and then the bread (although in 11:23-26 he will use the order bread, cup). This he does in order to smooth the way into an exposition of the bread in v. 17. "Cup" and "bread" serve as metonymy for participation in the rituals involving the said elements. They represent, moreover, the substance of a meal (or the substance of the "table"), the consumption of which unites the participant in fellowship with the one in whose honor the meal takes place.

Paul's idea of fellowship has both a vertical and a horizontal dimension: it consists in both unity with Christ and unity with fellow believers. Paul finds both dimensions present in participation in the Lord's Supper and so uses the word "body" in two different senses. (1) In v. 16, "body" refers to *Christ's* body, in the Eucharistic sense, just as "blood" refers to *Christ's* blood. (2) But in v. 17, "body" refers to the body of believers, whose unity is implied in the oneness of the loaf. The metaphorical nature of the image is evident insofar as the church is said to be *both* body *and* bread. Paul will develop the metaphor of the church as a "body" at length in 12:12-26.

Verse 18 offers a second example of the principle of participation, appealing now to "Israel according to the flesh." This designation refers to ethnic Israel, in contrast to spiritual Israel (cf. 10:1; Rom 2:25-29; Gal 2:29; Phil 3:3). The Israelites, too, when they ate of their sacrifices, were "sharers" in the altar (Deut 14:22-27).

Paul is now prepared to submit a heavy proposal. In his response to the Corinthians' affirmation that "an idol is nothing (*ouden*)" (8:4), Paul is not in fact affirming that an idol "*is* something (*ti*)" (10:19; cf. 3:7; Gal 5:6; 6:3, 15). He and the Corinthians are agreed on this point. He is suggesting, rather (*all*), that meat sacrificed to idols is in reality sacrificed to *demons* (alluding to Deut 32:17; Ps 106:37; Bar 4:7; cf. T. Job 2-5). Characteristic of Paul's apocalyptic worldview was a belief in a whole host of spiritual powers, many of which were evil (see on 8:1-6). In pagan thought, "demons" were divine powers of a class subordinate to the gods, and they could be either good or evil (see Plato, *Symp.* 202E; *SVF* 2.1101-5). In Jewish and early Christian literature, demons were invariably presented as being evil (LXX Deut 32:17; Tobit 3:8; Matt 7:22).

In other words, Paul suggests that while idols, as inert matter, are indeed "nothing," there is some spiritual reality *behind* them to which the sacrifices are devoted. In pagan ritual meals, participants placed sacrificial food before the statues of the gods honored to signify the latter's participation in the meal (Fotopoulos 2003, 162–69, 174–78). Paul suggests that partaking in the elements of the meal, i.e., the sacrificial meat, constitutes "participation" in the sacrifice, or rather *fellowship* with the deity honored. The allusion to Deuteronomy 32 shows that Paul equates this kind of participation with outright idolatry. Just as the Israelites sacrificed to "demons" (Deut 32:17; 1 Cor 10:20-21; see also LAB 25:9) and so provoked God to "jealousy" (Deut 32:21; 1 Cor 10:22), those who participate in pagan religious banquets provoke God to jealousy by diverting their worship to beings other than him. Although in pagan religious culture devotion to one deity did not preclude devotion to another, in accordance with Jewish monotheism Paul reaffirms that worship is owed exclusively to the Lord.

Seeking the Benefit of Others (10:23–11:1)

Discussion of sacrificial banquets breaks off and Paul begins to draw the discussion of idol-meat to a close. Without introduction, he reprises the Corinthian slogan of 6:12a (10:23a, c), citing it twice: "All things are permissible" (6:12a adds, "for me"). He responds each time in turn. His first response, as before, offers an answer focused on expedience: "but not all things are *beneficial.*" His second response is in the same spirit but uses language that anticipates chapter 14: "but not all things *edify*" (cf. 14:3, 4, 5, 12, 17, 26). *Whose* benefit Paul means is clarified in the maxim that follows: "Let no one seek their own interest but the interest of the *other*" (10:24). This maxim captures a common refrain in Paul's letters (cf. Phil 2:3, 4; 1 Cor 10:33; 13:5; Rom 15:1-2, 3; 2 Cor 8:9), but in this form it closely parallels a saying of the Greek moral philosophers (e.g., Musonius Rufus, *Diatr.* 13a; 14). Repeated in a different form in v. 33, the maxim forms an inclusio around the final paragraph, which functions as a summary of all that has been said since 8:7.

Before closing, Paul briefly addresses two further scenarios pertinent to the eating of idol-meat. Both involve situations in which the source of the food is unknown. The first situation addresses food purchased in the *macellum,* or "market" (v. 25). The *macellum* made available a variety of provisions, including meat (Fotopoulos 2003, 141). Archaeological evidence of the Corinthian *macellum* remains (Gill 1992). Often market-meat originated from sacrifices made in nearby temple ceremonies. Paul's recommendation that buyers not inquire into the meat's source implies that the status of market-meat—whether or not it had been consecrated to a god—would not always be apparent. He suggests that one should refrain from inquiring into its status "because of the conscience." He does not specify *whose* conscience is meant, but at least four points indicate that reference is to the conscience of some *other* person. First, protection of *another's* "conscience" has already been identified as a reason for curbing one's freedoms (8:10, 12). Second, the current scenario is quite apparently an application of the principle that encloses this section (vv. 24, 33), namely, that the interest or edification of the "other" takes precedence over one's personal freedom. Third, Paul here grounds permission to eat not in one's ignorance about the status of the meat but in the fact that "the earth is the Lord's, and the fullness thereof" (10:26; citing Pss 24:1; 50:12; 89:11); in other words, eating is *not* something that ought to inflict guilt on one's *own* conscience. Fourth, the directive of v. 25 is repeated in parallel form in relation to the scenario presented in v. 27 ("eat, not inquiring at all, because of the conscience"), where Paul unequivocally specifies that the conscience belongs to "the other" (v. 29).

The problem, then, is not necessarily that one commits idolatry by eating sacrificial meat with full cognizance that they are doing so. The problem is the effect that knowledge of the meat's status might have on the conscience of some *other* believer. There appears, then, to be some tension between the outlook expressed here and that expressed in 10:14-22. In vv. 14-22, Paul presented a sacramental understanding of eating, maintaining that partaking of the elements effects a real unity between the participant and the one honored. Now Paul sacralizes *all of creation*, so that the eating of idol-meat purchased in the market becomes permitted on the basis of God's sovereignty over all things. The difference between the two situations is not the status of the meat but the context in which it is eaten. Banquets in pagan temples are overtly religious occasions, being dedicated to purposes of worship (the worship occurs not in the act of eating but in the whole ritual complex). Such circumstances are absent in the eating of meat purchased from the market.

The second scenario involves the eating of idol-meat at a private dinner party of a nonbeliever (vv. 27-29a). In many situations, one would know that the meal was consecrated to a god: on holy days and feast days; at weddings, birthdays, occasions of thanksgiving, and funerals; and sometimes even at common meals (Gooch 1993, 31–38). In other situations, the meal might not be tied to religious rites. Paul recommends, as before, that one refrain from inquiring into the food's status. Yet he goes on to pose a counter scenario in which "someone" divulges that the food is in fact "consecrated" (*hierothyton*). Paul advises that in such cases one should refrain from eating "out of consideration for the one who informed you, and for the sake of conscience" (v. 28). This section raises several questions. (1) Is the "someone" a fellow believer or a nonbeliever? (2) Is the "informant" a fellow believer or a nonbeliever? (3) To whom does the "conscience" belong?

The scenario is best reconstructed as follows. The individuals in (1) and (2) are one and the same person (as the demonstrative pronoun [*ekeinon*] qualifying "informant" shows ["If *someone* says . . . do not eat because of *that* person"]). That the informant identifies the meat in connotatively positive terms—it is not "*idol*-meat" (*eidōlothyton*) but "*consecrated*-meat" (*hierothyton*)—identifies this person, and therefore also the "someone," as a nonbeliever, for Jewish and early Christian writings consistently use the pejorative term for such meat (e.g., 4 Macc 5:2; Acts 15:29; 21:25; Rev 2:14, 20), never the positive term. But why abstain "because of the informant" if the informant is a nonbeliever? *Not* so as to preserve the nonbeliever's *conscience* but so as not to flout what the nonbeliever clearly perceives to be a moral issue for the believer. Perhaps the believer does not want to appear (from the outsider's perspective) hypocritical or does not want nonbelievers to conclude that Christ-faith and paganism are compatible?

But to whom does the conscience belong? It can be neither one's own conscience nor the conscience of the nonbelieving someone/informant. The former is explicitly ruled out by Paul's clarification in 10:29, "I mean the conscience, *not of oneself* . . . ." Moreover, at least three pieces of evidence show that it is not the conscience of a nonbeliever that is meant but rather the conscience of some fellow believer. First, the "conscience" at issue in 8:9-13 was patently that of the believer and specifically that of the "weak" believer (esp. 8:10, 12) or "brother" (8:13). Second, the opening and closing sentences of the present paragraph (10:23, 24, 33) enclose a unit in which the concern is for the interest of one's fellow believers. Third, Paul does not say here, "because of the conscience of the informant" or "because of that person's conscience," but "because of the informant *and* because of the conscience." Paul, in other words, offers *two* reasons for abstaining, not one: "because of the informant *and* because of the conscience (of your fellow believer)." By what chance of circumstance does some other, presumably "weak," believer become aware that his brother has eaten idol-meat? Perhaps because he, too, is present or because rumor has carried it back to the church. Manifold scenarios are conceivable.

The meaning of v. 29b is much contested: "for why am I judged by another person's conscience?" Because this comment appears to about-face to the position of the knowledgeable after Paul has consistently taken up the cause of the weak, it could be regarded as another Corinthian slogan, spoken on behalf of the knowledgeable. This, however, is an unnecessary supposition. Verse 29b grounds what immediately precedes (v. 29a), elucidating why Paul has said that one need not be concerned with one's *own* conscience ("I mean not *one's own* conscience"). The first person singular, moreover, is meant in a universal sense ("I" = any person), indicating general application. The thought is: "Don't eat because of the conscience (v. 28), and I don't mean your *own* conscience (v. 29a), for why am *I* judged by another person's conscience (v. 29b)?" In other words, one should not fear the judgment of God on *oneself* simply because someone else's conscience is sensitive. This point does not fully advocate the position of the knowledgeable, for it does not advocate eating. Paul maintains that one should still accommodate their *behavior* to the values of the weak; yet he justifies the *principle* that, apart from the weak believer, one would indeed be free to eat.

Verse 30b stands parallel to v. 29b and reiterates the point: "Why am *I* blasphemed . . . ." The explicit first person pronoun *egō* establishes co-reference with the first person of the previous verse, so that the first person again indicates universal reference ("I" = any person). In sum, there occurs a chain of co-referents running from "one's *own* conscience" (v. 29a) to "*my* freedom" (v. 29b) and "*I*" (v. 30). To paraphrase: "Abstaining has nothing to do with *one's own* conscience (v. 29a). *My* conscience gives me no reason not to eat (vv. 29b), for if *I* eat with thanksgiving why I am blasphemed . . . ?" (v. 30). In short, vv. 29b-30 form not the final conclusion to the discussion running from 8:7 but only an addendum to v. 29a, elucidating why, despite abstaining for the sake of another person's conscience, one's own conscience might otherwise remain clean even if they had eaten.

Verses 10:31–11:1 form the proper conclusion to 8:1–11:1. Paul issues three commands. The first expands the principles of the preceding discussion into an all-encompassing ethic: "*Therefore* (*oun*), whether you eat or drink or whatever you do, do all things for the glory of God" (v. 31; cf. Col 3:17). Accommodating to others in matters of eating is but one expression of this principle. The second command enjoins the audience to be "blameless" toward Jews, Greeks, and the "church of God" (where the church is not identical with Israel; cf. 10:1). Here, "blameless" appears to be not objective but relative to the perceptions of different groups (v. 32), for Paul immediately juxtaposes his example of *accommodation* for the "benefit" of "the many," and this "in order that they might be saved." This point unmistakably echoes Paul's earlier description of his practice of personal *adaptation*, becoming to Jews "as a Jew," and to those under the Law as "under the Law," and to those not under the Law as "not under the Law," and to the weak as "weak" (9:19-23). By adapting to the (varied) ways of each group, he becomes "blameless" from the perspective of each. Finally, having offered his example, he appeals directly to the Corinthians to be his "imitators," though only as he himself is an imitator of Christ (11:1). Renunciation of personal interests for the benefit of others, as Paul has advocated throughout this section, is the epitome of cruciformity (cf. Rom 15:3).

Conclusion

First Corinthians 8:1–11:1 epitomizes Paul's approach to Christian ethics. Although he treats the eating of idol-meat as an ethical issue (because of the consequences it might inflict on other believers), he refrains from handling it by laying down concrete prescriptions or stipulations, and instead he offers an informative ethical *framework*. The constitutive principles of this framework include the exclusive lordship of Christ (cf. 10:14-22), the normativity of Christ's cruciform example (cf. 9:4-23; 10:23-24; 11:1), and the primacy of benefit to others over personal freedom (cf. 8:1; 10:23-24).

Although Paul unequivocally recommends abstaining from idol-meat, it is less clear from his discussion whether he believes that eating idol-meat is wrong *inherently*. Complicating this section is the fact that he seems to offer contradictory perspectives on idol-meat and that he seems to integrate Corinthian citations into the discussion without clearly marking them off from his own comments. Across 8:1–11:1, the chief tension is between the perspective apparent in 8:1-13 and that expressed in 10:14-22. In 8:1-13, Paul appears to agree that idol-meat is "nothing," since there is only "one God" (8:4), and to propose a policy of magnanimous abstention only as a measure to prevent scandalizing one's brother or sister (8:9-13). Yet in 10:14-22 he suggests that partaking of the sacrifices at the meal "table" is tantamount to fellowship with "demons." Is this blatant self-contradiction, or does some other explanation lie at hand?

This problem has a number of possible solutions (see Fotopoulos 2005, 613–14 for citations of the secondary literature): (1) 8:1-13 and 10:14-22 belong to originally separate letters, and Paul changed his thinking (or at least his policy) during the interval; (2) floundering for a solution to a community problem, Paul offers discursively inconsistent pragmatic (8:1-13) and theological (10:14-22) answers; (3) 8:1-13 constitutes the first step in a progressive argument, which begins with a stance of caution and climaxes with an absolute prohibition; (4) Paul in fact never agreed that an idol is "nothing," and this was affirmed by the Corinthians only; or (5) Paul addresses different situations in each context, and his instructions vary accordingly.

The first solution is rhetorically unnecessary and completely unsupported by the manuscript evidence. The second attributes to Paul an uncharitable level of confusion or at least significant rhetorical negligence. The third solution suffers a fatal flaw by failing to take into account Paul's central emphasis on self-limitation and *free* adaptability (8:9-13; 9:1-27; 10:23, 28-30), that is, his advice that one should surrender one's rights even though one does not *have* to. The fourth solution alleviates Paul of contradiction by attributing

8:4 to the Corinthians and postulating 10:14-22 as his response (Fotopoulos 2005); yet, like the third solution, this reconstruction implies that Paul was pressing toward a single, absolute theological principle all along and thus does not integrate well with Paul's discussion of free self-limitation.

The fifth solution explains the evidence most satisfactorily. Paul addresses several distinct situations in chapters 8–10:

   (1) reclining in a temple (and eating) (8:10)
   (2) participating in sacrificial banquets in pagan temples (10:14-22)
   (3) eating idol-meat sold in the market (10:25)
   (4) eating idol-meat served at private dinners (10:27)

His instructions vary according to the conditions. He permits the eating of idol-meat sold in the market and served at private dinners. While he grants permission provided that the source of the meat is not ascertained, the primary consideration seems to be the effect of eating on another person's conscience (10:25, 28-29). Comparison of the other two examples seems to present a more serious challenge. Both envisage the eating of idol-meat in pagan temples, and yet, while the first one focuses on its effects on another person's conscience (8:10), the latter presents such eating unequivocally as fellowship with demons. Despite this difficulty, it is unclear that the situation described in 8:10 is an idol *banquet*. It seems that Paul distinguished between eating, in a temple, food that happened to be idol-food and partaking of a ritual meal expressly devoted to some pagan deity (also Oropeza 2017, 133), and that the reason for his uncompromising stance in the latter case was the extreme similarity between such banquets and the Lord's Supper.

The chief point in favor of this interpretation is Paul's emphasis in chapter 9 on personal flexibility. Unmistakably, the point of chapter 9 is that he abstains *voluntarily*, that is, that he abstains from things in which he has every "*right*" to partake. The analogy to his personal example in 9:4-6 and following becomes pointless unless one attributes analogous framing to the issue of idol-meat. The point, in sum, is not that *all* eating of idol-meat is idolatry. Rather, Paul treats a range of situations, each with its own set of considerations. 10:14-22 suggests that in contexts of sacrificial meals, one should abstain *always*. 10:1-13 suggests that those who become unduly comfortable and hence insufficiently circumspect toward idol-meat run greater risk of transgression into situations of unambiguous idolatry. The remainder of chapters 8–10 suggests that believers in principle have a *right* to eat idol-meat, in certain contexts. In particular, Paul encourages those who are invited to private dinners with nonbelievers by all means to go; he would not have the church segregate from outsiders (cf. 5:9-10). Yet believers should abstain from eating in contexts where it would adversely affect another believer's conscience. All things are permissible, but not all things *edify* (10:23). The issue of idol-meat is one of several issues treated in the letter where Paul answers on the basis of the paramount principle of the edification of others (cf. 12:1–14:40).

Problems in Assembly for Worship

1 Corinthians 11:2–14:40

Paul is not finished. Adding to the long list of problems already discussed, Paul now opens a new major unit addressing further problems that are tearing at the community's fellowship. This unit treats three problems related to the church's gatherings for worship. The first relates to head-coverings practices (11:2-16), the second to the church's practice of the Lord's Supper (11:17-34), and the third to the exercise of spiritual gifts (12:1-40). An encomium of love amid the discussion of spiritual gifts provides a focal point to the section (13:1-13) and the antidote to the Corinthians' divisive practices.

Women Worshiping with Heads Uncovered (11:2-16)

Paul's warning to the Corinthians about the dangers of idolatry has reached an end (8:1–11:1). In 11:2, he takes a breath, as it were, and changes direction: "Now then" (*de*). Relenting from his chastisement, he lifts the Corinthians back to their feet by opening with a statement of praise. They have "remembered" the traditions that he passed down to them. But his praise is short-lived. An adversative statement immediately follows ("*But* I want you to know"), implying that their compliance with the tradition is imperfect at best.

What follows is a notoriously difficult passage. Paul's final point is that in contexts of public worship (note the "praying" and "prophesying" in the presence of other believers in vv. 4, 5) women should cover their heads and men should not. Implicitly, certain individuals have in some way violated this tradition. Otherwise several uncertainties remain. First, did the violations of the tradition concern men, women, or both? Second, why were people violating the tradition? Third, what kind of head covering was Paul referring to?

While Paul addresses men and women in somewhat complementary terms in this passage, several items reveal that his criticism is directed primarily toward the women. First, vv. 3-9 form a chiasm in which women figure at the center (Talbert 2002, 86):

> v. 3. The origin of woman
> > v. 4. Man/ head not covered
> > > **v. 5. Woman/ head covered**
> > > **v. 6. Woman/ head covered**
> > v. 7. Man/ head not covered
> vv. 8-9. The origin of woman

Second, although Paul treats men and women in complementary terms in vv. 4 and 5, he adds further comment only about women in v. 6. Third, there is no male complement to the warning to women about head covering in v. 10. Fourth, v. 13 asks whether it is fitting for women to pray or prophesy with head uncovered, although there is no parallel question about men. Fifth, the only imperatives in this unit are issued toward women (v. 6; *keirasthō, katakalyptesthō*). Sixth, *men . . . de* constructions ("on the one hand . . . on the other hand") often put "offline" material first (*men*) and the main "punch-line" second (*de*); thus, in vv. 14-15, "on the one hand, . . . man . . . on the other hand . . . *woman* . . . ."

Why were some women violating the tradition? They may have done so for theological reasons. Possibly they believed that in Christ gender distinctions had been effaced. Indeed, central to Paul's teaching was the conviction that the gospel destroyed ordinary social barriers. In Galatians (written sometime earlier), Paul had said that in Christ "there is no longer Jew or Greek, there is no longer slave or free," and likewise that "there is no longer *male and female*" (Gal 3:28). Tellingly, 1 Corinthians contains a similar mantra but drops any reference to male and female: "For in the one Spirit we were all baptized into one body—Jews or Greeks, slaves or free—and we were all made to drink of one Spirit" (1 Cor 12:13). This modification may suggest that the Corinthians misunderstood the thrust of his idea. The distinction between male and female has not been altogether erased. Male must act like male and female like female. Paul is intent on reinforcing these distinctions.

Sociological factors may also have played a role. In a male-dominated society, women had less opportunity for social advancement than men. The domain of the church, however, offered them an outlet where they could overcome traditional social strictures and achieve within the spiritual domain a higher status than they carried in society.

What kind of covering does Paul have in mind? This question captures one of the most debated aspects of this passage. Was Paul referring to an external covering like a veil or was he referring to long hair *as* a covering?

The issue is not as easily settled as it first appears. The language "veiled" and "unveiled," seen in vv. 5, 6, 7, and 13 of the NRSV translation, is interpretive and not a direct translation of the Greek text. Rather, the Greek expression "having down from the head" (*kata kephalēs echōn*) and the Greek words "cover" (*katakalyptetai*, vv. 6, 7) and "uncovered" (*akatakalyptōi*, vv. 5, 13) are in themselves ambiguous.

Strong arguments can be made for either view. The linguistic evidence supports the position that Paul referred to a veil, for some examples occur in Greek literature where *kata kephalēs* clearly means "having a veil on the head" (LXX Esth 6:12; Plutarch, *Mor.* 200f) and *katakalyptō* means to "cover with a veil" (Massey 2018, 504–505), while no unambiguous examples occur where this expression means "having long hair." However, sociological evidence is hard to square with the thesis that Paul is referring to veils. While Greek men did not wear head coverings in devotional contexts (Plutarch, *Mor.* 266C), Roman men did, drawing the toga up over their heads when praying or sacrificing (Oster 1988; Massey 2018). The following complication therefore ensues: if Paul *opposes* male head coverings, he is presupposing as the church's *accepted* custom exactly the opposite of the Roman tradition. That is, he is presupposing as an agreed premise that men should *not* wear veils. This is a strange supposition given that Corinth was a Roman colony (unless Paul had already taught against the common cultural practice). Moreover, archaeological evidence from excavations of Corinth frequently depict women as having their hair coiffured or rolled on the top of their heads, thus serving as a kind of covering. Only on special occasions did they let their hair down in public (Thompson 1988, 106–13). Furthermore, Paul unequivocally refers to hair in four places in 11:2-16: (1) an uncovered woman is one and the same as a "shaved" (*exyrēmenēi*) woman (v. 5); (2) if it is shameful for a woman to be "shaved" (*keirasthai*) or "shorn" (*xyrasthai*), her head should be covered (v. 6); (3) nature teaches that it is glory to a woman to grow her hair long (*komai*) (v. 14); and (4) "hair" has been given to woman *as* (*anti*) a covering (v. 15). Paul, then, may indeed be suggesting not that women should wear a material veil but that they should keep long hair, which itself serves as a covering.

Paul offers five separate arguments for his directive: an argument from the order of creation (v. 3), an argument from cultural conceptions of honor and shame (vv. 4-6), a second argument from the order of creation (vv. 7-10), an argument from nature (vv. 13-14), and an argument from the practice of the churches (v. 16).

The first argument states that man is "head" (*kephalē*) of woman/wife, just as God is head of Christ and Christ is head of man. Later in the passage "head" refers to the physical, anatomical head (vv. 4a, 5a, 7, 10). Here it refers either to one's "source" or one's "authority." Despite modern advocacy for the former meaning, nowhere in Greek literature does *kephalē* connote an individual as a source (though, "source" of a river in, e.g., Herodotus, *Hist.* 4.91). By contrast, *kephalē* frequently means "head" in the sense of a "ruler" or "leader" (e.g., Plato, *Tim.* 44d; Philo, *Spec.* 3.184; LXX Judg 11:11; 2 Sam 22:44; etc.). Moreover, just a few verses later, Paul says that woman is the source of *man* (v. 12). They would then apparently be sources of each other; however, if man is the source of woman and woman is also the source of man, is Christ, then, also the source of God, or man the source of Christ? Paul cannot have meant this.

As an alternative, some have taken *kephalē* to mean "that which is preeminent" (Perriman 2004). This sense highlights the head as that which is physically uppermost or in some sense most prominent. While this view is attractive in that it rightly avoids connotations of harsh or authoritarian mastery over another, one is nevertheless hard put to separate prominence from authority or rule (including benevolent rule). In any case, God does not just *represent* Christ as the more prominent of the two, but rather Christ is obedient or *submissive* to him. In short, much as this may clash with modern convictions, headship in this passage does imply some level of leadership or authority. However, more will be said about this as Paul proceeds (see below).

Paul's second argument for head covering is from cultural conceptions of honor and shame (vv. 4-6). Paul lived in an honorific culture. Honor was more to be sought than anything, and shame was most to be avoided. These values were reflected everywhere in the culture. Inscriptions covering the walls and streets of the city celebrated the merits of private individuals—those who funded building projects (*IKorinthKent* 314) or the renovations of public buildings (*IKorinthKent* 311); those who supplied food to the city in times of shortage (*IKorinthKent* 267); or those who had done the public some other service (*IKorinthKent* 248–49). The lust for honor manifested itself not only among elites but also among the lower classes, even slaves (Finney 2010, 28). Appealing to these values, Paul states that it is "shameful" for a man to pray or prophesy with his head covered, just as it is "shameful" for a woman to pray or prophesy uncovered (vv. 4-5). If Paul understands the covering to be long hair, then his remarks are consistent with the sentiments of his culture. Groups like the Nazirites, who refrained from cutting their hair (Judg 13:5), were the exceptions. So also those on the fringes of society like the unshorn philosophers and barbarians (Dio Chrysostom, *Or.* 35). Indeed, men with long hair were a frequent target of satire (Juvenal, *Satyr.* 2.96; Petronius, *Satyr.* 119). Ample evidence shows that short hair for men and long hair for women was the general expectation (Plutarch, *Mor.* 267B; Ps.-Phoc. 210-12; Pliny, *Nat. hist.* 7.59; cf. T. Job 24:9-10).

In vv. 4-6 "head" has double meaning. It stands in one sense for the physical head of the body but in a secondary sense for the respective metaphorical head that man and woman each have. That is, when a man prays or prophesies with his (physical) head covered, he shames both his physical head and his (authoritative) head—Christ—and when a woman prays or prophesies with her (physical) head uncovered, she shames both her physical head and her (authoritative) head—man. Paul elaborates only on the woman, declaring, with hyperbole, that an uncovered head, i.e., short hair, is as good as a "shaved" head (vv. 5, 6).

How these behaviors shame one's head is explained in Paul's next argument (vv. 7-10), which brings him back to the order of creation, now with allusions to Genesis 1 and 2. That man is the "image" of God (v. 7a) is an allusion to Gen 1:27. While Genesis does not describe Adam as the "glory" of God as Paul does here, texts of the Second Temple period, reflecting on the prelapsarian Adam, did attribute "glory" to Adam (1QS IV.23; CD III.20; H IV.15; cf. 2 Bar. 83:8-23). Reference to the origins of woman "from man" (v. 8) alludes to the formation of Eve from Adam's rib in Gen 2:18, 21-24. And the statement that she was made "because of man" (v. 9) derives from Gen 2:18, 20.

Verses 7-10 can be regarded as an elaboration on the claim that the "head of woman is the man" (v. 3). Paul says that woman is not only "from" man (v. 8) but that she exists "for the sake of" the man (v. 9). Here Paul also explains the claim that it is shameful for man to wear a covering (vv. 4). In covering his head man hides God's image and glory, and so brings God not glory but shame. The connective in v. 10 (*dia touto*) links this verse back with v. 7b: since the woman is the glory of man, she should wear a covering (the "symbol of authority" she has on her head); that is, when she does not wear a covering, she brings the man shame. How? Philo of Alexandria links head covering, or the lack thereof, with sexual activity, noting that women accused of adultery are stripped of the head covering that symbolizes their modesty (*Spec.* 3.56; cf. Sus 31). Paul may be striking a similar note. In support of this interpretation is Paul's reference to "the angels": it is "because of the angels" that the woman's being uncovered is problematic. The reference is obscure, but the angels are probably to be identified with the "sons of God" said to have lusted after the "daughters of men" in Gen 6:4 (cf. 1 En. 5:1-2). If this is the source of the allusion, Paul's meaning is that women shame men by removing their coverings and inviting angels to lust after them.

Several points reaffirmed in vv. 7-10 support the hierarchical reading of v. 3. First, while Paul says that the man was made in the "image" of God (v. 7), he makes no reference to the woman (tendentiously, since Gen 1:27 says that both male and female were made in his image). Second, Paul says that woman was created "from man" and "not man from woman" (v. 8). Third, Paul says that woman was made "because of man," not man because of the woman (v. 9).

In holding these views, Paul was well at home in his environment. The hierarchical nature of society and of the universe would have been anyone's natural assumption. Under the Roman Empire, states were not democracies but monarchies, tyrannies, aristocracies. Most philosophers conceived of the natural world as hierarchically ordered. The Stoics, maintaining that the lower things existed "for the sake of" the higher (Cicero, *Nat. d.* 1.154; cf. Epictetus, *Diatr.* 1.16.2-5; 2.8.7), set plants at the bottom, and above them, in order, animals, humans, and finally the gods (Seneca, *Ben.* 2.29.3; *Ep.* 113.17). Within the early church, the Apostolic Fathers adapted common (and especially Stoic) hierarchical notions to their Christian worldview. At the end of the first century AD, 1 Clement proposed that authority flowed down from God through Christ, to the apostles, and then to the bishops and deacons who succeeded them (1 Clem. 42:1-5). Ignatius (ca. AD 110) said that the church should be obedient to the bishops just as Jesus is obedient to the Father (Ignatius, *Smyr.* 8:2). The series laid out by Paul in v. 3 reflects a similar kind of universe. Christ "belongs" to God (3:23) and is "subject" to him (15:24, 27-28). Likewise, man is subject to Christ, who is "Lord over" all (Rom 10:12). Paul applied the hierarchy analogously to man and woman: woman is subject to man.

Despite the hierarchical thrust of these verses, Paul seems to have been motivated also by a competing ideology, which counteracts his tendency toward hierarchy. A close look at v. 3 shows that the series does not proceed in ascending or descending order but sets man and woman at the center, bracketed by Christ (Murphy-O'Connor 1988, 270): man | **Christ** | woman | man | **Christ** | God. This arrangement may be devised to put man and woman on equal footing as subjects of Christ. Moreover, Paul later pauses from his arguments for head covering, seeking (as if feeling he had gone too far) to qualify them from the order of creation. He makes two qualifying points. First, he states that, "in the Lord," neither is man "apart from" woman nor woman "apart from" man (v. 11). This reciprocal language resembles statements made in chapter 7: neither man nor woman is independent of the other; they share all things in common (7:4). Second, Paul states that both man and woman owe their existence to God (v. 12; cf. 3:21-23; 8:6; Rom 11:36). These two qualifications serve to relativize hierarchy.

By appearances, Paul does not resolve the tension (Newberry 2019), and so this conclusion seems unavoidable: that this section "contains two competing arguments based on two distinct pictures of the order of creation" (Sampley 2015, 800).

In vv. 13-15, Paul returns to his argument that women should cover their heads. Here he appeals to the Corinthians' own sense of judgment (cf. 10:14; Phlm 14), posing two rhetorical questions. The first (v. 13) asks them to consider what is "fitting" (*prepon*). This term has philosophical resonances; in Stoic philosophy, it designated what was "in accordance with nature." Paul's second question appeals to nature itself: does not "nature" (*physis*) teach that a man should have short hair and a woman long hair (vv. 14-15)? Paul's argument is non-intuitive, for hair grows equally on men and women (on the head at least), its length determined not by nature but by human device (i.e., shears). But the term "nature" should not for that reason be taken to mean "convention." Of course, many people would simply have assumed that their convention actually reflected nature. Among the educated, however, "nature" and "convention" were carefully distinguished (Sextus Empiricus, *Prof.* 11.140; Cicero, *Off.* 3.17.16; Pseudo-Socrates, *Ep.* 39, 7-8). It was recognized that convention varied from one city and one ethnic group to another. By contrast, nature was that which reflected the very order of the universe and did not change according to public opinion. In every other instance where Paul employs the term "nature," he means it in this sense (Rom 1:26; 2:14, 27; 11:21, 24; Gal 2:15; 4:8; Eph 2:3; and the adjective *physikos* in Rom 1:26, 27). Using a version of the hair argument, the Stoics pointed to facial hair as a sign given by nature of the difference between the sexes (Epictetus, *Diatr.* 1.16.9-14).

However, it seems that Paul is wary of his own argument. In appealing to nature in the form of a rhetorical question ("Does not nature itself teach you . . . ?"), he appears to distance himself from the implied conclusion, while hoping that the argument will carry weight for the Corinthians themselves (Brookins 2017a). If the Corinthians had Stoic leanings, Paul may be trying to paint them into a corner: you who identify with the Stoics, will you not accept an argument from nature?

For good measure, Paul closes (v. 16) with an argument from convention (*synētheia*). "If anyone is minded to be contentious" means "if anyone remains unconvinced." Paul snuffs out any remaining dissent with this plain declaration: both the apostles and all of God's churches practice as he has advised. This, of course, is the bottom line. Under different circumstances,

Paul might have advised about head coverings differently. Here, his main purpose is to put an end to practices that disturb the church's fellowship. If appeal to the conventions of culture (what brings honor and shame), to arguments from the order of creation (that he himself may doubt), or to the traditions of the church can restore the church to unity, his purpose has been achieved.

Abuses at the Lord's Supper (11:17-34)

Paul now transitions to a second problem afflicting the church's gatherings for worship, namely their manner at the Lord's Supper. This unit falls into three sections: a statement of the problem (11:17-22), a recitation of the institution of the Lord's Supper (11:23-26), and an exhortation for proper observance of the Supper (11:27-34). The unit opens and closes with reference to the church's "coming together" (vv. 17, 34), underscoring the irony of the fact that divisions manifest themselves in a ritual centering on unity.

11:17-22

The opening statement looks back to the affirmation that opened v. 2:
    Now I commend you . . . (v. 2)
    But in this I do *not* commend you . . . (v. 17)

The contrast reflects the dual purposes of epideictic rhetoric: praise and blame (Ps.-Cicero, *Rhet. Her.* 1.2.2). Paul does *not* commend them because when they come together, they "come together (*synerchesthe*)" not "for the stronger (*kreisson*)" but "for the weaker (*hēsson*)." One can better appreciate the phrasing, and the irony, of Paul's expression when its military connotations are recognized. The same word is used when military forces "come together," or unite, in battle (Herodotus, *Hist.* 4.120; Euripides, *Phoen.* 462; Plato, *Charm.* 157e; Aristotle, *Pol.* 1278b; Demosthenes, *Cor.* 18.19; Plutarch, *Mor.* 481c); they unite to become "stronger," not "weaker." Yet the Corinthians have done the latter.

Several details about the circumstances can be determined. First, "divisions" have occurred when the church has come together for the Lord's Supper (v. 18). Although the word used here is *schismata* ("schisms"), these are not "splinters" off of the church but divisions internal to it (cf. 1:10). Second, when the church meets for the Lord's Supper, some people are eating ahead (*prolambanein*) of others (v. 21). This naturally disrupts unity of fellowship. Third, some people have more than enough to eat while others have too little. Fourth, the problem does not seem to be one incidental to particular meetings but to a more perennial problem of "haves" and "have-nots" (v. 22).

It may be possible to reconstruct a more specific social setting accounting for this set of details. One reconstruction focuses on limitations of space (Murphy-O'Connor 1983, 153–61). A dining room (*triclinium*) in a modestly sized villa might have seated nine people comfortably. Since the Corinthian church consisted of fifty or more individuals (see introduction), the remaining individuals would be displaced to the atrium, where thirty to forty people might crowd together, either sitting on the hard floor or standing up. The prime seats available in the dining room would be awarded to the "first-class believers" (158–59). These would include the more affluent members of the community, including the host, who had offered up his size-able home, and his closest associates. The host of the Corinthian assembly may have been one such as Gaius, whom Paul identifies in his letter to the Romans as the host of the "whole church" during his stay in Corinth (Rom 16:23).

But how is it that one goes "hungry" and another one gets "drunk" (v. 21)? The following scenario could offer an explanation (Theissen 1982). When Paul says that "each one goes ahead with *his own* supper," he implies that some within the church began taking a private meal prior to partaking in the congregational meal, that is, the Lord's Supper proper. Perhaps the private meal consisted of food set aside from the Supper for select members of the congregation. Two traditions common at formal meals in the Greco-Roman world would support this explanation. First, the dinner host commonly offered larger portion sizes to himself and his friends (e.g., *CIL* XIV 2112). Second, the food that the host allotted to himself and his friends was often of higher quality (Pliny, *Ep.* 2.6; Martial, *Epigr.* 3.60; 1.20; Juvenal, *Epigr.* 3.60; 4.85). Who would have been the beneficiaries? Those who had made the meal possible by their generous hospitality, i.e., the wealthier members of the church.

While this explanation has some sense, it probably does not best account for the details of the passage. The phrasing of v. 21 seems not to incriminate the host but the very people who were eating. Paul emphasizes their individualistic tendencies: "Each person (*ekastos*)" takes their "own (*idion*)" meal ahead of others (v. 21). This phrasing suggests that the verb (*prolambanein*) has an active ("takes") rather than a passive ("receives") meaning. If this is right, then one is not to imagine guests "receiving" varying portion sizes dealt out selectively by the host but actively "taking" some certain portion.

It may be that individuals brought "their own" meals from home, consuming them on their own initiative, before grace, so to speak. This, however, could not explain the whole issue. It is not just that they do not eat together; it is that some do not get to eat enough. It seems better, then, to suppose that the community met together for a prepared meal and that certain individuals proceeded through the line first (so to speak), taking more than their fair share, leaving too little for the others.

The problem goes even deeper than this. Some do not get enough, and at the *Lord's* Supper of all places. Paul indicates that there is a more permanent, socioeconomic problem at issue: the very people who are getting more than their fair share also "have homes to eat and drink in," while others "do not have (homes to eat and drink in)" (v. 22). Most likely, this does not mean that the latter were homeless but that they resided in small, likely *rented* quarters like apartments, workshops, shops, and bars, as most people did (Oakes 2009). In any case, Paul's purpose is to make a contrast between "home" and "church (*ekklēsia*)." The assembly of believers should be a gathering where people look out not for their own interests (as at home) but for the interests of the whole church assembly.

Even while Paul is deploring the "schisms" that split the church assembly, he somewhat puzzlingly suggests that "factions (*haireseis*)" are "necessary (*dei*)" (v. 19). This statement most likely alludes to a saying of Jesus not recorded in the Gospels but recorded in several other early Christian texts (Justin Martyr, *Dial.* 35; Ps.-Clementine, *Homily* 16.21.4), in which Jesus predicts that "factions" will arise in the end times. Paul views this prospect with a sense of resignation but focuses somewhat sarcastically on the positive outcome: factions throw the differences between people into relief, so that the "approved" stand out clearly from the disapproved. That is, those who are approved by God will become "manifest" on the day of judgment (cf. 3:13; 4:5). The term "approved"—which can also mean "distinguished"— probably originated with the Corinthians and parallels their self-ascription as "wise," "spiritual," and "knowledgeable" people. Here, then, Paul has again appropriated a Corinthian catchword and turned it against those who used it. Those who fancy themselves "distinguished" should beware lest they turn out to be disapproved at the judgment.

Paul closes off the section by echoing his opening words: "Should I commend you?" (v. 34; cf. v. 17, "I do *not* commend you"). He answers directly: he will not.

11:23-26

Here is found the earliest extant attestation in history of the Lord's Supper ritual. The institution itself grounds Paul's declaration that he will *not* praise the Corinthians (vv. 17, 22). Their behavior is at odds with the institution. They exhibit disunity in practicing a ritual signifying unity.

In describing the transmission of the institution, Paul uses the language of tradition ("received," "delivered"; cf. 11:2; 15:1, 3; Herodotus, *Hist.* 2.51). The Corinthians received from him what he had received from the Lord—not directly, but through others (possibly through Peter or James; Gal 1:18-19). While the Supper tradition is found in all three of the Synoptic Gospels (Matt 26:26-29//Mark 14:22-25//Luke 22:14-20), Paul's rendition most approximates that found in Luke, except that he reverses the order of the elements, matching Matthew and Mark in naming the bread first followed by the cup (although 1 Cor 10:16-17 has cup followed by bread, as in Luke).

Paul's recital of the institution reads like fixed church liturgy. The unit opens with the setting as described in the Gospels: the Supper occurred on the night on which Jesus was betrayed. Following are two parallel parts, each consisting of an action of Jesus, followed by an explanation of an element (bread, cup), then a command. The liturgy closes with an exhortation to practice the Supper until Jesus "comes."

The content is dense. "Handed over" (v. 23) may refer either to Jesus' betrayal by Judas (Matt 20:18; 26:15; Mark 10:33a; 14:10; Luke 22:4, 6; John 19:11) or to his handing over according to God's sovereign plan (Rom 8:32), or to both (cf. Acts 2:23; 4:27-28). "For you" (v. 24) indicates substitution ("in your place"; 15:3; Rom 5:6, 8; 2 Cor 5:15, 21; Gal 2:20; 3:13), or at least advantage (cf. Rom 8:31, "If God is *for us*"). "In remembrance of me" (vv. 24-25) recalls the Passover meal, which Jews observed in remembrance of their deliverance by God from Egypt (Exod 12:14; Deut 16:2-3); Christian theology had already connected Jesus with the Passover lamb as seen elsewhere in 1 Corinthians (1 Cor 5:7). "The new covenant" (v. 25) refers to the new covenant foretold by the prophets (Jer 31:31-34; Ezek 36:25-27), although here the covenant is said to have been established specifically by Jesus' blood.

Jesus' death and return bracket the unit. This arrangement indirectly "reminds readers that they live between the times" (Perkins 2012, 144). Such a reminder contextualizes the audience's lives within a narrative that both begins and ends with Jesus. The reference to Jesus' return also sounds a warning that the Corinthians ought to test themselves (vv. 27-34). It is to this point that Paul now turns.

11:27-34

Following the recitation of the Lord's Supper ritual, the discussion takes a turn towards judgment. Verses 27-34 are rife with forensic language: "answerable" (v. 27), "examine" (v. 28), "discerning," "judgment" (v. 31), "judged," "disciplined," "condemned" (v. 32), "condemnation" (v. 34). In short, whoever does not take the Lord's Supper "in a worthy manner" will be "answerable for the body and blood of the Lord" (v. 27), "eats and drinks judgment on himself" (v. 29), and will be "condemned along with the world" (v. 32). Paul refers not to eschatological judgment but to judgment in the present tense. Some have already "fallen asleep," or died (cf. 10:1-13). In suggesting that judgment functions for believers as discipline, Paul echoes the traditional Jewish idea that God disciplines those whom he loves but judges in a final sense those whom he hates (2 Macc 6:12-17; cf. Deut 8:5).

As the pieces of this section are put together it becomes apparent that to eat "in an unworthy manner" means (1) to eat and to drink without "examining" oneself (v. 28); and (2) to eat and to drink "without discerning the body" (v. 29). Two interconnected principles explain the logic.

First, participation in the Supper signifies personal participation with Christ. One must "examine" oneself, then, so as to discern rightly what one *is*, that is, a participant with Christ (cf. 2 Cor 13:5). To take the Supper without recognizing this is to miss the most fundamental characteristic of one's identity.

Second, those who participate in Christ participate with each other. The term "body (*sōma*)" has three possible meanings in this passage (Fitzmyer 2008, 391): (1) literally, the historical body of Christ crucified (Rom 7:4); (2) analogously, the ecclesiastical body of Christ (1 Cor 12:27; cf. Eph 4:12); and (3) liturgically, the eucharistic body of Christ (1 Cor 10:16; 11:27). In short, it means Jesus, or the church, or bread. In v. 27 Paul refers clearly to the literal body of Jesus, for he suggests that those who take the elements unworthily are liable for "the body *and* the blood" of the Lord; i.e., they are responsible for his execution (cf. Deut 19:10). In v. 29 Paul drops reference to the blood and refers only to the body. This change suggests that Paul now refers to the eucharistic bread as body, which in turn serves as a figure for the ecclesiastical body of which church members are fragments. In other words, those who disrespect the body (or the bread that represents Christ) disrespect the unity of the body (or the church). To rightly "discern" the body, then, means to view the bread as representative of the unity that the body's members share with each other. To take the bread as less than this—as just the bread of an ordinary meal—is to treat the body in an unworthy way.

Paul draws things together by alluding again to the Corinthians' discordant participation in the meal. In response to those who "take their own supper beforehand" (v. 21), he now implores, "wait for one another" (v. 33). In sum, if the meal is a symbol of unity, they should take their meal together.

In his final statement Paul intimates that he intends to visit again (v. 34). At that time, he will give the church further instructions about the Supper. Unfortunately, he gives no indication what these instructions might concern.

Abuses of Spiritual Gifts (12:1–14:40)

In the lengthiest unit in the letter, Paul treats the issue of spiritual gifts, the third and final problem addressed in connection with dissension in the church's gatherings for worship. The unit as a whole counters an attitude that views manifestations of the Spirit as tokens of superiority, presenting them instead as gifts, distributed to all believers alike, in accordance with the will of the Spirit, and for the common benefit. Abuse in the deployment of tongues seems to have been the chief problem. The term *glōssa* ("tongues") appears twenty-one times in this unit, occurring in all three lists of spiritual gifts (12:8-10, 28-30; 13:1-3) and always at or near the end; in the final section (14:1-33) tongues is set in direct comparison with prophecy, to which it is proposed to be inferior.

12:1-3 provides a short introduction to the unit. 14:36 offers a conclusion. Enclosed are three parts, structured in an A-B-A pattern:
A. Diversity of gifts (12:4-30)
    B. Love vs. gifts (12:31–13:13)
A′. Prophecy vs. tongues (14:1-33)

Part A affirms the diversity of gifts and their common source in the Spirit. The final part presents prophecy as superior to tongues owing to its greater potential to build up the community. At the heart of the unit appears an encomium of love, in which Paul presents love as superior to the gifts and as the antidote to the community's divisive use of the gifts.

While Paul presents his comments in this section as authoritative (14:38), he generally refrains from imperatives. Rather, he makes abundant use of rhetorical questions (twenty rhetorical questions appear in chapters 12 and 14), relying instead on the power of suggestion, and appeals to example, not least his own (14:18-19).

12:1-3
The formula "Now concerning" (*peri de*) recurs (7:1; 8:1), signaling a transition to another new topic, that of "spiritual things" (*pneumatika*). That this means "spiritual *gifts*" (so English translations) is shown by the substitution of the word "gifts" (*charismata*) in v. 4 and by Paul's exhortation to "strive for the greater gifts (*charismata*)" in v. 31.

Paul suggests indirectly that the Corinthians are "ignorant" (v. 1), reminding them of their days when they "were Gentiles" and were led away to "mute" idols. Herewith Paul addresses the church as if it consisted primarily of non-Jews. The suggestion that they are Gentiles no longer may imply (Hays 1997, 209) that in Christ they have been "grafted on" to the olive tree of Israel (Rom 11:17-24), although Paul has not formulated things in these terms in this letter, and in chapter 10 he distinguished the "church of God" from "Jews" and "Greeks" (10:32). That idols were "mute" or "dumb" was a stock Jewish critique of idols. Idols were nothing but brass, wood, stone, and clay, made with human hands, helpless and lifeless in themselves (Deut 4:27-28; Pss 115:5; 135; Isa 44; 46; Jer 10:2-15; 29; Hab 2:18; Wis 13:10; 14:1; Ep Jer 6:8; Apoc. Ab. 3:8–4:6; Let. Aris. 135–138; Jos. Asen. 11:8; 12:5, 11). Gentiles in the church who were more philosophically minded might have concurred with Paul's assessment even as Gentiles, for pagan philosophers were often equally critical of divine images (Epicurus in Cicero, *Nat. d.* 1.123; Seneca in Augustine, *Civ.* 6.10). Yet Paul depicts the Corinthians as all equally deceived in their past. When he says that they were "led away" by idols, he refers not to possession under ecstatic influence (Horsley 1998, 168) or to procession to the site of an idol (Paige 1991) but simply to being "led astray," that is, away from the true God.

Verse 3 establishes a conclusion based on what precedes: Paul now "makes known" the truth about the Spirit in response to the Corinthians' presumed ignorance (vv. 1-2). It is not that the Corinthians had never learned this truth but that they were not living in recognition of it; Paul "makes known" this truth as a reminder (cf. 15:1). The truth is that all who declare Jesus as Lord, and not just the few, have the Spirit and from the Spirit spiritual gifts.

The term "Lord" (*kyrios*) is the same term as that used in the Septuagint to translate YHWH. The declaration that "Jesus is Lord" would be heard as a declaration of exclusive loyalty to Jesus, precluding assent that "Caesar is Lord" (*Mart. Pol.* 8.2; cf. Epictetus, *Diatr.* 4.1.13) or that any other is Lord. The counter declaration, that "Jesus is cursed (*anathema*)," is a declaration that Jesus is accursed by God. The word "anathema" refers to something "set up" or, hence, "consecrated" to a god. Such could be considered holy or, conversely, "accursed," in the sense of being taboo. Some Jews must have made a connection between the affirmation in Deuteronomy that anything hanged on a tree (or a cross) is accursed by God on the one hand, and the crucifixion of Jesus on the other (Deut 21:23; Gal 3:13). However, it seems unlikely that members of the Corinthian church believed anyone would utter "Jesus be accursed" when speaking in the Spirit. Rather, the declaration is contrived by Paul so as to create an antithesis between a life that declares the lordship of Jesus and one that does not.

The function of this introduction is to present a theological framework for the ensuing discussion about spiritual gifts. When the Corinthians were still practicing idolatry, they were ignorant of spiritual gifts and ignorant of Jesus' lordship. When they converted, they became Spirit people and could declare the lordship of Jesus. Declaring the lordship of Jesus, in other words, goes hand in hand with life in the Spirit. The conclusion is that all who declare Christ as Lord have the Spirit. And if all have the Spirit, all play a part in building up the body of the church. No one in the church is unspiritual. Each person has their own gift.

12:4-11

This new section consists of two smaller units (vv. 4-6, 7-10) and a summary (v. 11). Verses 4-6 affirm that while there are many gifts, they are all the work of the same God. The switch from "spiritual things" (*pneumatika*) in v. 1 to "gifts" (*charismata*) in v. 4 highlights the nature of spiritual phenomena as gifts from God and not as personal achievements. Moreover, these gifts belong to all who declare Jesus as Lord (v. 3; or in v. 7, to "each" person who declares Jesus as Lord).

Verses 4-6 constitute a tricolon structured around the Spirit (the Holy Spirit), the Lord (the Son), and God (the Father), thus reflecting an incipient Trinitarianism. Within this structure the repetition, symmetry, and emphasis on *oneness* and *all things* has a resemblance to philosophical descriptions of God (cf. Marcus Aurelius, *Med.* 7.9: "there is both one Universe, made up of all things, and one God immanent in all things, and one Substance, and One Law . . . ," etc.; cf. Eph 1:23).

The emphasis on oneness underscores the purpose of the gifts (v. 7): "the good" (*sympheron*). That this refers to the "common good," or the benefit of the community, is assured by the context of chapters 12–14 (esp. 14:4-5, 12, 17, 31). Earlier, Paul had used the same word in response to the Corinthian slogan "all things are permissible" (6:12a/10:23a): "but not all things are *beneficial* (*sympherei*)" (6:12b/10:23b). There he had focused on the surrender of one's rights for the benefit of others. Now he focuses on use of the spiritual gifts for the benefit of the community.

Verses 7-10 affirm that the Spirit distributes different gifts to different people. Apparently the gifts are not necessarily received at conversion, for Paul later says that one can "strive after" the greater gifts (12:31a) and advises that the Corinthians should "*seek* to prophesy" (14:1). While here Paul assigns a single gift to each person, later discussion suggests that a person may possess more than one gift. One who speaks in tongues may pray "also that he or she may interpret" (14:13). Paul himself exhibited many gifts: he spoke in tongues (14:18); he did "signs and wonders and powers" (2 Cor 12:12; cf. Rom 15:19); he imparted prophetic revelations (Rom 11:25-26; 1 Cor 15:51-52; 1 Thess 4:15-17); he was also an apostle (12:28, 29). He says, nevertheless, that one cannot have all the gifts (vv. 28-30).

The list of gifts is selective rather than exhaustive, for non-identical lists occur in 12:28-30; Rom 12:6-8; and Eph 4:4-12. This list is evidently tailored to the situation in Corinth. The first two gifts play on Corinthian catchwords—"word of *wisdom*" (cf. 1:17-3:23) and "word of *knowledge*" (cf. 8:1-13)—and do not appear in lists outside of 1 Corinthians. The protracted treatment of prophecy and tongues in 14:1-40 shows that these gifts, or at least one of the two, had engendered problems in Corinth. These and the other gifts mentioned seem to fall into an intentional arrangement. Apart from "faith," the other six gifts fall into pairs: "word of wisdom" and "word of knowledge," "gifts of healings" and "works of miracles," and "kinds of tongues" and "interpretation of tongues." Alternatively, Paul may have arranged the list so as to distinguish gifts of teaching (word of wisdom, word of knowledge), miraculous gifts (faith to move mountains, gifts of healing, works of powers), and inspired speech (kinds of tongues, interpretation of tongues). Paul offers no definitions of the gifts, and as later discussion shows, there is some overlap among them (e.g., 14:6).

Finally, after repeated but varied expressions of the Spirit's agency in distributing the gifts ("through the Spirit . . . according to the same Spirit . . . by the same Spirit . . . by the one Spirit"), Paul concludes with a recapitulative summary, affirming that "the one and the same Spirit works all these things" (v. 11). Lest anyone think that they have earned the gifts, Paul adds, "as it [the Spirit] wills."

12:12-26

Paul illustrates the principle of unity in diversity with the analogy of a body. The opening verse (v. 12) states the main idea. The next verse (v. 13) establishes the means through which this reality came to be. Then follow three elaborations of the main idea (vv. 14-20, 21-24, 25-26).

Verse 12 proposes that the church (for which Paul substitutes the word "Christ"), like a body, is both one and has many parts (cf. Rom 12:4-5). While the same principle presumably applies to the universal church, Paul has in mind the Corinthian church in particular. Appeal to the body as an analogy for the principle of unity in diversity was widespread in the ancient world (Lee 2006). The Stoic philosophers used the idea to describe the universe

(Marcus Aurelius, *Med.* 4.13, 40; Seneca, *Ep.* 65.19; Diogenes Laertius, *Vit. phil.* 7.87-88). Stoic-influenced political treatises used the image to describe the city (Cicero, *Off.* 3.5.22-23; Hierocles//Stobaeus, *Anth.* 3.39.34-35). Several ancient historians record an instance in which the Roman consul Menenius Agrippa used a "fable" about the body to capture the relationship between the Roman Senate and the plebeians (Dionysius of Halicarnassus, *Rom. Ant.* 6.86.1-5; Livy, *Hist.* 2.32; Plutarch, *Cor.* 6.3-4). Paul seems to be aware of the body trope, but he adapts it so that it applies not to the world or to the city but strictly to the church.

Verse 13 presents the church's unity not only as a social reality but also as a metaphysical reality. The church became one through baptism in the Spirit (cf. 10:2-3). This verse may contain the outline of an early church liturgical formula used at baptism. Indeed, the unity of Jew and Greek, slave and free, in association with baptism, is also affirmed in Gal 3:27-28. Moreover, the verse here describes unity in summary, listing not all possible pairs but two representative pairs: one ethnic (Jew and Greek) and the other social (slave and free). Standing out is Paul's omission of the pair male and female, which Gal 3:28 includes. If the Corinthian women believed that in Christ they had transcended gender distinctions (see 11:2-16), Paul may have omitted the male-female pair so as to preclude a misapplication of his teaching (Wire 1990, 137–38).

Paul's first elaboration of the analogy (vv. 14-20) focuses on the point that *the body does not consist of just one part.* Paul states his premise in v. 14 and then illustrates it with reference to particular body parts. He personifies the foot and the ear (vv. 15-16) so that the foot implies that the hand makes up the whole body, and the ear that the eye makes up the whole body. Paul then speaks in his own voice, reproving the foot and the ear by asking if the whole body can really be just one part, since other parts also seem to be necessary (v. 17, 19). God designed the body to have multiple parts. Things are as he willed them at creation (v. 18). The final verse offers a correction to the notion that one part could constitute the whole body: "but as it is, there are *many* parts, but one body" (v. 20).

The second elaboration (vv. 21-25a) illustrates the point that *all the parts are necessary.* Paul's affirmation that the head needs the feet harks back to the discussion of heads in 11:3 and offers an important qualification. If the "head of every woman is man," still man cannot say to the woman, "I do not have need of you." In a radical move, Paul goes even further. Appealing to the Corinthians' sense of honor, he affirms that the less honorable parts are actually worthy of the greater honor, as people adorn those parts of the body that are uncomely but leave unadorned those parts that are comely (cf. Cicero,

Off. 1.35). This application of the analogy is atypical in its ancient context. The analogy was often used to reinforce social hierarchies. Paul comes very near to reversing them (cf. Martin 1995, 40–42).

First Corinthians 12:12-26, like 11:3-10, reflects a strong tension in Paul's theology. On the one hand, he affirms a hierarchical view of headship, and he will later suggest that some gifts possess greater importance than others, even while all the gifts are necessary. On the other hand, he affirms the interdependence of man and woman, and of all the parts of the body. This passage, then, is perhaps best characterized not as anti-hierarchical but as anti-elitist. Some parts may have more foundational significance, and some gifts may be more beneficial than others, but all of them contribute something of importance. Paul ends with a fine balance. God has made things in such a way as to preclude a "split" in the body (v. 25). He has bestowed greater honor on the inferior members ("that which is lacking"), so that the otherwise honored members might not set themselves above them. Each part has a kind of honor of its own. Thus, the parts cannot stand that far apart; and a split cannot occur.

The third elaboration of the initial premise emphasizes that *each of the parts should feel what the others feel* (vv. 25b-26). They should care about the same things; they should suffer together; they should rejoice together (cf. Rom 12:15). The Greek word here translated "suffers together" (*sympaschei*) was used in Stoic philosophy to indicate a literal sympathy between the parts of the universe: the parts were so interwoven that each experienced what the others experienced (Philo, *Migr.* 180//*SVF* 2.532; Hierocles// Stobaeus, *Anth.* 4.84.20; Epictetus, *Diatr.* 1.14.5-6; cf. *SVF* 2.546, 1013). Paul uses the verb in the same way, but specifically with reference to the relationship between Christ-people. The principle of sympathy prevents anyone from standing out, above or below others. One cannot be elevated without the others rejoicing together with them, and one cannot suffer without the others suffering with them.

12:27-31a

Paul restates his original premise, but now he reveals explicitly the identity of the body: while he had begun, "so also is the *Christ*" (v. 12), he now says, "And it is *you* [emphatic] who are the body of Christ" (v. 27). This statement introduces a final elaboration of the principle of unity in diversity. Here Paul returns from the gifted to the gifts, thus bending the chapter into a ring structure (Talbert 2002, 104):

    A. The variety of gifts (vv. 4-11)
        B. The one body (vv. 12-27[28])
    A'. The variety of gifts (vv. [27]28-30)

In v. 28, Paul renames some but not all of the gifts mentioned in vv. 8-10. Now he adds that God has appointed some people to be apostles, some to be prophets, and some to be teachers. He also adds the gifts of "helps" and "administrations" (NASB), while omitting "words of wisdom," "words of knowledge," and "discernment of spirits." In vv. 29-30, he repeats more or less the same list through a series of rhetorical questions, organized into two sets of three. The gifts that appear in all three lists (vv. 8-10, 28, 29-30) appear in the same order in each of them: powers, healings, and tongues.

The ordinal adverbs "first," "second," and "third" undoubtedly establish a ranking of offices (apostles, prophets, teachers). But this is no ordinary hierarchy, for Paul has already presented the apostles as "weak" (4:9), as ministers and stewards (4:1), and as subservient to the church (3:22). The apostles are perhaps first in the sense that their work is foundational (cf. Rom 10:15: "And how are they to hear without someone to proclaim him? And how are they to proclaim him unless they are *sent* [*apostalōsin*]?"). Thereafter, the switch from ordinal numbers to the adverb "then" suggests that the ensuing gifts follow the first three in rank; yet Paul now strings the gifts together in a series, giving no indication of their rank, unless by their written order. Since Paul compares tongues unfavorably to prophecy in chapter 14, it seems no accident that tongues comes "at or near the bottom" in all three lists, and that in each of its appearances prophecy comes "near the top" (Sampley 2015, 817).

Paul's alternation between people and gifts makes it difficult to determine whether he thinks of gifts as permanent or temporary endowments. He seems to think of the offices of apostle, prophet, and teacher as permanent. At least he viewed his role as apostle in this way.

The first half of 12:31 anticipates chapter 14, where Paul sets prophecy and tongues in juxtaposition. Although all the gifts can serve the common benefit, some are "greater" than others. The imperative "*strive after* the greater gifts" contains double entendre. In Greek the verb "strive after" (*zēloute*) is based on the same root as the noun "rivalry" (*zēlos*)—the noun that Paul had used in 3:3 to refer to "strife and *rivalries* among you." Thus Paul alludes to the Corinthians' enthusiasm for rivalry while trying to redirect it toward more noble ends: the building up of the church. To paraphrase, "Do not strive *with one another* but rather strive *after the greater gifts.*"

12:31b–13:13

Dividing the discussion of spiritual gifts in chapters 12 and 14 is an encomium of love. In ancient rhetorical theory, an encomium was an expository composition that artistically described the excellence of some person or thing (Hermogenes, *Prog.* 7; Aphthonius, *Prog.* 8; Nicolaus, *Prog.* 8). Encomiastic discourse was closely related to the epideictic kind of rhetoric, which served the purpose of either praise or blame and highlighted what was either honorable or disgraceful. The final purpose of such discourse was to exhort the audience toward either imitation of or aversion to the person or thing described. Although 1 Corinthians as a whole could be characterized as a piece of deliberative rhetoric (M. M. Mitchell 1993, 1), chapter 13 is no intrusion. Rather it is the focal point of the discussion comprising 12:1–14:40. The focus on love serves a subtle rhetorical purpose. It enables Paul to critique the Corinthians indirectly by presenting a model to which they plainly were not conforming, rather than confronting them directly and risking dismissal.

Verse 12:31b introduces the topic. 13:13 offers a concluding statement. Between, the chapter breaks down into three sections: vv. 1-3 (the gifts are nothing without love), vv. 4-7 (those who have love exhibit the named characteristics), and vv. 8-13 (love will not pass away). Paul has not elaborated on love to this point in the letter (but cf. 8:1-3), but love can be regarded as another name for that death-to-self-for-the-benefit-of-others that he has been talking about all along.

The chapter as a whole is stylistically elevated and can be considered hymnic. It contains artfully arranged and carefully varied clauses. It contains clear structural parallelism, as for instance in the threefold repetition of "If . . . but love I have not" (vv. 1-3). It contains numerous instances of word repetition: the threefold repetition of "and if . . . and if . . . and if" (v. 8); the fourfold repetition of "a child . . . a child . . . a child . . . a child" at the end of successive clause (v. 11); and the fivefold repetition of "and" (vv. 2-3). It exhibits several parallel antitheses: "all . . . all . . . all . . . *nothing*" (v. 2); "all . . . *nothing*" (v. 3); "now . . . but *then* . . . now . . . but *then*" (v. 12). And in its Greek form it exhibits multiple instances of alliteration (vv. 12, 13). While the hymn is exceptional compared to Paul's usual style and could have derived from a different author, the hymn is so well integrated with the rest of the letter that it seems best to conclude that it was composed by Paul for just this occasion (Corley 2004).

The transition from the topic of spiritual gifts into the hymn of love happens in two quick steps. After establishing that there are a variety of gifts (12:1-30), Paul urges the Corinthians to "strive after the *greater* gifts"

(12:31a). Then, in a second step, he offers to show them a way better than the greater gifts themselves (12:31b). This is the way of love, as described in 13:1-13.

Paul describes this way as "more excellent" (NRSV) or, literally, a way "according to excess" (12:31b). Nowhere else does Paul use this expression adjectivally. Here Paul may intend to echo philosophical tradition. According to Aristotle, ethical decisions were to target the "mean" between "deficiency" and "excess" (*Nic. eth.* 4.1.1-2). For instance, "liberality" was the desired mean between the aberrant dispositions of "meanness" (defect) and "prodigality" (excess). Paul may mean to flout this ethical system: in the case of love, one does not want to aim at moderation, but indeed excess!

The first section of the hymn reiterates that spiritual gifts exercised empty of love are useless (vv. 1-3). Paul speaks in the first person, drawing examples that could be hypothetical but that are also to some extent autobiographical. Two of the examples may allude to Jesus tradition: reference to "faith to move mountains" (Matt 17:20) and reference to the giving away of one's possessions (Mark 10:17-22, 23-30). The full set of examples moves toward a climax, from marvelous acts of spiritual prowess to extreme acts of self-denial culminating finally in death. All such acts, performed without love, are useless. The refrain "I am nothing . . . I profit nothing" recalls the affirmation in 1:28 that God chose those who "count for nothing" (NAB); ironically, those who seek to elevate themselves through displays of spiritual prowess make themselves "nothing" once again (Gardner 2018, 564).

Paul selects as examples several of the gifts named in 12:8-10: tongues, prophecy, knowledge, and faith. He refers to two kinds of tongues, the "tongues of men" and "(the tongues) of angels." The first expression could at first notice be taken as a reference to eloquent speech. However, since Paul is speaking with reference to spiritual gifts, the phenomenon should be seen as a spiritual endowment and could consist in inspired preaching or teaching. The tongues of angels could correlate with the phenomenon described in the Testament of Job where the daughters of Job receive the ability to speak in the language of the angels (T. Job 48:1–50:3). The hymn, however, is poetic, and Paul's expression need not be taken as a literal reference to "the language that angels speak." More likely, Paul has in mind spiritually inspired utterance, unintelligible to humanity and therefore of a "higher" kind (see 14:1-40). Paul's comparison of tongues to cacophonous cymbals fits with the larger point of 12:1–14:40, namely that the body should work together in a way that creates harmony in the whole. Indeed, cymbals were not meant to be played solo but contributed in an ensemble to a harmonious blend of sounds (Portier-Young 2005).

Among the gifts named in v. 2, prophecy will later be discussed as one of the greater gifts (14:1-40). Knowledge of "all the mysteries" recalls the language of Jewish apocalyptic (where a heavenly intermediary imparts secrets of the heavenly realm and the end times to some human recipient) or at least refers to some kind of inspired knowledge of truth (1QS IV.6). While in 8:1-3 Paul had set love in contrast with knowledge, it is evident now that love and knowledge are not mutually exclusive, but rather that knowledge can be applied either with love or without it. Paul's description of faith as faith "to move mountains" shows that the gift called "faith" earlier (12:9) is not saving faith but rather a situational faith.

Paul finishes by naming two extreme acts of self-denial. Voluntary surrender of all one's possessions was indeed exceptional, although it was not without parallel in the ancient world. Famous for their ascetic lifestyle, the Cynic philosophers characteristically owned nothing but a single cloak, a staff, and a wallet (Diogenes Laertius, *Vit. phil.* 6.13, 22-23; Lucian, *Dem.* 5; *Peregr.* 15). Paul, however, may have in mind the disciples of Jesus, who "left everything" to follow him (Mark 10:28).

Instances of voluntary capitulation to death are well documented in ancient sources (Murillo 1954), and victims are usually lauded as examples for imitation, although some denigrated them as mad or merely obstinate (Epictetus, *Diatr.* 4.7.6; Pliny, *Ep.* 10.96; Marcus Aurelius, *Med.* 11). Some translations of v. 3 judge that Paul here anticipates giving up his body in order that he might "boast" (NAB, NIV). Other translations follow manuscripts that read "in order that I might *burn*" (KJV, NKJV, RSV, ESV). While there is no record of the immolation of Christians this early in history (see Tacitus, *Ann.* 15.44), death by immolation was common enough and it is recounted in both Jewish and Greco-Roman sources (Daniel 3; 2 Macc 7:5; 4 Macc 9:22; 10:14; Seneca, *Ep.* 7.4, 5; 14.2). Which of the two readings is correct here is very difficult to decide (Malone 2009). Still, Paul's main point is clear: even the most extreme forms of self-denial count for nothing if they are performed absent of love.

In the second part of the hymn (vv. 4-7), Paul personifies love as a human agent. As such, Paul's encomium of Love resembles Plato's encomium of *Erōs* (*Symp.* 197c-e), Seneca's encomium of Reason (*Ira* 1.17.7), and the encomium of Truth found in 1 Esdras (4:34-40).

Paul arranges this section into a pair of positive affirmations ("love is patient, is kind"); a series of eight negative affirmations, each repeating "not"; and four final affirmations, each led by the word "all" and together forming an AB//BA chiasm in which the first and last terms are synonymous ("*bears*

. . . believes . . . hopes . . . *endures*"). In all, this section contains "fourteen descriptive statements in pairs" (Robertson and Plummer 1914, 292).

Most of the *negated* verbs overtly allude to actions that Paul has previously associated with the Corinthians. While Love is not, *they* are "envious" (3:3); *they* boast and are "boastful" (4:6, 7, 18, 19; 5:2; cf. 8:1); *they* are vindictive and commit "wrongs" against each other (5:1-13). As Love does not "seek" its own benefit, they should not "seek" their own benefit but rather the benefit of others (10:24, 33).

The words "Love never fails" set off the final portion of the hymn (vv. 8-13). The theme of this part is the antithesis between the transience of spiritual gifts and the permanence of love. The list of spiritual gifts—prophecy, tongues, and knowledge (cf. 12:8, 10)—is selective and representative. These will pass away just as "the present form of this world is passing away" (7:31). But Paul correlates several other antitheses with the main one: along with the contrast between the transient and the permanent (v. 8) are contrasts between the partial and the complete (vv. 9-10), the immature and the mature (v. 11), and the indirect and the direct (v. 12).

transient	permanent
partial	complete
immature	mature
indirect	direct

These contrasts are further expressions of the contrast between the spiritual gifts and love. The spiritual gifts yield only a fragmentary grasp of God. Love embodies God in his fullness. Now the spiritual gifts are present. At the eschaton, love will arrive in its fullness. In this way Paul identifies love as the "perfect" (*teleion*) thing (v. 10). The "perfect" is the same word that the Greek philosophers used to describe the highest goal of human life. Each of the philosophical schools identified this goal differently. For Aristotle the highest goal was happiness (Aristotle, *Nic. eth.* 1.4.1-2); for the Epicureans it was pleasure (Cicero, *Fin.* 1.29-39); for the Academics it was suspension of belief (Sextus Empiricus, *Pyr.* 1.8); for the Stoics it was life according to nature (*SVF* 3.2-19). Paul identifies the highest goal—the "perfect" thing—as love.

From here Paul illustrates the contrast with two analogies. The first appeals to the stages of human maturation (v. 11). Here again Paul appeals to himself as an example (cf. 2:1-5; 3:5–4:5, 16; 7:7, 8; 8:13; 9:1-27; 10:33–11:1). He once spoke, thought, and reasoned like a child. He has now put away childish things.

There are two ways to take this analogy. First, the analogy could be seen as breaking from the present-future pattern of the other antitheses.

Accordingly, Paul would be saying not that the gifts *will* come to an end but that he has *already* matured beyond them. If this is his point, then he is evidently speaking of the gifts not in their purer form (for he does still practice the gifts) but in the sense in which he refers to them in vv. 1-3, that is, as faculties exercised without love. The implication would be that the Corinthians, who so value spiritual things, are again acting as "children" (3:1), emphasizing the gifts but not practicing them in love. Alternatively, Paul could be suggesting not that his practice of the gifts *has* come to an end but that, just as childhood gives way to maturity, so the spiritual gifts *will* give way to love in the *end*. This would maintain the present-future pattern of the other antitheses.

The second analogy compares manifestations of spiritual gifts to images seen in a mirror. Philo of Alexandria uses the analogy of a mirror to describe the way in which humans access the transcendent, that is, indirectly (*Dec.* 105; *Migr.* 190; *Fug.* 213). Paul's contrast between seeing "in a mirror, dimly" and seeing "face to face" shows that he is using the analogy similarly, although he draws the image specifically from Num 12:8 and Deut 34:10, where Moses, in contrast with the other prophets, is presented as having the ability to converse with God face to face (Hollander 2010). Paul's epistemological humility is paralleled by philosophers like Seneca, who maintained that we now see as through a "mist" and will not know all the secrets of the universe until we die (*Ep.* 102.28). In short, for Paul the spiritual gifts yield indirect knowledge of God, while love creates a direct bond with him. We do not know God but have been "known" by him. God revealed himself when no one was looking for him. He reached out to humanity, "knew" *us*, when humanity did not really know *him*. Paul, however, returns summarily to the first person plural: while he has not known God fully, he *will* know him. The word that Paul uses here for "knowing" is different than usual (*epiginōskein* vs. *ginōskein*) and indicates knowledge in a complete sense (Aristotle, *An. post.* 2.99b-100b; *SVF* 2.35).

In a poetic conclusion characterized by several types of alliteration in the original Greek (Smit 1991, 205), Paul elevates faith, hope, and love above the spiritual gifts (v. 13). This triad appears in at least loose association in several other places in Paul's letters (Rom 5:1-5; Eph 4:2-5; Col 1:4-5; 1 Thess 1:3; 5:8). Since Paul has focused here on the contrast between the transience of the gifts and the *permanence* of love, and since Paul now states that these three, in contrast with the gifts, all "*abide*," Paul must mean that all three of these, not just love, are permanent. In this sense, faith is that which "characterizes a life lived for all eternity in the sphere in which Christ's salvation is known and experienced and in which he continues forever to be acknowledged as Lord" (Gardner 2018, 581). And hope "presupposes and expresses a genuine and therefore unalterable truth about God . . . God is our hope; that is, one in whom hope is properly reposed" (Barrett 1968, 309). Love, however, is the greatest since God himself possesses this. Believers are to love as God loves.

14:1-40

In chapter 14 Paul works out a comparison between two of the gifts, namely, tongues and prophecy (in chapters 12–14 the singular "tongue" occurs eight times, and the plural "tongues" occurs twelve). Some in the church have put tongues on display when gathered for worship, apparently viewing tongues as an indicator of high spiritual status. Paul proposes that the gift of prophecy is greater than the gift of tongues, since the former builds up the church while the latter builds up only oneself. The noun "upbuilding" and its verb cognate "build up" occur seven times in this chapter, reprising the references to upbuilding found earlier in the discussion of idol-meat (8:2; 10:23). Paul's main thesis here is that, when the church assembles, the gifts should be used for the upbuilding of the church (14:3, 4, 5, 12, 26) or at least of some other member (14:17).

The chapter opens and closes with an exhortation to strive after prophecy (vv. 1, 39). Inside are three sections. The first explains why prophecy is superior to tongues (14:1-19). The second explores the effects of tongues and prophecy on nonbelievers (14:20-25). The third urges believers to practice the gifts in orderly fashion (14:26-40).

The first verse of the chapter reverses the steps taken in 12:31a and b. There Paul had urged the Corinthians to strive after the greater gifts (12:31a) and then introduced the "more excellent way" of love (12:31b). Then followed a description of love. A reverse image of 12:31, 14:1 now urges the Corinthians to "pursue love" (14:1a) and then to "be zealous for spiritual things" (14:1b).

    A. strive after the greater gifts (12:31a)
        B. the more excellent way of love (12:31b)
            C. love (13:1-13)
        B'. the pursuit of love (14:1a)
    A'. zeal for spiritual things (14:1b)

In this way, Paul transitions from love back to the spiritual gifts.

14:1-19

Within 14:1-19, verses 1c-5 constitute the first of three paragraphs. Verse 1c introduces Paul's chief exhortation, that the Corinthians should strive "that [they] may prophesy." Verse 5 closes the paragraph with the same words, "that you may prophesy." The paragraph opens up a direct comparison between prophecy and tongues, wherein Paul commends the former over the latter. The comparison was anticipated in chapter 12, where "prophets" ranked just after the "apostles" (12:28). Tongues had ranked at or near the end in all the earlier lists (12:10, 28, 30).

Here in 14:2-5, Paul explains, in a series of parallel antitheses, that prophecy is "greater" than tongues since the former edifies the church. Seven times in this chapter Paul identifies the edification of the church as a criterion for the value of a spiritual gift (vv. 3, 4, 5, 6, 12, 17, 26).

Paul refrains from offering detailed descriptions of the gifts, although chapters 12–14 offer clues about how he understood them. Regarding tongues, at least four points can be made. First, tongues give expression to "mysteries" (v. 2). Second, tongues are not ordinarily intelligible either to the mind of the speaker or to others (vv. 14-15). Third, the meaning of what is expressed in tongues can be understood through interpretation (v. 13). Fourth, the speaker can control their use of tongues (v. 28).

Beyond this it is not clear what, in Paul's view, the phenomenon of tongues consists in. Three options are usually identified. (1) Tongues could consist in the ability to speak foreign languages by the inspiration of the Spirit. Yet several points militate against this option. First, while Acts 2:1-13 may appear to describe something like this, what it actually describes is the ability of people to *hear* in their own language (2:11), not the ability to *speak* in the language of others. Second, Acts gives no indication that the phenomenon was something over which hearers had any control, while Paul suggests that tongues remain under the speaker's control (14:28). Third, although the ability to speak foreign languages could theoretically serve an important missionary purpose, Paul nowhere associates tongues with this purpose; rather he sets the value of tongues in their potential to edify, chiefly oneself (v. 4). Finally, it is far from evident why someone would need to speak a foreign language "to God" (v. 2), or how doing so would edify the speaker (v. 4).

(2) A second possibility is that tongues refers to angelic speech. In favor of this option is Paul's reference to the "tongues . . . of angels" in 13:2 and evidence in the pseudepigraphical book the Testament of Job where Job's daughters are said to speak in the language of angels (T. Job 48:1–50:3). However, Paul's reference to the "tongues . . . of angels" is a rhetorical

counterpart to the "tongues of men" and should probably not be taken literally. Moreover, one should not expect the tongues of angels to cease (Gardner 2018, 596), as tongues will (13:8). Nothing else in chapters 12–14 identifies tongues specifically with angels.

(3) A third possibility is that tongues refer to "ecstatic" speech—ecstatic, that is, not in the sense that the speaker loses control (v. 28) but in the sense that the speaker "has an experience of God that appears to be direct and immediate, that is, more spontaneous than planned or prepared" (Gardner 2018, 598). The plural "tongues" (12:30; 13:1, 8; 14:5 [x2], 6, 18, 22, 23, 39), or "kinds of tongues" (12:10, 28), would then imply that the coding is different in different acts of expression or for each individual speaker. Such an understanding could correlate partially with the phenomenon of "ecstatic" speech said to have been practiced among pagan oracles (see below).

Paul's understanding of prophecy comes into focus by contrast. Unlike tongues, prophecy offers encouragement (v. 3). Unlike tongues, prophecy is readily intelligible (vv. 2-5). Paul gives no indication whether prophecy involved messages of condemnation or predictions of future events. Prophecy as it is known from the Jewish scriptures, however, must have helped to shape his views. In the OT a prophet was one who spoke under divine inspiration (1 Sam 10:10; 1 Kgs 22:24) or directly on behalf of God (Jer 1:2, 4; Ezek 1:3). The classical prophets, like Isaiah and Jeremiah, not only preached repentance but also predicted specific future events (*ABD* 5:483). During the Second Temple period, views on prophecy varied. The author of 1 Maccabees maintained that prophecy had ceased (4:45-46; 9:27; 14:41) but anticipated that it would return (4:45-46; 14:41). The continuation of prophecy is well attested in other sources. The Qumran community believed that their "Teacher of Righteousness" offered inspired interpretations of the scriptures (1QHab 2:2-3). Both Philo (*Heres.* 259) and Josephus (*J.W.* 3.400-402; 6.300-309) make reference to contemporary prophets. Many Jews of the period viewed the Spirit as a source of wisdom, as an ecstatic power, or as a source of inspiration (Levison 2009, 118–53, 154–77, 178–201), thus associating the spirit with prophetic activity. Later, rabbinic writings attest to the view that prophecy had ceased and would not return until the eschatological age (Song of Songs Rab. 8.9-10; Num. Rab. 10.10; b. Yoma 9b, 21b; t. Sota 13.2; 'Abot 1).

Prophecy was not restricted to the Jews. Greek and Roman poets depicted themselves as inspired by the Muses (Pindar, fr. 150; Ovid, *Metam.* pr.) and could be designated by the term "prophet." In Greek the term "spirit" (*pneuma*) could be used with reference to inspired speech (Plato, *Ax.* 370c; Plutarch, *Mor.* 605). Plato believed in an inspired form of speech that exceeded the grasp of ordinary intelligence (*Tim.* 71E). It was often said that prophets prophesied from a state of ecstasy, or a trancelike state, in which they lost control of themselves, even raved, and became nothing more than instruments for the divine voice (Plato, *Phaedr.* 244A-B; *Tim.* 71E; *Ion* 534C-D; Cicero, *Div.* 1.2.4). Paul probably had such prophets in mind when he worried that outsiders would think that Corinthian church members who spoke in tongues were "out of their minds" (14:23). Like Plato, Philo of Alexandria maintained that prophecy transcended reason, or rather grasped what reason could not (*Mos.* 2.6). Sharing the Hellenistic view, he recounted that the translators of the Septuagint became "possessed" and wrote what God dictated, word for word (*Mos.* 2.34-40); he also claimed that Moses, on certain occasions, became "possessed" and in this way delivered the Law to Israel (*Mos.* 2.188).

Hellenistic sources also describe a kind of prophecy that excluded the element of trance. Plutarch suggested that the reason the style of oracles at Delphi changed over time is that "the god" imparted only the ideas, while the prophets themselves determined the words (*Mor.* 397C; 404B-405D). Similarly, Philo recounts that Moses sometimes spoke not under dictation but as God's "interpreter" (*Mos.* 2.188). In short, while Hellenistic sources usually depict prophets as prophesying from a state of trance, they do not always do so (Callan 1985). In the case of Hellenistic Jews like Philo, the influence of the OT caused a shift of meaning in the Greek term *prophētēs*, so that the element of trance was deemphasized (Callan 1985, 134).

Reportedly, prophetic utterances were often unintelligible. It was not uncommon for messages to come out confused (Lucian, *Alex.* 22, 49). Plutarch reports that the Pythia at Delphi uttered unintelligible messages that were then translated by the so-called prophets (*Mor.* 431D-438E). At other times, messages resembled something akin to gibberish. Sources describe strange sounds (Herodotus, *Hist.* 8.135; Plutarch, *Mor.* 412A; Dio, *Or.* 10.23-24; Apuleius, *The Golden Ass* 8.27), messages made to sound like known languages (Lucian, *Alex.* 13), and meaningless sequences of letters (Lucian, *Alex.* 51, 53). In the opinion of Lucian, such nonsense exposed the prophet as a charlatan (Lucian, *Alex.* 13, 22, 49, 51, 53).

Little is known about early Christian prophecy. Chronologically, John the Baptist is the first prophet known from the NT (Matt 3:1-12//Mark 1:4-8//Luke 3:2-18). In a break from Second Temple Judaism, early Christianity came to associate prophecy with the permanent filling of the Spirit experienced by Christ believers (Levison 2009, 238). The prophetic gift is mentioned in 1 Thessalonians (5:19-20), Paul's earliest letter and the earliest writing in the NT (AD 50).

As Paul describes them, the distinction between tongues and prophecy does not seem to be absolute. In Hellenistic sources, ecstatic prophecy involving confused chatter or inarticulate sounds could be associated with the phenomenon that Paul calls tongues. If the Corinthians shared the culture's understanding of prophecy, they may not have seen a distinction (Callan 1985). Even for Paul, tongues and prophecy could overlap. He suggests, for instance, that one could speak tongues "in a prophecy" (v. 6), with the result that one spoke in tongues and prophesied at the same time. Paul, however, ultimately insisted on a difference.

Paul further elaborates on the difference in vv. 6-12, where he reiterates that, if one's message is to edify the church, it needs to be intelligible. He illustrates with two analogies (vv. 7, 8) followed by an application (v. 9) and then a third analogy (v. 11) followed by another application (v. 12).

The first analogy takes the example of musical instruments (v. 7). Paul borrows a commonplace observation that inanimate things, like the flute and the lyre, make their own distinct sounds, which when emitted in orderly patterns of rhythm and pitch can be intelligibly processed as the playing of a flute or a lyre and not as just random noise (cf. Cicero, *Nat. d.* 2.146-150; Aristotle, *An.* 420B). The second analogy makes the same point. A trumpet must produce the distinct sound of a trumpet, in a meaningful pattern, if people are to heed its signal at the critical moment of battle (v. 8). The application establishes that the words of a spoken message must make articulate sense. The addendum—that if what is spoken cannot be understood, one is "speaking into the air"—sounds like a blanket rejection of tongues; however, this characterization only parodies tongues, not private use of tongues.

In v. 11 Paul describes the kind of misunderstanding that occurs between people who speak different languages. This is not evidence that Paul conceived of tongues as a foreign language. Rather, following the previous two analogies, Paul now cites a third analogy: the speaker of tongues is *analogous* to a "barbarian" in the eyes of the person who does not understand. The term "barbarian" originated as an onomatopoeic term for the sound of foreign speech as Greeks perceived it (cf. the English word "babble"). By extension the term came to mean "non-Greek" and thus, by connotation, "uncultured." The Corinthians, who evidently spoke Greek, would be familiar with the experience of encountering non-Greek speakers on the streets, in the marketplace, and in other public spaces, and they would know well the frustration of hearing a language that made no sense to them.

Paul's application of the analogy to the Corinthians in v. 12 ("so also you") follows from the analogy only loosely: *since* they are "zealous of spiritual (gifts)" (NASB), they ought, through spiritual gifts, to strive for the edification of the church (and not to sound like barbarians!). The noun "zealots" is cognate with the word that Paul used earlier when he said, "there is *jealousy* among you" (3:3). Earlier he used the verb cognate to urge the Corinthians to "strive after" the greater gifts (12:31; cf. 14:1). Here again there is a hint of sarcasm. They are zealous for spiritual things, yes, but their zeal has been misdirected.

Verses 13-19 offer a second round of arguments. First, Paul states a conclusion: the one who prays in a tongue should also seek an interpretation. In fact, the speaker himself or herself should pray that he or she might interpret. Each person, it seems, is not limited to one gift.

Paul's next point is that people should speak so as to engage both their spirit and their mind (vv. 14-17). In general, Paul uses the words "spirit" (*pneuma*), "mind" (*nous*), "soul" (*psychē*), and other anthropological terms without technical consistency (Jewett 1971). However, his use of a spirit/ mind dichotomy here may have been taken over from "contemporary theorizing about prophetic activity" (Martin 1995, 100). Only, his understanding of the relationship between the spirit and the mind stands in noticeable contrast with the view taken by some theoreticians. Plato and others viewed inspiration as a means of achieving knowledge *higher* than that which could be grasped by the rational faculties. Paul suggests that because glossolalia engages only the spirit, it is fruitless. In other words, while Plato subordinates the mind to the spirit, Paul subordinates the spirit to the mind (Martin 1995, 96–101). It is possible to read this relation as an analogue to Paul's understanding of relationships within the church. That is, just as the ordinarily higher part, the spirit, should submit to the lower part, the mind (Martin 1995, 101), so also it should be in the body of the church: the higher should submit to the lower.

In his concern for intelligibility, Paul takes special consideration for a figure in the assembly that he calls the *idiōtēs*. Renderings of this word in English translations vary ("outsider," ESV; "unlearned," KJV; "uninstructed," NAB; "ungifted," NASB; "inquirer," NIV), due to the puzzling nature of this figure's description. Apparently, the *idiōtēs* is not identical with the nonbeliever, with whom the *idiōtēs* appears side by side in vv. 23, 24. This figure is welcome in the assembly (v. 16) and is expected to say "Amen" when church members pray in thanks to God (v. 16). On the other hand, the *idiōtēs* is yet to be convicted in heart, to fall on their face and worship God, and to declare that God is truly present (vv. 24-25), and it is expected that the figure will view glossolalists as being out of their minds (v. 23). Moreover, Paul's concern that gifts should be used to "instruct others" (v. 19) probably suggests that the *idiōtēs* is not yet educated in the faith.

It may be that the *idiōtēs* possessed an official *status* as *idiōtēs* in the church, for it should be noticed that Paul does not refer to the figure only as an *idiōtēs* but as a person "in the position of" (NRSV) the *idiōtēs* (v. 16). While there is no evidence that the church yet had an extensive "catechetical" curriculum, it could be that the *idiōtēs* maintained their status as such until instruction was complete (or until baptism?). Since the figure is not expected to understand tongues (vv. 16, 23) and is expected to be impressed by prophecy (vv. 24-25), the figure was probably not yet seen as being gifted by the Spirit. In short, the *idiōtēs* seems to have been a figure welcome in the church, sympathetic to the church, and in attendance in assembly for worship, but not yet having full status as either a gifted or an educated believer. Hence, there is good justification for the varied renderings "unlearned" (KJV), "uninstructed" (NAB), "ungifted" (NASB), "inquirer" (NIV).

Paul concludes the paragraph by appealing again to his personal example (vv. 18-19). He himself can and does speak in tongues, and he does so "more than all" of the Corinthians. While this apparent boast seems to revert to the status-wielding behavior that Paul has sought to quash throughout the chapter and throughout the letter, two points clarify that his tone is less boastful than it may seem. First, he credits God for his ability ("I give thanks to God"). Second, the statement itself is an exaggeration serving rhetorically to enlarge the magnanimity of his decision *not* to use tongues publicly. That is, while he speaks in tongues more than anyone, he is willing not to do so at all in the interest of clear instruction or benefit to others. He does not, like others, wish to draw attention to himself. His qualification "in assembly" is important. He wants to limit himself only in public, for the benefit of others. In private his practice may have continued unhindered.

14:20-25

The first main part of the chapter comes to a close. Verses 20-25 shift to a new concern: the effects of tongues and prophecy on nonbelievers. Paul prefaces with an exhortation for the Corinthians not to be childish but to be mature in their thinking (v. 20). Although this language clearly echoes two earlier passages (3:1; 13:10), it may draw inspiration from the context of the quotation that follows (v. 21), where Paul quotes from Isa 28:11, 12. That is, v. 20 seems to allude to the material just preceding, in Isa 28:9.

v. 20, allusion to Isa 28:9
v. 21, quotation of Isa 28:11, 12

In Isa 28:9 the prophet chides the Israelites for their failure to heed God's oracles, saying, "To whom will he teach knowledge, and to whom will he explain the message? *Those who are weaned from milk, those taken from the breast?"* (NRSV). Implicitly, Paul's warning not to be children in thinking constitutes an exhortation for the Corinthians not, like children, to misevaluate the purpose of tongues.

Verse 21 cites Isa 28:11, 12, with changes. Paul changes the third person plural to the first person singular and adds "the Lord says," so that God, as it were, speaks directly to the Corinthians. Since Paul introduces Isaiah as "the Law," he must mean "Law" in a sense that encompasses the Jewish scriptures generally (cf. Rom 3:10-19).

Here in Isaiah God says that he will speak to his addressees "with foreign tongues," "with the lips of others," since they have failed to heed him. In the original context, the addressees represent unbelieving Israelites and the tongues/lips belong to the Assyrians. In Paul's application, the addressees represent outsiders and the tongues/lips belong to the Corinthians. Verse 22 explains the meaning. Because the Israelites failed to listen to the simple message of the prophets, they are now left to listen to an unintelligible message. This unintelligible message (or tongues) is a "sign" of God's judgment, that is, a sign that God has given them over to judgment by their enemies. In this sense, "sign" means an "indication of God's attitude" (Gardner 2018, 613), and in this case a negative attitude.

In contrast to nonbelievers, believers get prophecy, to which they, as believers, will listen. In short, believers get prophecy because they are sure to heed its message, and nonbelievers get tongues because they fail to listen to prophecy. Hearing tongues as "foreign," then, is a sign that one is not in good standing with God; tongues are "for" outsiders in this *negative* sense.

Paul elaborates his point in vv. 23-25, but now he seems to contradict himself. Here he says not that tongues are for nonbelievers and prophecy for believers but that tongues drive away nonbelievers and prophecy attracts them. One way of dealing with the shift is to view vv. 21 and 22 as the *Corinthians'* viewpoint and vv. 23-25 as Paul's response to it. This supposition is unnecessary (nor is it likely given the conjunction "therefore" at the opening of v. 23). Rather, tongues serve a different role in each scenario. In the quotation from Isaiah, tongues played the *negative* role of signifying that the listener was not in good standing with God. What Paul now says is entirely consistent with this: the *idiōtēs* or the nonbeliever will see those speaking in tongues and think that they are out of their minds; that is, outsiders (still) do not understand tongues and tongues (still) do not serve a positive purpose for them. Conversely, Paul does not now say that prophecy is "for" nonbelievers in the sense that it builds them up though it can make believers out of them, and at that point the prophecy functions "for" them as for believers.

The scenario given in vv. 23-25 helps paint a picture of the problem that Paul is opposing. Reference to the gathering of the "whole church" and the depiction of "all" the church as speaking in tongues brings to the imagination a picture of chaos. Again, it is not glossolalia that Paul opposes but meaningless noise. The scenario also illustrates that Paul expects the doors of these assemblies to be open to outsiders. The church is not like the Greco-Roman associations dedicated to patron gods or goddesses, which were exclusive and often secretive (Ascough 2003, 87–91). The church should welcome outsiders and be sensitive to the way things may appear to them.

14:26-40

The emphasis now shifts from a concern with meaningfulness to a concern with order. This section opens with a depiction of disorder (v. 26) and closes with the affirmation that all aspects of the Corinthians' worship services should be executed appropriately and *in* order (v. 40). Enclosed are four parts. In vv. 27-28 Paul treats guidelines for tongues. In vv. 29-32 he treats guidelines for prophecy. He then backs his guidelines in two ways, first with appeal to the customs of all the churches (vv. 33b, 36) and second with the weight of his personal authority (vv. 37-38).

Previously Paul had said that tongues should be accompanied by some revelation or knowledge or prophecy or teaching (v. 6). Now it appears that the Corinthians do impart teachings and revelations, only they all do so at the same time (v. 26). The word "each" emphasizes the Corinthians' individuality, and the fivefold repetition of "has" highlights the plurality of competing messages.

In countering disorder, Paul remains focused on tongues, proposing three restricting guidelines for their use (vv. 27-28). First, only two or at most three should speak at one time. Apparently this means that two or three at a time may speak *quietly*, for the second guideline stipulates that these two or three should speak aloud *one* at a time. The third guideline is that one person should interpret. The point is not only that there should *be* an interpreter but also that there should be *only one* interpreter and not a cacophony of interpreters speaking over each other. If no interpreter is present, the speaker should communicate silently. Although no one else hears, they do speak "*to God.*"

Complementing these guidelines are three guidelines for prophecy (vv. 29-30). Only two or three should speak (or stand ready to speak?) at once, and each in order. Whereas for tongues Paul said that someone should interpret, for prophecy he says that others should "evaluate" (cf. 1 Thess 5:20-21). Reference to the evaluators as "*the* others" could indicate "the other *prophets,*" but the verb used for "weigh" (*diakrinein*) is cognate with the noun "discernment" (*diakriseis*), which was used earlier in reference to the gift called "discernment of spirits" (12:10). Paul may consider this a different gift from the gift of prophecy.

Verse 31 emphasizes the potential for "all" people to prophesy. While Paul does not mean "all" absolutely (for in 12:29 he said that all are *not* prophets), this statement nods back to his earlier directive for the church to "*strive* that [they] may prophesy" (v. 1; cf. v. 39). The threefold repetition of "all" underscores the participation of the whole community, if not in manifesting the gift then in benefiting from it. Since all "learn" and all "are encouraged" by prophecy, the goal of the gifts—that is, to build up the church—is achieved.

The next verse ("and the spirits of prophets are subject to the prophets") is somewhat obscure. The sentence is succinct and contains alliteration of both the *p* sound and the *t* sound in the original Greek, perhaps indicating that this was a proverb. The meaning is perhaps elucidated by the structure of the section. That is, vv. 30-31 could be seen as an elaboration of v. 29a ("And let two or three prophets speak") and v. 32 an elaboration of v. 29b ("and let the others weigh").

If v. 32 is indeed an elaboration of v. 29b, then the meaning of v. 32 would be that the prophecies of prophets are subject to the *evaluation* of other prophets.

v. 29b: "and let the others weigh what is said"

v. 32: "and the spirits of prophets are subject to the prophets"

Alternatively, the meaning would be that the prophets can *control* themselves when they prophesy, unlike the ecstatic prophets of pagan religion. The verse that follows may recommend this as the more likely meaning: "God is not a God of disorder but of peace" (v. 33).

A new paragraph ensues, but the placement of v. 33b is subject to question. The KJV, NKJV, and NASB, following the Textus Receptus and WH, link this verse with vv. 32-33a, while the RSV, NRSV, ESV, NIV, and REB, following the UBS[5]/NA[28], link it with v. 34. Complicating matters is the question of the originality of vv. 34-35. While stylistic arguments may offer some basis for seeing these verses as Pauline (Jervis 1995, 52–59), strong arguments suggest that they are likely the result of interpolation. There is some discrepancy in the manuscript tradition, with some manuscripts placing these verses not after v. 33 but after v. 40. This point is not decisive, but textual criticism has revealed that variable placement of text in the manuscripts can be a sign that the material originated as a scribal note and that it was later inserted by different scribes at different points in the text (Parker 2008, 276). However, other problems present themselves as well. First, the author's comments in these verses are hard to square with Paul's comments about women elsewhere. While here women "are not permitted" to "speak," in 11:5 Paul seems to accept the legitimacy of prayer and prophecy by women in contexts of worship. Moreover, women played an important part in Paul's wider missionary efforts (Rom 16:1-3; Phil 4:2-3; Phlm 2), and it is hard to imagine that such individuals, dispatched as emissaries to other churches, played no role in instructing men. Second, if vv. 34-35 are original, there results a redundancy of "in all the churches" (v. 33b) and "in the churches" (v. 34a). Third, v. 36 does not logically connect with v. 35; yet it makes good sense directly after v. 33b.

If vv. 34 and 35 constitute an interpolation, then self-evidently v. 33b should not be seen as introducing them. Instead, v. 33b should be understood in connection with what precedes, as part of the same paragraph. The primary assertion is that "spirits of prophets are subject to prophets" (v. 32). Next, "For God is a God not of disorder but of peace" (v. 33a) offers a parenthetical aside that elaborates on v. 32. Verse 33b then fits directly with v. 32. The flow of thought is similar to that found elsewhere in the letter, where Paul grounds what precedes by appealing to the practices of the churches or to his own practice in all the churches (4:17; 7:17). To summarize, "Prophets have control of themselves (for God is a God not of disorder but of peace), as is true in all the churches."

Verse 36 ("Or did the word of God originate with you? Or are you the only ones it has reached?") responds directly to v. 33b. There are prophets everywhere and they conduct themselves in orderly fashion in every other place; why should the Corinthians' disorderly practice be normative? So concludes the paragraph.

A new paragraph offers backing for the guidelines that precede by calling attention to Paul's authority (vv. 37-38). "If anyone thinks he is a prophet or spiritual" (NASB) is somewhat derisive. Paul used the same formulation earlier ("If anyone thinks . . ."), where he seemed to be citing Corinthian catchwords: "If anyone thinks he is a *wise man*" (3:18); "If anyone thinks they have *knowledge*" (8:2). Implicitly, the Corinthians are claiming to be "prophets" or "spiritual." In response, Paul presents his words as "a commandment of the Lord." Since this pronouncement comes in response to the Corinthian claim that they are prophets or spiritual, the "commandment" must refer specifically to Paul's words about spiritual gifts, and perhaps more specifically to his words about tongues and prophecy (14:1-36). He does not simply refer to the fact that he "has the Spirit of God" (7:40), for here he claims to have authority over and above the "spiritual" person. Most likely, he refers to his authority as the Corinthians' apostle.

An intriguing alternative is that the "commandment" refers to some commandment of the historical Jesus. In light of Paul's oration about love in chapter 13, it would not be too far-fetched to suppose that is referring here to the "love commandment" (cf. Matt 22:39; Mark 12:31; Luke 10:27; John 13:34).

In the next verse Paul suggests that those who do not recognize his words as authoritative are "*ignorant*" (NKJV). No doubt this remark is calculated to sting those who pretend to "have *knowledge*" (8:1). The verse represents a complete conditional construction, including both protasis ("if") and apodosis ("then"). Apart from the NKJV ("ignorant"), most translations render the protasis "if anyone does not *recognize/acknowledge* this." Although the protasis contains the active form of the verb, the apodosis contains the passive: "he *is* not recognized/acknowledged." In the repetition of the verb, Paul employs a play on words: "If anyone is *ignorant*, that person is *not known*." In other words, the ignorant person should not be known, or recognized. The implied agent is either the church ("that person is not, on principle, recognized by the church") or God ("that person is not recognized by God"). Thus, under threat of ostracization, Paul ensures that the church will comply.

"Therefore" (v. 39) introduces the final conclusion to the discussion of tongues and prophecy (14:1-36). The words "strive to prophecy" close off an inclusio that opened in v. 1, thus bringing the discussion full circle. Next to these words, "*do not hinder* speaking in tongues" seems an understatement, although it unequivocally sanctions the practice, reinforcing the fact that Paul sees benefit in it, even if only for the individual.

On the whole, this passage should not be seen as a rejection of tongues but rather as a rejection of its abuse. Paul wants "everyone" to speak in tongues (v. 5), as he himself speaks in tongues (v. 18). He says that those who speak in tongues "speak to God" (v. 2) and "build themselves up" (v. 4). He acknowledges (even if it is somewhat sarcastic) that those who pray in tongues "give thanks well" (v. 17). Moreover, he places restrictions not only on the use of tongues (vv. 27-28) but also on the use of prophecy (vv. 29-30), and he implies that tongues are not inferior to prophecy provided that someone interprets (v. 5). He concludes with an admonition not to prohibit speaking in tongues (v. 39). These are important qualifications to an otherwise negative evaluation of tongues, and these qualifications show that Paul's restrictions have much to do with the specific situation in Corinth.

As Paul opened the paragraph by depicting disorder in the Corinthians' worship services (v. 26), he closes with the statement that everything should be done appropriately and *in* order (v. 40). This directive offers an apt conclusion not only to the paragraph but also to 11:2–14:40, for here Paul's discussion of problems in the Corinthians' worship assemblies comes to an end.

Conclusion

Paul's concerns with church order and with the relative value of the church's individual members in 1 Cor 11:2–14:40 raise perplexing questions about his orientation toward hierarchy. On the one hand, he establishes man as head of woman, and he ranks some gifts ahead of others. On the other hand, he states that men and women are interdependent, and he affirms that all the gifts serve to benefit the whole. Moreover, he subsumes hierarchy within a structure that he likens to a body: as in a body all the parts are necessary and the well-being of each is entangled with the well-being of the others, so it is in the body of Christ.

In some ways, Paul's sentiments in this passage could even be considered "anti-hierarchical." Distinct from non-hierarchy, anti-hierarchy preserves hierarchy but reverses its traditional ordering. For instance, in his analogy of the body, Paul states that the "weaker" and "less esteemed" members have the *greater* honor. Likewise, Paul reverses the status of the self-proclaimed "spiritual" and "mature" (2:6-16) and casts them as unspiritual and childish (3:1-3; 14:20), depicting the lowly as those whom God has chosen (1:26-31). Moreover, while Paul ranks the apostles "first" among church offices, he also describes the apostles as weak (4:10-12), as ministers (4:1), and as subservient to the church (3:21-22).

This theology follows after the pattern modeled by Jesus: the first shall be last and the last shall be first. In the terms in which Paul expresses it, this means that those who edify others—who put the interests of others above the interests of themselves—are the "greater." However, when all so conduct themselves, all are simultaneously both lesser and greater; the world's hierarchies are shaken up; and the church is built up.

Resurrection

1 Corinthians 15:1-58

Paul saves for last his discussion of the resurrection, not because it was the least significant issue but because it was the most significant of all. Spanning 15:1-58, this unit contains three main sections: vv. 1-11 (the foundation of the gospel on the resurrection of Christ), vv. 12-34 (the certainty of the resurrection of the dead), and vv. 35-58 (the nature of the resurrection body).

The issue that sets this discussion off, as v. 12 reveals, is that "some" of the Corinthians had come to believe that there would be no resurrection of the dead. That is, they denied the general resurrection of the *body* at the end of the age. The basic philosophical framework that led them to this position was the same one that motivated other problems addressed in the letter. They devalued the body, prioritizing the intellectual and relegating bodily matters to the category of indifference. This is the same group that fancied themselves "spiritual," that claimed to be "mature," and that pretended to "have knowledge." In short, it is the same group that divided the believing community into tiers, tearing the community in two.

The Resurrection of Christ (15:1-11)

Before introducing the key issue, Paul reviews the gospel message that both he and the apostles preach and that the Corinthians heard and believed. He presumes upon their agreement on this message. Thus, this section serves as a common reference point that Paul can leverage later in his argument against the Corinthians' denial of the general resurrection.

Verses 1-11 contains three subunits. Verses 1-2 sketch a climactic summary of the chain of events that runs from Paul's initial proclamation of the gospel to the Corinthians' present status in Christ: "I preached . . . you received . . . you stand . . . you are being saved." Although they have already heard his message, Paul states that he now "makes known" the gospel (cf. 12:3). This may suggest that the Corinthians were wavering in their faith and that Paul felt some uncertainty over them (Coppins 2010). Indeed, a danger of lapsing is implicit in Paul's use of the present tense "are *being* saved," and explicit in his qualification "*if* you hold fast." In any case, he expects that they agree with the message that he will now review.

Verses 3-8 contain the basic confession that formed the core of both Paul's proclamation and the Corinthians' faith. The confession spans multiple generations. Paul passes on to the Corinthians what he had received from others. He handed on this confession presumably during his eighteen-month stay in Corinth in the early 50s (Acts 18:1-17). He himself must have received the confession in the 40s at the latest, probably from the apostles in Jerusalem, and the content would have been formulated still earlier. The tradition may go back to the earliest months or years after Jesus' resurrection and probably constituted the content of the earliest Christian preaching (Hengel 2001, 122).

Symmetrical in structure, the confession has the earmarks of a creed. "That" occurs four times in parallel clauses, once with each new verb ("that he *died* . . . that he was *buried* . . . that he was *raised* . . . that he *appeared*"). In each clause the subject comes first and, in the list of appearances, the recipient of the appearances comes last. While vv. 3c-5 contain a number of "non-Pauline" expressions ("for our sins," "in accordance with the scriptures," "buried," "raised," "the third day," "the Twelve"; so Jeremias 1966, 101–105), vv. 6-8 sound distinctly Pauline. This could suggest that the original creed consisted of vv. 3c-5. However, vv. 3-8 are tightly structured, and if vv. 6-8 did not originally form a part of the creed, Paul has integrated them well. Indeed, in the series of four occurrences of "appeared" the recipient comes last in each clause (". . . to Cephas . . . to the Twelve . . . to more than five hundred brothers at once . . . to James . . . to all the apostles"), and together vv. 3-8 form a concentric pattern (Talbert 2002, 122):

> *appeared* to Cephas
>> *then* to the Twelve
>>> *then he appeared* to more than five hundred
>>> *then he appeared* to James
>> *then* to all the apostles
> *appeared* to me

Paul states twice that the named events happened "according to the scriptures." No text in the OT plainly states that the "Christ" would "die for our sins" or that he would "rise on the third day." But early Christians interpreted the scriptures Christologically, reading "backwards" from the Christ event (Hays 2014). The notion of death on behalf of others' sins may be rooted in Christological readings of texts like Isa 53:3-5 (as 1 Pet 2:22-25 shows). LXX Jonah 1:17, where Jonah is said to have been "in the belly of the sea monster three days and three nights," seems to have been viewed as a figurative reference to Christ's burial and resurrection; Jesus interprets the text in this way in Matt 12:39-40. Reference to some kind of restoration on the "third day" occurs in Hos 6:2. The Gospels as well as Acts show that "on the third day" was a standard formula within early Christian discourse (Matt 16:21; 20:19; Luke 9:22; 24:46; Acts 10:40).

Paul makes no explicit mention of an empty tomb. While the sequence "buried" and "was raised" could imply that the tomb was empty, one could conceivably interpret "raised" to mean that Jesus' soul ascended while the corpse remained in/on the ground. However, several pieces of evidence confirm that an empty tomb is presupposed. First, a failure to mention the empty tomb need not imply ignorance of it. Luke omits reference to the empty tomb from confessional summaries of the resurrection in the book of Acts, although the Gospel of Luke shows that he was well aware of the empty tomb tradition (Ware 2014, 480). Second, the idea of physical resurrection was well established in both the Jewish and Greco-Roman cultural encyclopedia (Cook 2017). Third, a thorough semantic analysis of the word "raised" (*egēgertai*) shows that this word always implied physical upward movement and was never used with reference to the ascent of souls (Ware 2014; Cook 2017).

The list of appearances is organized in chronological sequence ("then . . . then . . . then . . . then . . . last"). Although according to the Gospels Jesus appeared first to Mary Magdalene (John 20:14-17); or to Mary Magdalene and "the other Mary" (Matt 28:1); or to Mary Magdalene, Mary the mother of James, and Salome (Mark 16:1), the creed here makes no mention of the women, undoubtedly reflecting a bias against women as credible witnesses. The creed tallies with the Gospel account that Jesus appeared to Cephas (Peter) privately before appearing to the other disciples (Luke 24:34). The group of "the Twelve" includes Peter, for Paul does not say "then to the *rest* of the disciples." It is remarkable that this group is still known under the designation "the Twelve" despite having lost Judas (cf. Matt 27:3-8; Acts 1:18-19); Matthias (Acts 1:21-26) is not included in the number, for the creed refers to the appearance to the eleven as seen in the Gospels (Matt 28:16; Luke 24:36-43; John 19:23), prior to the selection of Matthias as Judas's replacement. Although Matthew refers to the "eleven" (Matt 28:16), "the Twelve" could have remained a well-established designation for the group.

Here is the only reference in the tradition to an appearance "to more than five hundred brothers at once." It may be notable again that Paul refers to "brothers" but makes no mention of women. Paul's appeal to the five hundred as living witnesses (having seen Jesus all "at once") confirms that he viewed forensic verification of the resurrection to be important.

Here also is the only reference in the tradition to an appearance to James. This is not James the son of Zebedee, who is by now deceased (Acts 12:1-2). This is James the brother of Jesus (Gal 1:19). The Gospels offer no evidence that James had been a follower of Jesus during Jesus' earthly ministry, and indeed he seems to have found Jesus something of an embarrassment (cf. Matt 13:55; Mark 3:21, 31-32; 6:1-4; John 7:5). Both Acts (1:14; 12:17; 15:13-22; 21:18) and Paul (Gal 1:19; 2:9) depict him as a prominent leader in the Jerusalem church following the resurrection. Josephus depicts him as a believer and a martyr (*Ant.* 20.200).

Next to last, Paul refers to an appearance to "all the apostles." This refers to a group larger than the group of Twelve who followed Jesus, for Paul has already used the term "Twelve" to refer to that group, and "all" seems to expand the group to a larger number. Moreover, Paul does not restrict the term "apostle" to the Twelve only (Rom 16:7; 1 Cor 9:5; 12:28; Gal 1:19; Phil 2:25; 1 Thess 2:7).

The switch in v. 8 to the first person singular signals that the creed has ended, or at least that Paul has modified it. Last of all, Christ appeared to Paul. Paul's self-characterization is variably translated in English renderings: "as to one untimely born" (ESV; NASB), "as to one born abnormally" (NAB; NIV), "it was as though I was born when no one expected it" (JB), "though this birth of mine was monstrous" (NEB). This variation reflects the difficulty of Paul's expression. The underlying term (*ektrōma*) normally referred to an "untimely birth," or a miscarriage. Paul's meaning, then, would seem to be that he came to know Christ at the wrong time. However, as things were, he came to know Christ *late*, whereas miscarriages occur early. Thus, it may be better to take the term as a description of Paul's *self-evaluation*: he depicts himself as tossed aside as worthless (M. W. Mitchell 2003). Although the term may have arisen as an aspersion from opponents who viewed his apostolic credentials as suspect (M. W. Mitchell 2003), he himself connects his status with the fact that ("because") he "persecuted the church of God." His letters suggest that he was haunted by the fact that he had done so (Gal 1:13; Phil 3:6-8), and he seems to have carried in himself a certain degree of self-loathing (remembered in 1 Tim 1:15). Because of his actions he viewed himself as the "*least* of the apostles." (It is perhaps also in this sense that he calls himself "*last* of all.")

Verses 9-11 trail into a discussion of Paul's value as an apostle. While he views himself as the least of the apostles in worthiness, he considers himself perhaps the most significant in impact. As always, he credits the grace of

God (cf. 3:10; 14:18). His boast that he "worked harder" than all the other apostles only magnifies God's grace, for it was through this that his working "harder" was accomplished. Verse 11 states a conclusion to the first ten verses of the chapter: the message that Paul preaches is the same message that the other apostles preach, and it is the same message in which the Corinthians originally put their faith. All are in agreement. Thus, Paul nails down a firm foundation on which to build his subsequent argument.

The Resurrection of the Dead (15:12-34)

Here the topic shifts from Jesus' resurrection to the general resurrection of the dead. This unit contains three parts. Verses 12-19 explore the implications of the premise that "there is no resurrection of the dead." Verses 20-28 offer a sketch of the eschatological events that follow from the resurrection of Jesus. Verses 29-34 propose that certain Christian practices and indeed Paul's whole manner of life find justification only if a general resurrection awaits.

15:12-19

The connecting word "proclaim" links this section with the previous one. Having reviewed the gospel that he and the other apostles "proclaim" and that the Corinthians "believed" (vv. 1-8), Paul now explores the implications of this proclamation. If Christ is "proclaimed" as having been raised from the dead, how can some of the Corinthians say "there is no resurrection of the dead"? While Paul has cited the Corinthians at several points in the letter (cf. 6:12a, 13a, 18; 7:1; 8:1, 4, 5-6, 8), only here does he attribute words to them explicitly. Whether the Corinthians had made this claim in the letter they sent him (cf. 7:1) or it was reported to Paul by Chloe's people (cf. 1:11) cannot be known for certain.

In denying a "resurrection of the dead," the Corinthians denied not Christ's resurrection but the traditional belief, held by many Jews, of a "general resurrection"—the belief that at the end, before the final judgment, God would raise the righteous, restoring their bodies and rewarding them in an afterlife for their faithfulness.

Views on the afterlife were many in the ancient world, and Paul does not clearly reveal the viewpoint taken by the Corinthian naysayers. While groups like the Pharisees (Josephus, *Ant.* 18.11-25), perhaps among others (2 Macc 7:1-38), believed in a resurrection of the dead, with the exception of only a few texts (Dan 12:1-3; cf. Ezek 37:1-14; Hos 6:1-3; Isa 26:19), the Hebrew Bible reflects no such view. Taking their cues from the Torah, the Sadducees, conservatively, denied a general resurrection (Mark 12:18//Matt 22:23//Luke 20:27; Acts 4:1-2; 23:6-8; Josephus, *Ant.* 18.11-25). Apart from the Sadducees many Jews apparently viewed death as the end of existence (1 Macc 2:62; Tob 3:6; Sir 14:19). Reportedly, the Essenes believed in an afterlife in the form of immortality of the soul (Josephus, *Ant.* 18.11-25). Under the influence of Greek philosophy, other Jews took this view as well (Wis 2:22; Philo, *Abr.* 258).

Greek and Roman philosophers in general viewed death as a separation of the soul from the body. The Epicureans were exceptions, believing that the soul dissolved at death (Lucretius, *Rer. nat.* 3.417-829). Plato believed that the soul survived forever, traveling from one body to another (*Resp.* 620A-D; *Phaed.* 80D-E). Traditionally, the Stoics believed that the soul could survive into the afterlife, but only for a time (Diogenes Laertius, *Vit. phil.* 7.157), and they debated whether a person maintained self-consciousness (Seneca, *Brev.* 18.5; *Polyb.* 5.2; 9.2; *Ep.* 54.4; 109.30). The intelligentsia tended to disbelieve the traditional myths about an afterlife in the Underworld (Seneca, *Ep.* 24.18; 82.16; Cicero, *Tusc. disp.* 1.6.11; Lucretius, *Rer. nat.* 3.629-32, 979-1022; Lucian, *Philops.* esp. 149), although some held out hope of a blessed haven for the virtuous as a remote possibility (Cicero, *Tusc. disp.* 1.40.98).

Among the general public, the whole range of views found representation (Lucretius, *Rer. nat.* 1.111-27). Stories of the resurrection of individuals to life on earth are abundantly attested (Cook 2017, 62–73), although such cases were exceptional. Elite sources claim that most people believed in an afterlife as depicted in traditional mythology (Plato, *Resp.* 599A; Augustine, *Civ.* 6.6; Lucian, *Lover of Lies; On Funerals*). Certain burial rituals indeed indicate that people believed in a life beyond the grave (Hope 2009, 102; Lucian, *On Funerals*). Epitaphs variably indicate expectations of either afterlife or annihilation (Hope 2009, 111–15).

Several pieces of evidence suggest that the Corinthians who denied the general resurrection believed in the immortality of the soul. First, the view that the soul was immortal was widespread among the first-century Greco-Roman population (Seneca said that it was the "general opinion of mankind"; *Ep.* 117.6). Second, Paul intimates later that the Corinthians did believe in an afterlife of some kind (15:29). Third, clues elsewhere in the letter suggest that the Corinthians' problem was not with the possibility of an afterlife but with the inferiority of the body (see 6:12-20); thus, as the inferior part of the person, the body could not ascend to the celestial sphere. In this belief, they followed philosophers of a Stoic and Platonic bent.

Certainly their view was not that "the resurrection has already happened" (see 2 Tim 2:17-18). Indeed, their argument is not that it has happened already but that there is "no" resurrection of the dead.

After presenting the basic Corinthian claim in v. 12, Paul works out, in a highly repetitive section, the theological implications entailed by their position. If there is no general resurrection, neither was there a resurrection of Christ (vv. 13, 15, 16); the apostles' preaching is in vain (v. 14); the apostles are false witnesses (v. 15; cf. Exod 20:16); the Corinthians' faith is in vain (vv. 14, 17); they are still in their sins (v. 17); and those who have fallen asleep in Christ have perished (v. 18). The Corinthians cannot have thought, or realized, that their position entailed these points, but Paul's purpose is to show them that it did. While the Corinthians both believed in Christ's resurrection and denied the general resurrection, Paul suggests that this is a theological inconsistency, because one thing entails the other.

The series of negative outcomes described culminates in the woeful conclusion that, "If for this life only we have hoped in Christ, we are of all people most to be pitied." This does not mean, "If we have *only hoped*" in resurrection but will not actually experience it. Rather, it means that believers are pitiable if they have *only this life* (similar to 2 Bar. 21:13; cf. 19:5-8). Paul's conclusion does not indicate that the Corinthian believers denied the afterlife. They did not *think* that they had hope in Christ in this life only any more than they thought their faith was vain (vv. 14, 17) and they were still in their sins (v. 17); Paul only suggests that this, like his other points, follows naturally and logically from their denial of a general resurrection.

15:20-28

Verse 20 reformulates the idea behind vv. 12-13 (cf. 15d-e, 16): Christ's resurrection entails the general resurrection, for his resurrection was the first act of a larger drama. Here Paul begins to offer a response to the Corinthian position that he reduced to absurdity in vv. 13-19.

Christ's resurrection set in motion an inexorable series of eschatological occurrences. Christ was a "first fruit" of the resurrection. The first gathering of the year's harvest, a "first fruit" indicated what could be expected of the season's yield as a whole (Exod 23:19). In the same way, Christ's resurrection (as first fruit) served as a sign of a larger resurrection (harvest) to come.

Christ's resurrection, however, was not just *earlier* than the general resurrection; somehow it also *set it into effect*. Paul compares—or rather contrasts—Christ's work with that of Adam (vv. 21-22; cf. 15:42-49; Rom 15:12-21). Since death was "through a man" (Adam), so also "through a man" (Christ) is resurrection of the dead. And just as "in Adam" all die, so also "in Christ" all will be made alive.

Although Paul formulates the comparison in syntactically parallel clauses, the substance of the clauses does not entirely match. In the first place, it is not clear that the work of Adam and Christ, respectively, are effective for people in exactly the same way. Jewish texts lay the blame for the entrance of sin into the world on various agents. Fourth Ezra and 2 Baruch blame Adam (4 Ezra 7:118; 2 Bar. 48:42-43; 56:6). Other texts blame Eve (LAB 18:1; Sir 25:24). Some blame rebellious angels (1 En. 6:1-16:4; 69:11; 2 En. 18). Yet many texts affirm that people are responsible for their own sins. Second Baruch identifies each of us as "our own Adam" (2 Bar. 54:19). Sirach says that people sin by their own free choice (15:11-20). Paul may be closest to 2 Baruch, for while he blames Adam as the first sinner, he does not make people culpable for Adam's sin, only for their own (cf. Rom 5:12). The work of Christ is different. People do not make themselves alive in the same way that people commit their own sins. Christ makes them alive.

Moreover, even though Paul parallels "*all* die" with "*all* will be made alive," he cannot, in the latter instance, mean "all" absolutely, for he maintains elsewhere that some will be disqualified from the kingdom (6:9, 10), "are perishing" (1:18), and will be destroyed (8:11) or condemned (11:32). Furthermore, while Paul mentions the resurrection of those "in Christ" (v. 23), he never mentions the resurrection of nonbelievers. It is not clear whether this means that nonbelievers will be annihilated, although some Jews believed that the wicked would receive this fate (Wis 5:14; LAB 16:3).

Following the comparison between Adam and Christ, Paul enumerates a series of eschatological occurrences (vv. 23-28): Christ's resurrection, Christ's return, and Christ's victory. This section makes abundant use of the language of warfare. The orders of the resurrection are likened to ranks drawn up in battle: the first-fruit Christ, then those who belong to Christ, whose resurrection occurs at Christ's coming, or *Parousia*. In political contexts, the word *parousia* often referred to the "coming" of a high-ranking person such as an emperor or a king (BDAG, 781), especially after a victory in battle; thus, reference to Christ's "coming" could be seen as a challenge to the rule of the emperor (Wright 2007, 136–49).

After the Parousia and general resurrection comes the "end," when Christ "hands over the kingdom to the God and Father, when he abolishes every rule and every authority and power." In Jewish apocalyptic literature, it is often predicted that God (1 En. 38:3; 46:5; 48:8; 53:5; 54:2), or else the Messiah (2 Bar. 40:1-4), would destroy the rulers of the world at the time of judgment. Like others, Paul links the rulers with the demonic powers (1 En. 55:4). Thus, the rulers, authorities, and powers are not just the human powers that be but also evil, or at least rebellious (Wasserman 2017), agents active in the heavenly regions (see 2:6-8).

Paul makes no mention of a future millennial reign (Rev 20:2-7; cf. 4 Ezra 7:28; 2 Bar. 40:3) but depicts Christ as ruling now from heaven (v. 25). Despite his present rule, his enemies have not all been subdued, or at least none of them have been subdued entirely. Death will be defeated last of all (v. 26). While Christ's resurrection has set the powers of life in motion, Death is still at work and will continue to nag until the end. The ages overlap—"this age," during which sin and death reign on the one hand, and the age to come, during which God rules over all on the other. At the end, God will reestablish his rule over creation, which in the meantime other powers have claimed for themselves. God will subject all things to Christ (cf. 3:23; 8:6). Then Christ will subject himself to God (cf. 3:23).

Finally, God will be "all in all" (cf. Eph 1:23). This affirmation echoes the Stoic view that at the end all the elements that comprise the universe would mix together and reduce to God (*SVF* 3.302; Seneca, *Ep.* 9.16; 71.12-14). While Paul's expression could be taken to mean that everything will become ontologically identical to God, as in Stoicism, it is hard to see how that view would fit with Paul's otherwise transparently theistic theology. Rather, he means that everything will participate in God's life and rule.

15:29-34

Verses 29-32 offer two further grounds for the affirmation that there is a general resurrection (v. 20). First, Paul argues from a Corinthian practice that, he suggests, implies belief in a general resurrection, viz., baptism for the dead (v. 29). The practice to which he refers remains a mystery. On the face of it, it appears that the Corinthians made it a practice to have themselves baptized somehow for the benefit of the deceased—presumably deceased believers who had passed away before being baptized. While Paul does not unequivocally endorse the practice, he uses the Corinthians' belief in its validity to advance his argument for the resurrection.

Second, Paul argues from his personal commitment to the cause of the gospel (vv. 30-32). Working on behalf of the gospel, he risks peril at every moment (cf. 4:10-12; Rom 8:31-39; 2 Cor 4:7-12; 6:1-10; 11:21b-29). Why take this risk if there were no resurrection? "I die every day" may be another echo of the philosophers. Seneca maintained that people should not fear death, since we are dying every day; death is just the last moment in a process that afflicts us at every moment (*Ep.* 1.2; 24.20; 120.14). However, when Paul refers to daily death, he refers to death to self for the benefit of others, after the pattern of Christ (cf. 2 Cor 4:10). He boasts that the Corinthians are the fruit of his toil, the life generated from his death.

As an example of his hardship Paul offers the fact that he "fought wild beasts in Ephesus." It is unlikely that Paul, as a Roman citizen (Acts 16:37-38; 22:25-29; 23:27; 25:10-12), would have been condemned to fight beasts in the arena, nor should he, as an untrained man, have been expected to survive had he done so. Rather, as the words "humanly speaking" (ESV) indicate, Paul speaks figuratively (cf. Rom 6:19; Gal 3:15; 4:24; Plato, *Crat.* 392b; *Phaedr.* 246a; Aristobulus, *fr.* 2; Philo, *Sacr.* 1.101; *Opif.* 4-6; Ignatius refers to his stand against his Roman opponents as fighting against "wild beasts": Ign. *Eph.* 1:2; 7:1; *Smyrn.* 4:1). In ancient sources, the fight for personal mastery against pleasure, or those who promote pleasure, is sometimes described as fighting against "beasts" (Malherbe 1968). This idea fits the context here, for Paul promptly concludes that, if there is no resurrection of the dead, one should indeed resort to a life of pleasure. While he quotes from Isa 22:13 (cf. Eccl 2:24; 3:12)—"Let us eat and drink, for tomorrow we die"—the same sentiment was traditionally associated with Epicurean philosophy (Malherbe 1968, 76–77).

Paul concludes with three directives: "do not be deceived" (v. 33); "come back to your senses"; and "sin no more" (v. 34). The directive not to be deceived follows with a quotation from the comic poet Menander (fr. 187.1/218.1): "bad company ruins good morals." Besides the quotation of Epimenides in Titus 1:12, this is the only recognizable quotation from a non-Jewish source in the entire Pauline corpus. The saying may have been in common currency, so Paul need not have read Menander. In any case, the saying resonates with a common message of the philosophers, who warned against consorting with the unvirtuous. People corrupt each other as a live coal sets alight a dead one (Epictetus, *Diatr.* 3.16.2) or as a man covered in soot smears those whom he touches (Epictetus, *Diatr.* 3.16.3). Here Paul applies the saying particularly to the issue of the resurrection. Echoing the Corinthian slogan cited in 8:1 ("We all *have knowledge*"), Paul now declares that "some *have ignorance.*" By "some" he means those who deny the resurrection of the dead. The Corinthians should be especially wary of consorting with such people.

The Resurrection Body (15:35-58)

Having shown that there is a general resurrection, Paul now explains the nature of the resurrection body: it will not be like the present body, for believers' bodies will be "changed." In vv. 36-41 Paul offers two analogies that explain the difference between these bodies. In vv. 42-49 he then applies these analogies to the resurrection of the dead. Finally, in vv. 50-58 he offers a summary reaffirming the fact that believers will receive new bodies and death will be defeated.

15:35-41

In v. 35 Paul anticipates an objection to the general resurrection: "*Someone will ask, 'How are the dead raised? With what kind of body do they come?'*" These need not be real questions asked by a specific person. Rather, in the tradition of diatribe (see introduction), Paul is invoking an imaginary interlocutor into whose mouth he can place anticipated objections, affording himself an opportunity to reply before a real person is able to make the relevant objections (e.g., Seneca, *Ben.* 5.20.6). Still, the presumption behind the interlocutor's question tallies with the Corinthian position that "there is no resurrection of the dead," and it articulates precisely *why* they might have objected to the resurrection. The second question clarifies that the first is about the feasibility of a resurrection of the kind of body such as we currently have. Some Jewish texts depict the resurrected body as an exact restoration of the pre-resurrected one (2 Macc 7:1-38). Others do not. In 2 Baruch the eponymous prophet asks a pair of questions similar to the one stated by Paul's interlocutor here: "In which shape will the living live in your day? Or how will remain their splendor which will be after that?" (2 Bar. 49:2). While *2 Baruch* makes no explicit mention of a resurrection *body*, it does affirm that in the coming age the righteous will take on a more glorified form (2 Bar. 51:1). A Greek philosophical perspective precluded the possibility of heavenly resurrection. Philosophy generally distinguished between the ethereal and the sub-ethereal regions and maintained that the sub-ethereal elements, of which the body consisted, could not rise to the ethereal region (Asher 2000, 15). If the Corinthians took an analogous position, then their objection to the resurrection would have been that *this* kind of body, physically speaking, could not enter the heavens; that only the soul could do so.

Paul's harsh rejoinder—"Fool!"—continues to reflect the diatribe style and is still directed at an imaginary opponent (singular). Paul answers the interlocutor's questions with two analogies. First, he offers the analogy of the seed (vv. 36-38). A seed (body) dies after it is sown, and life (a restored body) springs up again. Moreover, a *person* sows the seed, but *God* gives it a body. The subject stays the same throughout this process. That is, x is not raised as y; although x is changed, it is still raised as x (Ware 2014, 486–87); it is the "same" body.

In vv. 39-41, Paul switches the analogy. Just as there are different kinds of flesh among created things, so there are different kinds of bodies. He illustrates the point with observations about created things on earth and in heaven. First, each thing *on earth* has its own kind of flesh. Alluding to the creatures created in Gen 1:20-25, but in reverse order (Gardner 2018, 707), Paul names humans, beasts, birds, and fish. Second, things *on earth* have different kinds of flesh from things *in heaven*. According to Greek philosophy, the heavenly bodies consisted of a kind of "ethereal" material, distinct from the elements that existed on earth (Aristotle, *Cael.* 290a9; Plutarch, *Mor.* 928a-29a). Paul may have shared this view. Third, each thing in heaven has *its* own kind of flesh. Even each star differs from each other star (cf. Marcus Aurelius, *Med.* 6.43).

While some ancient people believed that the stars were heavenly beings (Philo, *Spec.* 2.255), and perhaps even deified human beings (Seneca, *Ben.* 3.20.1; *Cons. Poly.* 9.2-4; *Ep.* 86.1; Jewish texts use this language figuratively: Dan 12:1-3; Sir 44:21; 50:5-11; Wis 3:7; 2 Bar. 7:124; 51:10; 1 En. 104:2), Paul does not advocate here for the transformation of human bodies into "astral" bodies. He names multiple kinds of bodies (not just human and heavenly) only to illustrate that not all kinds of bodies are the same. Just as there are many kinds of bodies in the universe, analogously there is more than one kind of human body.

15:42-49

"So" in v. 42 indicates that vv. 36-41 functioned as the front end of an analogy. Paul now applies the analogy to the resurrection, picking up specifically from the analogy of the dying and rising seed (vv. 36-38).

The difference between the pre- and post-resurrection bodies is now illustrated through a series of nine antitheses. First comes a set of four antitheses (vv. 42-44). The first three involve contrasts that were common in apocalyptic thinking of Paul's day: the body is sown in corruptibility, dishonor, and weakness; it is raised in incorruptibility, glory, and power (cf. 4 Ezra 7:112-5; 2 Bar. 44:8-13). This language is not only material but also ethical and sociological. That is, the present body is subject to decay, but the resurrection body will not be (this is the material dimension). Somatic nature, moreover, correlates with ethical ability (this is the ethical dimension), and ethical behavior redounds to one's reputation before God and humanity (the sociological dimension).

The fourth antithesis, between the "natural" and the "spiritual" body, creates a transition back to the comparison between Christ and Adam (vv. 45-49). The language of this antithesis is not traditional, and it may reflect Corinthian terminology (see 2:6-16). Paul had used the term "natural" earlier as a virtual synonym for "fleshly," or "sinful" (cf. 2:15–3:3). Here it indicates a "living" body. (The NRSV translation "physical" is misleading, as this could imply a contrast between "material" and "immaterial"; on the contrary, both are "bodies"). Its counterpart, the "spiritual" body, is a body characterized by Spirit. While this could mean that the body *consists* of Spirit, it is not clear how this would integrate with Paul's otherwise theistic distinction between humanity and God. It may be better to see Paul's description as indicating a body fully *inhabited, possessed,* or *directed* by the Spirit.

Verse 45 follows from vv. 42-44 as the resolution of another simile ("so also," NASB). The application comes via an adapted quotation of Gen 2:7. Adding the words "first" and "Adam," Paul creates a contrast between the "first man Adam" and the "last Adam" (or Christ), thus resuming the comparison between Adam and Christ posed earlier (15:20-22). The contrast between the "natural" and the "spiritual" continues, but now with cognate terminology: Adam was a "*living* being" but Christ is a "life-giving *spirit.*" Verses 46-49 offer a midrashic development of the contrast based on the description of Adam in Gen 2:7 as made "from the dust of the ground." The antitheses of vv. 46-49 apply the distinction between Adam's body and Christ's body to the bodies of believers: they have Adam's kind of body prior to the resurrection, and they will have Christ's kind of body after it.

A distinction between two Adams also occurs in the writings of Philo. Paul's treatment, however, is different from Philo's in one very important respect. While Philo depicts creation of a heavenly man first, followed by creation of an earthly one (*Opif.* 134; *Leg.* 1.31, 53, 88-95; 2.4), Paul makes the earthly man first, then the heavenly. Conceptually, Paul's treatment of Adam may have more in common with the theology of the Dead Sea Scrolls (Maston 2016). The Qumran Hymns (*Hodayot*) present human sinfulness as a close correlate of the fact that humans have "dusty" bodies (cf. 1 Cor 15:48), and present the "Spirit" as an enlightening and purifying power that overcomes Adam's dusty nature. Similarly, Paul presents Adam as a "dusty" person and the Spirit as a power that transforms the dusty body (yet, while Paul presents Adam as having been created this way, in the Hymns Adam is originally glorious). While Paul does not draw a direct *causal* ethical connection between the body and sin, for Paul the type of body that one has does correlate with the "age" in which one lives—whether the age of *sin* and death on the one hand, or the age of *righteousness* and life on the other.

15:50-58

The final section of the chapter divides into three parts (vv. 50-53, 54-57, 58). In vv. 50-53 Paul restates his preceding point but in different words: the body will be changed at the resurrection. In parallel clauses, Paul refers to the present body with the synecdochic expression "flesh and blood" and with the metonymic term "perishable (thing)" (v. 50). This body cannot inherit the kingdom of God. "Inherit" is an economic metaphor pertaining to the transference of property from one party to another. The idea has roots in the OT idea that Israel would inherit the land (Deut 4:21). Paul replaces the land with the "promise" of the gospel (cf. Gal 3:18) or, as he puts it here, with the "kingdom of God" (cf. 1 Cor 6:9, 10; Gal 5:21). The kingdom is fully realized when Christ subdues every enemy and God becomes all in all (15:23-28).

Paul characterizes his remarks about the resurrection as a "mystery." While in Paul's writings the articular expression "*the* mystery" usually refers to the revelation of the gospel itself, here Paul refers to "*a* mystery." Therewith he claims, in the manner of a prophet, to have been the recipient of a more specific revelation about the nature of the resurrection body. His use of the first person plural places him in the company of his addressees: expecting Christ to return soon, he anticipates that some of his generation will be living when the Parousia occurs. Yet his chief point is that, at the Parousia, "we all will be changed." It was a doctrine of the Stoic philosophers that the universe was always changing (Seneca, *Ep.* 36.11; Marcus Aurelius, *Med.* 6.4); that it would come to an end (Seneca, *Marc.* 21.2; 26.6-7; *Ep.* 71.13); and that it would be renewed again (Marcus Aurelius, *Med.* 9.28). Paul maintains that the world will indeed come to an end and that creation will be renewed, but he avers that the new creation will be different and more permanent. "The present form of this world" is passing away (7:31), and both the world (Rom 8:18-39) and believers (2 Cor 3:18) are being renewed in a process of a transformation. The final transformation will be instantaneous. Employing stock apocalyptic imagery (1 Thess 4:16; Rev 11:15; Sib. Or. 7.115; 8.239; 4 Ezra 6.23), Paul places the instant of transformation at the sound of the "last trumpet". His continuing use of the first person plural shows that he refers specifically to the transformation of believers; again he says nothing of the fate of nonbelievers (cf. 15:23-24).

Verse 53 switches the metaphor. Now it is not a "*change*" but a change of *clothing*, as believers "put on" incorruptibility and immortality. The metaphor should not be pressed too far; the corruptible body does not remain present "beneath" the incorruptible.

Paul gives no indication of what happens to believers between death and the general resurrection (cf. 2 Cor 5:6-9; Phil 1:21-24). Many Second Temple texts imagine temporary separation of the soul from the body, with the souls being stored away in a special place until the time of the resurrection or final judgment (LAB 21:9; 23:13; 33:3; 1 En. 22:9-14; 4 Ezra 4:42-43; 7:32, 78; 2 Bar. 21:22-23; T. Abr. 19:3; 20:9-12; recension B, 7:16). Given his belief that Christ could very well return during his lifetime, Paul perhaps found little reason to speculate.

Paul's emphasis changes slightly in vv. 54-57, as he moves from discussion about bodily transformation to an affirmation that death will be defeated (cf. v. 26). Thus, having reiterated the facticity of Christ's resurrection (15:1-12), having established the facticity of the general resurrection, and having clarified the nature of the resurrection body (15:13-53), Paul proceeds to a climax, boldly declaring death's defeat. Here he joins LXX Isa 25:8 with LXX Hos 13:14 in a composite citation based on the linking word "death." In citing Hos 13:14, he changes the word "Hades" to "Death" in the second instance of "Death," and the word "penalty" to "victory" to match the wording of the quotation from Isaiah. This is the only instance in Paul's letters where he quotes scripture as having its fulfillment in the future (Gardner 2018, 727). Victory over death happens in the general resurrection itself. As use of the indefinite relative conjunction shows ("when"), the timing of the event is unknown.

Greco-Roman philosophy offered ways to help people come to grips with death. The Epicurean philosophers maintained that death was a means of curtailing life's sufferings (there was no afterlife and so no postmortem suffering). The Stoic philosophers stifled fear of death by declaring that it was "no evil," that it was only a matter of indifference. Paul's solution is different: God is bringing death itself to an end.

Paul personifies death as a kind of beast fitted with a "stinger," as of a wasp or a scorpion (cf. Rev 9:10). The stinger is sin itself, the instrument by which the agent death (cause) brings about spiritual death (effect)—just as in the Grim Reaper metaphor, death comes to the door to summon people to death, so that "death" is at once a cause and an effect (see T. Abr. 16:1ff).

In an unexpected tangent, Paul declares the power of sin to be "the Law." Although he does not develop the idea here, his letter to the Romans suggests that the power of sin is the Law in the sense that the Law increases sin (Rom 5:20). While the Law is "good" (Rom 7:12), it is too weak to overcome the flesh (Rom 8:3), and sin draws it into alliance with itself to create further opportunity for sin (Rom 7:7-25). As in Romans 7, Paul concludes here with an impassioned declaration of thanks to God for the victory that God is providing through Jesus Christ (1 Cor 15:57; Rom 7:25). Use of the present tense shows that God *is* providing the victory but that the victory is not complete. Reference to Jesus as "Lord" continues to evoke the idea of God's kingdom, reclaimed for God from the powers of sin and death.

Verse 58 offers a practical conclusion to the theological discussion that precedes. Just as the work of the apostles would be in vain if Christ were not raised (15:10, 14), so the work of believers would be in vain if the dead are not raised. Believers can remain steadfast in their work ("your" plural emphasizes collective community effort) since they can rest assured that death will be defeated. Or put negatively, having the victory does not give them license to do nothing (Sampley 2015, 854).

Conclusion

First Corinthians 15 should not be considered in isolation from the preceding fourteen chapters of the letter. While Paul makes mention of the resurrection of believers in only one verse prior to chapter 15 (6:14), the present chapter has several other links with preceding portions of the letter. Themes treated here and elsewhere include the kingdom of God (6:10; 15:24, 50), the Lordship of Christ (8:6; 12:3; 15:24-27), God's grace (1:4; 3:10; 4:18; 15:10; cf. 1:5, 7, 29-31; 2:12; 3:10, 21-23; 4:7), Paul's sufferings for the gospel (4:10-13; 15:30-31), the danger of bad associations (5:6-13; 15:33), knowledge and ignorance (8:1-13; 15:34), and the "spiritual" (2:15; 12:1; 14:1, 37; 15:44-46).

Still, these are only minor connections. Chapter 15 ties in with what precedes more at the level of Paul's underlying theological framework. The resurrection validates the "wisdom of God," or the way of the cross, the way of self-sacrifice for the benefit of others, a way that heals divisions because it builds others up. Just as God raised the one who set this cruciform example, so he will raise those who live in imitation of it (like Paul and Apollos!). Moreover, the gospel, including the promise of resurrection, is transformative, and it requires and even enables a reorientation of one's life. Because there is a resurrection, one should labor for the Lord all the more.

Conclusion

1 Corinthians 16:1-24

In a chapter that by itself approximates the typical length of an ancient private letter (Perkins 2012, 195), this lengthy letter begins to draw to a close. Paul concludes with instructions about a "collection for the saints" (vv. 1-4), a preview of his and his associates' travel plans (vv. 5-12), some final exhortations (vv. 13-18), closing greetings (vv. 19-21), and a postscript consisting of a curse (v. 22) and a benediction (vv. 23-24).

The Collection (16:1-4)

Having addressed the problems contributing to the Corinthians' "divisions" (1:10), Paul shifts now to matters of business. He asks the Corinthians to begin saving for "the collection for the saints" and to select delegates to deliver the gift to Jerusalem (thus, "the saints" = believers in the Jerusalem church). Although discussion of the collection constitutes a dramatic and sudden change of topic from the preceding discussion of God's defeat of death, Paul's appeal to the Corinthians to give flows naturally from the preceding chapter's final exhortation (15:58), that they would abound "in the work of the Lord" (Gardner 2018, 735).

Paul's introduction of the new topic with the frequently repeated formula "now concerning" (7:1, 25; 8:1; 12:1; 16:12) need not imply that the Corinthians had inquired about the collection in their letter to him, although it does imply that the Corinthians were familiar with the initiative (M. M. Mitchell 1989). The initiative seems to have extended over a period of several years, as Paul refers to it in several of his letters (Rom 15:25-32; 1 Cor 16:1-4; 2 Cor 8–9; Gal 2:10). He recruited participation from the churches in Galatia (1 Cor 16:1; Gal 2:10), Philippi, and Thessalonica (2 Cor 8:1; 9:2-3), as well as from the church in Corinth (1 Cor 16:1-4; 2 Cor 8–9). According to Romans, the purpose of the collection was to betoken the Gentile believers' gratitude for the spiritual—or salvation-historical—

debt that they owed to the Jews (Rom 15:25-32). When Paul wrote Romans, he was preparing to travel to Jerusalem to deliver the gift (Rom 15:25-27).

Several items about Paul's instructions for the collection are noteworthy. First, he addresses not just the affluent but "each" person. Second, he does not stipulate a fixed percentage but prevails upon them to give "whatever extra" they earn, presumably meaning whatever remains after they have met their needs. The wording is vague in itself and leaves to the audience to decide where to draw the line between need and surplus. Third, Paul asks that they store their offering in their savings "on the first day of every week." The reference is to Sunday, likely implying that the church's meetings took place on the day of the resurrection (see also Rev 1:10; Justin Martyr, *1 Apol.* 67), not on Saturday, the Sabbath. Fourth, Paul wants the Corinthians to begin saving now. Saving little by little, they would be able to store away more than they could scrounge up upon an impromptu visit from Paul.

Although Paul's letter to the Romans indicates that he delivered the gift himself (Rom 15:25-27), it is apparent here that the mode of delivery had not yet been decided. Paul is open to having the Corinthians deliver their own contribution, through delegates of their choosing. These delegates he would send with letters of recommendation (cf. Acts 9:2; 22:5; 2 Cor 3:2). Since connections between the churches were of a personal rather than an institutional nature, an introduction of the delegates through letters would be necessary.

Travel Plans (16:5-12)

Looking to the near future, Paul addresses the possibility of visits from himself (vv. 5-9), from Timothy (vv. 10-11), and from Apollos (v. 12).

He himself intended to visit after passing through Macedonia (presumably to visit the Philippian and Thessalonian churches). Currently in Ephesus (v. 8), he would therefore have to cut a course from Asia and through Macedonia by land. This itinerary is hard to square with the movements recounted in 2 Corinthians, where Paul recollects that he had visited the Corinthians on the way to Macedonia before making his way back to Ephesus (2 Cor 1:16), thus reaching Achaia by sea (perhaps) and traveling in the opposite direction. After visiting Macedonia, his intention had been to travel back to Corinth. He admits that he did not do so. The change of plans shows that his travel plans were often tentative. Indeed, when discussing his travel plans he often set conditions on them ("if the Lord wills," 4:19; "if the Lord permits," 16:7) or left them indeterminate ("wherever I go," 16:6). Thus, there is no way to know if the plans indicated here came to fruition.

At this point his intention was to remain in Ephesus until Pentecost (or the Feast of Weeks, a Jewish holiday that took place the day after seven weeks after Passover, thus "fifty" days after Passover) and then to take up residence in Corinth for the winter. Thus, he makes clear that he did not intend simply to make Corinth a convenient stop but wished to spend some length of time with them. His purpose, however, also turns out to have been somewhat practical. He wants the Corinthians to "send" him on his way, that is, to send him off with provisions to his next destination. This objective shows that, although he was disinclined to accept support from them while he ministered *among* them (9:1-27), he was willing to allow them to participate in supporting his missions abroad.

Paul notes that although God had granted him promising evangelistic opportunities in Ephesus (an open "door"), he encountered much opposition. Acts 19:21-40 recounts an incident in which a silversmith named Demetrius incited the city against him. The opponents mentioned in this passage may very well be the "wild beasts" that Paul referenced in 1 Cor 15:32.

Still wrapping up, Paul alerts the Corinthians of a possible visit from Timothy (vv. 10-11). According to Acts 19:22, Paul sent Timothy and Erastus ahead from Ephesus to Macedonia, planning to remain longer in Ephesus before moving on to Macedonia himself, and then from there to Achaia (Acts 19:21). Having followed his plan, he arrived in Achaia and makes what appears to be his second and final visit to Corinth (Acts 20:2-3; cf. 18:1-18). Timothy accompanies him when he departs and so Timothy must have been present with him in Achaia for some period of time (Acts 20:4). The difficulty with this account is that it seems to conflict with the circumstances envisaged in 1 Corinthians. In 1 Cor 16:10 Paul indeed sends Timothy ahead, but to Corinth, of which nothing is said in Acts. Moreover, Paul awaits completion of Timothy's voyage and his arrival in Ephesus "with the brothers," not intending to travel to Corinth until he has reunited with Timothy and the brothers in Ephesus. Hence, if Acts 20:2-3 does refer to the visit to Corinth anticipated here, then one must suppose *either* that Timothy and the brothers indeed traveled to Macedonia (Acts 19:22), and did so on their way to Corinth (1 Cor 16:10-11), but returned to Paul in Ephesus before Paul himself departed (1 Cor 16:11), and that Paul is silent on the first of these points and Acts on the third, *or* that Paul changed his plans, and he did not wait until the arrival of Timothy and the brothers before leaving Ephesus but moved on to Corinth while Timothy was still there. If in one way or the other the two accounts can be reconciled, then the group of "brothers" said to be traveling with Timothy would likely have included

Erastus, who according to Acts accompanied Timothy to Macedonia (Acts 19:22).

Excursus

Paul's remarks in 2 Corinthians and Romans introduce further difficulties with this itinerary. In 2 Corinthians Paul recounts that he had made a second, "painful" visit to Corinth (2 Cor 2:1, 5; 7:12; 13:2) and later anticipates a final, third visit (2 Cor 12:14; 13:1), which his letter to the Roman church later shows that he did in fact make (Rom 15:25-27; 16:23). However, Acts depicts only two visits to Corinth (18:1-18; 20:2-3), the second of which seems to correlate with the plans anticipated in 1 Cor 16:5-11 but does not reflect the movements recounted in 2 Corinthians (where he moves from Ephesus directly to Corinth), and which does not appear to be a "painful" visit, and which turns out to be Paul's final visit to Corinth rather than his second. Thus, the plans anticipated in 1 Cor 16:5-11 are not in fact (fully) fulfilled as the events play out in Acts 19:22–20:4. Rather, Luke has fused Paul's second and third (final) visits, reflecting the dispatch of Timothy to Corinth (via Macedonia) prior to Paul's second visit (1 Cor 16:10) but omitting Paul's change of plans and his second ("painful") visit, and finally recounting Paul's trip to Corinth via Macedonia for his third and final visit (2 Cor 12:14; 13:1; Rom 15:25-27; 16:23).

As stated in 4:17, Paul sends Timothy to Corinth as a surrogate for himself. His exhortation to the Corinthians to give Timothy nothing to fear and not to despise him may show that their relationship with Timothy—or else the one whom he represented—was currently under strain.

While a visit from Timothy could imply that Timothy was the letter's carrier (Talbert 2002, 132), Paul's wording here precludes this possibility. The Corinthians are to receive Timothy "*if* Timothy comes" (16:10). Paul would not have put Timothy's arrival in question if the Corinthians' receipt of instructions about Timothy required delivery of the letter and delivery of the letter depended on the arrival of Timothy himself.

Finally, Paul addresses the question of a visit from Apollos (v. 12). Paul had wanted him to visit the Corinthians "with the brothers" (that is, probably with Timothy and the brothers with him). Although Paul introduces the topic of Apollos with the formula "now concerning," again, this need not imply that the Corinthians had inquired about Apollos in their letter (cf. 7:1), much less requested a visit from him (M. M. Mitchell 1989, 256n120). Paul's remark implies only that the Corinthians know Apollos (as indeed 3:4–4:5 shows) and care enough to have interest in the question of a visit. It could have been Paul, more than the Corinthians, who wanted Apollos to visit (indeed, Paul implored him to go): just as he wanted Timothy and the brothers to visit, Apollos too could serve as a surrogate for himself.

Final Request and Greetings (16:13-24)

The last unit of the letter consists of several short components. First is a set of final exhortations, as often come at the conclusion of Paul's letters (cf. Rom 16:17; 2 Cor 13:11; Gal 6:14-16; 1 Thess 5:12-21).

The exhortation section comes in two parts (vv. 13-14 + 15-18). The first part (vv. 13-14) contains five commands. The first four commands utilize military language (cf. Gal 5:1; Eph 6:10-18; Phil 1:27; 4:1) to exhort the Corinthians to stand against sin (cf. Acts 20:31; 1 Pet 5:8; Rev 3:2): "Keep alert, stand firm in your faith, be courageous, be strong" (v. 13). The exhortation to "stand firm in the faith" recalls Paul's earlier warning that the audience is *being* saved "if" they hold fast (15:2). The fifth command, "Let all that you do be done in love" (v. 14), forms a fitting conclusion to the letter. This is not a standard Pauline closing, and it is adapted specifically to the situation in Corinth. The church is divided. The exhortation is virtually synonymous with one asserted earlier: "Let all things be done for *building up*" (14:26). The exhortation also recalls the hymn of love that formed the centerpiece of chapters 12–14.

In the second part of the exhortation (vv. 15-18), Paul urges the Corinthians to subject themselves to their leaders. He mentions specifically the household of Stephanas (see 1:16), "the first converts in Achaia" (NASB, "the first fruits of Achaia"). A Roman province, Achaia comprised much of geographical Greece. According to Acts, Paul had converted Dionysius the Areopagite, Damaris, and "others" from Athens—also in Achaia—before coming to Corinth (Acts 17:34). How then was Stephanas the "first fruit" of Achaia? It could be that Stephanas was a believer prior to Paul's arrival; indeed, when Paul arrived, it seems that there may already have been believers there (see Acts 18:1-2). It seems most likely that Stephanas was in fact a convert of Paul himself since Paul claims to have baptized him (1:16). Paul, then, probably means that the household of Stephanas was "*a*" (rather than "*the*") first fruit of Achaia (thus the lack of the article in Greek).

Paul does not identify Stephanas or those in his household with any church "office" (cf. 1 Thess 5:13). Nor were they appointed to their position. On the contrary, they "appointed" ("devoted," NRSV) themselves. Thus, the leadership structure apparent in the Corinthian church contrasts with the structure seen in the synagogues or in the private associations (where laws administered by elected officials governed affairs) and in the church as reflected in later Christian writings (1 Clem. 42:1-5; Ign. *Phld.* 8:2; *Trall.* 7:2; *Smyrn.* 12:2; *Pol.* 6:1; *Rom.* 4.1; 7.1). It is remarkable that, although Paul commands the Corinthians to "be in subjection" (NASB) to Stephanas and his household, Paul commends the latter for their "service," not for their high social standing (Gardner 2018, 748). Given Paul's high accolades for Stephanas, most likely he was not among the "wise" people responsible for so many of the church's problems.

Stephanas and two other Corinthians— a certain Fortunatus and Achaicus—are now present with Paul in Ephesus. The names Fortunatus and Achaicus are typical slave names, and these individuals may have been servile members of Stephanas's household. Paul views these three as surrogates for the Corinthians, just as he viewed Timothy as a surrogate for himself (4:17; cf. Ign. *Eph.* 1:3; 2:1). These are most likely the carriers of the letter from the Corinthians (cf. 7:1), and it makes the most sense to suppose that they also delivered Paul's letter of response when they returned to Corinth.

Following his final exhortations, Paul issues a series of greetings (vv. 19-21). Such greetings were standard in ancient letters, as they are in Paul's (Rom 16:16, 21, 23; 2 Cor 13:12; Phil 4:21; Col 4:10-14; 2 Tim 4:21; Phlm 23). Since travel was expensive—to say nothing of writing and delivery—conveying greetings from multiple parties was a more affordable and effective way of maintaining long-distance relationships. Paul sends greetings first from "the churches of Asia." Located in the province of Asia (western Asia Minor, or modern-day Turkey), Ephesus claimed one of apparently many churches in the region. Next Paul mentions Aquila and Prisca "together with the church in their house." Aquila and Prisca (known in Acts as Priscilla; Acts 18:2, 18, 26) were close associates of Paul (see also Rom 16:3; 2 Tim 4:19) and according to Acts "tentmakers" like him (Acts 18:2-3). They were apparently already believers when Paul arrived in Corinth (Acts 18:1-3). They had been displaced to Corinth when the emperor Claudius expelled the Jews from Rome (AD 49). Now it seems that they are residents of Ephesus. Later they returned to Rome, where they hosted another house-church (Rom 16:3-5a).

Next Paul sends greetings from "all the brothers." This designation may refer to his coworkers, since he has already sent greetings from the local churches (Horsley 1998, 226).

It is curious that Paul urges the Corinthians to greet "each other" with a "holy kiss" (v. 20). This exhortation appears at the end of several of Paul's letters (Rom 16:16; 2 Cor 13:12; 1 Thess 5:26; cf. Phil 4:21). Possibly he intended for the believers to carry out the kiss at just this point in the public reading of the letter. In any case, greetings from the author to a third party were conventional in ancient letters, and Paul may simply be asking the Corinthians to greet each other (and other local believers?) on his behalf (cf. Klauck 2006, 373). Greeting with a kiss was common in the ancient Near East (Gen 29:11; Mark 14:45; Acts 20:37), yet the greeting here serves as a symbolic bond that cuts across social and economic divides and unites specifically those of the believing community. The gesture became common practice in early Christianity (see also 1 Pet 5:14; Justin Martyr, *1 Apol.* 65.2). It is "particularly appropriate in a letter directed to a community that had experienced tensions and divisions (cf. 1:10)" (Collins 1999, 609).

Finally, Paul sends greetings from himself (v. 21). Reference to his own "hand" comes at the close of several of his letters (1 Cor 16:21; Gal 6:11; Col 4:18; 2 Thess 3:17; Phlm 19). It would be known from the address line that he was the author (1:1), so the purpose of the reference would be to indicate that he used a scribe up to this point (Rom 16:22 explicitly identifies his scribe), as was common even for educated writers (Klauck 2006, 55); and that he is now signing off on the work, as was also conventional (Klauck 2006, 16).

The postscript consists of a curse (v. 22) and a benediction (vv. 23-24). The curse is severe and somewhat unexpected in the context: "Let anyone be accursed who has no love for the Lord" (cf. 12:3). Paul uses here a more common, and weaker, word for "love" (*philein*). The idea may be that, if anyone does not have *even this* kind of love for the Lord, they certainly do not belong to him. Summarily following is an originally Aramaic expression that means "O Lord, come!" In Greek the expression is juxtaposed with the word "accursed," which contains the same consonant sounds (*anathema*, *maranatha*) and creates an obvious play on words. The expression represents, in perhaps a liturgical form, the all-important expectation of Christ's return (cf. 1:8; 4:5; 11:26). It may also be intended as an exhortation to a life such as might be considered worthy of Christ at the judgment.

Paul concludes with a two-part benediction. The first part consists in a formula that appears at the conclusion of every letter in the Pauline corpus: "The grace of the Lord Jesus be with you" (cf. Rom 16:20; 1 Cor 16:23; 2 Cor 13:13; Gal 6:18; Eph 6:24; Phil 4:23; Col 4:18; 1 Thess 5:28; 2 Thess 3:18; 1 Tim 6:21; 2 Tim 4:22; Titus 3:15; Phlm 1:25). Yet the expression takes on special significance in the context of this letter. Although the Corinthians have boasted in their spiritual status, Paul has emphasized their immaturity (2:14–3:3). It is by God's grace that they are what they are and by God's grace that they will reach maturity. In the second part of the benediction, Paul declares—in an irenic gesture—that his love is with them. This not only recalls the theme of love made front and center in chapter 13; it also shows that although Paul has been severe with them (cf. 4:21), he does not want to end his letter without making absolutely clear that he has said all things in love and for their edification.

Works Cited

Ascough, Richard S. 2003. *Paul's Macedonian Associations: The Social Context of Philippians and 1 Thessalonians.* WUNT II 161. Tübingen: Mohr Siebeck.

Asher, J. R. 2000. *Polarity and Change in 1 Corinthians 15: A Study of Metaphysics, Rhetoric, and Resurrection.* Tübingen: Mohr Siebeck.

Balch, David L. 1983. "1 Cor 7:32-35 and Stoic Debates about Marriage, Anxiety, and Distraction." *JBL* 102: 429–39.

Barclay, John M. G. 1992. "Thessalonica and Corinth: Social Contrasts in Pauline Christianity." *JSNT* 47: 49–74.

Barclay, John M. G. 2015. *Paul and the Gift.* Grand Rapids: Eerdmans.

Barclay, John M. G. 2016. "Apocalyptic Allegiance and Disinvestment in the World: A Reading of 1 Corinthians 7:25-35." Pages 257–73 in *Paul and the Apocalyptic Imagination.* Edited by Ben Blackwell, John Goodrich, and Jason Maston. Philadelphia: Fortress.

Barclay, John M. G. 2001. "Matching Theory and Practice: Josephus's Constitutional Ideal and Paul's Strategy in Corinth." Pages 139–64 in *Paul Beyond the Judaism/Hellenism Divide.* Edited by Troels Engberg-Pedersen. Louisville: Westminster John Knox.

Barrett, C. K. 1968. *The First Epistle to the Corinthians.* Harper's New Testament Commentaries. New York: Harper & Row.

Baur, F. C. 1831. "Die Christusparti in der korinthischen Gemeinde, der Gegensatz des paulinischen und petrinischen Christentums in der ältesten Kirche, der Apostel Petrus in Rom." *Tübinger Zeitschrift für Theologie* 4: 61–206.

Bradley, Keith R. 1987. *Slaves and Masters in the Roman Empire: A Study in Social Control.* Brussels: Collection Latomus, 1984; Oxford: Oxford University Press.

Bradley, Keith R. 1994. *Slavery and Society at Rome.* Cambridge University Press: Cambridge.

Bradley, Keith R. 2011. "Resisting Slavery at Rome." Pages 62–84 in *The Cambridge World History of Slavery; Volume 1: The Ancient Mediterranean World.* Edited by Keith Bradley and Paul Cartledge. Cambridge: Cambridge University Press.

Brookins, Timothy A. 2010. "Rhetoric and Philosophy in the First Century: Their Relation with Respect to 1 Corinthians 1–4." *Neot* 44: 233–52.

Brookins, Timothy A. 2014. *Corinthian Wisdom, Stoic Philosophy, and the Ancient Economy.* SNTSMS 159. Cambridge: Cambridge University Press.

Brookins, Timothy A. 2017a. "Economic Profiling of Early Christian Communities." In *Paul and Economics.* Edited by Thomas Blanton and Ray Pickett. Philadelphia: Fortress.

Brookins, Timothy A. 2017b. "'Natural Hair': A 'New Rhetorical' Assessment of 1 Cor 11:14-15." Pages 181–206 in *Paul and the Greco-Roman Philosophical Tradition.* Edited by Andrew Pitts and Joseph Dodson. LNTS. London: T & T Clark.

Brookins, Timothy A. 2020. "Reconsidering the Coherence of 1 Cor 1:10–4:21." *NovT* 62/2: 139–56.

Bultmann, Rudolf. 1910. *Der Stil der Paulinischen Predigt und die kynisch-stoische Diatribe.* Göttingen: Vandenhoeck & Ruprecht.

Byron, John. 2003. "Slave of Christ or Willing Servant?: Paul's Self-description in 1 Corinthians 4:1-2 and 9:16-18." *Neot* 37: 179–98.

Callan, Terrance. 1985. "Prophecy and Ecstasy in Greco-Roman Religion and in 1 Corinthians." *NovT* 27: 125–40.

Campbell, Constantine. 2012. *Paul and Union with Christ: An Exegetical and Theological Study.* Grand Rapids: Zondervan.

Caragounis, Chrys C. 2006. "What Did Paul Mean?: The Debate on 1 Cor 7,1–7." *ETL* 82: 189–99.

Chester, Stephen J. 2003. *Conversion at Corinth: Perspectives on Conversion in Paul's Theology and the Corinthian Church*. Studies of the New Testament and Its World. New York: T & T Clark.

Chow, John. 1992. *Patronage and Power*. JSOTSup 75. Sheffield, Eng.: JSOT.

Clarke, Andrew. 1993. *Secular and Christian Leadership in Corinth: A Socio-Historical and Exegetical Study of 1 Corinthians 1–6*. New York: Brill.

Collins, John J. 1963. "Chiasmus, the 'ABA' Pattern and the Text of Paul. Pages 575–84 in *Studiorum Paulinorum Congressus Internationalis Catholicus*. Rome: Biblical Institute Press.

Collins, Raymond. 1999. *1 Corinthians*. SP 7. Collegeville, MN: Liturgical Press.

Cook, John Granger. 2008. "1 Corinthians 9:5: The Women of the Apostles." *Bib* 89: 352–68.

Cook, John Granger. 2017. "Resurrection in Paganism and the Question of an Empty Tomb in 1 Corinthians 15." *NTS* 63: 56–75.

Coppins, Wayne. 2010. "Doing Justice to the Two Perspectives of 1 Corinthians 15:1-11." *Neot* 44: 282–91.

Corley, Jeremy. 2004. "The Pauline Authorship of 1 Corinthians 13." *CBQ* 66: 256–74.

Coutsoumpos, Panayotis. 2015. *Paul, Corinth, and the Roman Empire*. Eugene, OR: Wipf & Stock.

Dahl, Nils. 1977. "Paul and the Church at Corinth According to 1 Corinthians 1:10–4:21." Pages 40–61 in *Studies in Paul: Theology for the Early Christian Mission*. Minneapolis, MN: Augsburg.

de Vos, Craig Steven. 1999. *Church and Community Conflicts: The Relationships of the Thessalonian, Corinthian, and Philippian Churches with Their Wider Civic Communities*. SBLDS 168. Atlanta: Scholars.

Deming, Will. 2003. "Paul and Indifferent Things." Pages 384–94 in *Paul in the Greco-Roman World*. Edited by J. Paul Sampley. London: Continuum.

Deming, Will. 2004. *Paul on Marriage and Celibacy: The Hellenistic Background of 1 Corinthians 7*. Grand Rapids: Eerdmans.

Derrett, J. Duncan M. 1991. "Judgment and 1 Corinthians 6." *NTS* 37: 22–36.

Doughty, Darrell. 1975. "The Presence and Future of Salvation in Corinth." *Zeitschrift für die neutestamentliche Wissenschaft und die Kunde der älteren Kirche* 66: 61–90.

Dutch, R. S. 2005. *The Educated Elite in 1 Corinthians: Education and Community Conflict in Graeco-Roman Context.* JSNTSup 271. New York: T & T Clark.

Fee, Gordon. 1980. "1 Corinthians 7:1 in the *NIV.*" *JETS* 23: 307–14.

Fee, Gordon. 1987. *The First Epistle to the Corinthians.* NICNT. Grand Rapids: Eerdmans, 1987.

Finney, Mark T. 2010. "Honor, Rhetoric and Factionalism in the Ancient World: 1 Corinthians 1–4 in its Social Context." *BTB* 40: 27–36.

Fiore, Benjamin. 1985. "'Covert Allusion' in 1 Cor 1–4." *CBQ* 47: 85–102.

Fitzgerald, John T. 1988. *Cracks in an Earthen Vessel: An Examination of the Catalogues of Hardships in the Corinthian Correspondence.* SBLDS 99. Atlanta: Scholars.

Fitzmyer, Joseph A. 2008. *First Corinthians.* AB 32. New Haven: Yale University Press.

Foerster, Richard. 1915. *Libanii Opera, Vol. IIX: Progymnasmata. Argumenta Orationum Demosthenicarum.* Leipzig.

Fotopoulos, John. 2003. *Food Offered to Idols in Roman Corinth: A Socio-Rhetorical Reconsideration of 1 Cor 8:1–11:1.* WUNT 2/151. Tübingen: Mohr Siebeck.

Fotopoulos, John. 2005. "Arguments Concerning Food Offered to Idols: Corinthian Quotations and Pauline Refutations in a Rhetorical *Partitio* (1 Corinthians 8:1-9)." *CBQ* 67: 611–31.

Friesen, Steven J., Daniel N. Schowalter, and James C. Walters, editors. 2010. *Corinth in Context: Comparative Studies on Religion and Society.* NovTSup 134. Leiden: Brill.

Gardner, Paul D. 2018. *1 Corinthians. Exegetical Commentary on the New Testament.* Grand Rapids: Zondervan.

Gill, David W. J. 1992. "The Meat-Market in Corinth (1 Corinthians 10:25)." *TynBul* 43: 171–79.

Gill, David W. J. 2017. "Early Christianity in Its Colonial Contexts in the Provinces of the Eastern Empire." Pages 68–85 in *The Urban World of the First Christians*. Edited by Steve Walton, Paul R. Trebilco, and Gill W. J. David. Grand Rapids: Eerdmans.

Gooch, Peter D. 1993. *Dangerous Food: 1 Corinthians 8-10 in Its Context*. Waterloo, Ont.: Wilfrid Laurier University Press.

Goodrich, John. 2012. *Paul as an Administrator of God in 1 Corinthians*. SNTSMS 152. Cambridge: Cambridge University Press.

Gormanchael J. 2001. *Cruciformity: Paul's Narrative Spirituality of the Cross*. Grand Rapids: Eerdmans.

Goulder, M. D. 1991. "Σοφία in Corinthians." *NTS* 37: 516–34.

Grindheim, Sigurd. 2002. "Wisdom for the Perfect: Paul's Challenge for the Corinthian Church (2:6-16)." *JBL* 121: 689–709.

Gupta, Nijay K. 2010. "Which 'Body' is a Temple (1 Corinthians 6:19)?: Paul beyond the Individual/Communal Divide." *CBQ* 72: 518–36.

Harrison, James R., and L. L. Welborn, editors. 2016. *The First Urban Churches 2: Roman Corinth*. WGRWSup 8. Atlanta: Society of Biblical Literature.

Hays, Richard B. 1997. *1 Corinthians*. Louisville: John Knox Press.

Hays, Richard B. 2014. *Reading Backwards: Figural Christology and the Fourfold Gospel Witness*. Waco: Baylor University Press.

Hengel, Martin. 1995. *Studies in Early Christology*. Edinburgh: T & T Clark.

Hengel, Martin. 2001. "Das Begräbnis Jesu bei Paulus und die leibliche Auferstehung aus dem Grabe." Pages 119–83 in *Auferstehung–Resurrection*. Edited by F. Avemarie and H. Lichtenberger. WUNT 135. Tübingen: Mohr Siebeck.

Hollander, Harm W. 2010. "Seeing God 'in a Riddle' or 'Face to Face': An Analysis of 1 Corinthians 13.12." *JSNT* 32: 395–403.

Hope, Valerie M. 2009. *Roman Death: The Dying and the Dead in Ancient Rome*. London: Continuum.

Horsley, Richard. 1976. "Pneumatikos vs. Psychikos: Distinctions of Spiritual Status among the Corinthians." *HTR* 69: 269–88.

Horsley, Richard. 1998. *1 Corinthians*. Nashville: Abingdon.

Hurd, J. C. 1965. *The Origin of 1 Corinthians*. New York: Seabury.

Jeremias, Joachim. 1966. *Eucharistic Words of Jesus*. Translated by Norman Perrin. New York: Scribner.

Jervis, L. Ann. 1995. "1 Corinthians 14:34-35: A Reconsideration of Paul's Limitation of the Free Speech of Some Corinthian Women." *JSNT* 17: 51–74.

Jewett, R. 1971. *Paul's Anthropological Terms*. Arbeiten zur Geschichte des antiken Judentums und des Urchristentums 10. Leiden: Brill.

Kerferd, George B. 1990. "The Sage in Hellenistic Philosophical Literature." Pages 320–28 in *The Sage in Israel and Ancient Near East*. Edited by John G. Gammie and Leo G. Perdue. Winona Lake, IN: Eisenbrauns.

Klauck, Hans Josef. 2006. *Ancient Letters and the New Testament: A Guide to Context*. Waco: Baylor University Press.

Kuck, D. W. 1992. *Judgment and Community Conflict: Paul's Use of Apocalyptic Judgment Language in 1 Corinthians 3:5–4:5*. NovTSup 66. Leiden: Brill.

Kugler, Chris. 2020. *Paul and the Image of God*. Lanham, MD: Fortress Academic/Lexington Books.

Lee, Michelle V. 2006. *Paul, the Stoics, and the Body of Christ*. SNTSMS 137. Cambridge: Cambridge University Press.

Letteney, Mark. 2016. "Toward a New Scribal Tendency: Reciprocal Corruptions and the Text of 1 Corinthians 8:2-3." *JBL* 135: 391–404.

Levison, John. 2009. *Filled with the Spirit*. Grand Rapids: Eerdmans.

Litfin, Duane. 1994. *St. Paul's Theology of Proclamation: 1 Corinthians 1–4 and Greco-Roman Rhetoric*. SNTSMS 79. Cambridge: Cambridge University Press.

Long, A. A. 1982. "Soul and Body in Stoicism." *Phronesis* 27: 34–57.

Long, A. A., and D. N. Sedley. 1987. *The Hellenistic Philosophers*. 2 volumes. London: Cambridge University Press.

Lütgert, W. 1908. *Freiheitspredigt und Schwarmgeister in Korinth*. Göttingen: C. Bertelsman.

Lutz, Cora E. 1947. *Musonius Rufus: The Roman Socrates*. YCS 10. New Haven: Yale University Press.

Malherbe, Abraham J. 1968. "The Beasts at Ephesus." *JBL* 87: 71–80.

Malherbe, Abraham J. 1983. *Social Aspects of Early Christianity.* Philadelphia: Fortress.

Malherbe, Abraham J. 1994. "Determinism and Free Will in Paul: The Argument of 1 Cor 8 and 9." Pages 231–55 in *Paul in His Hellenistic Context.* Edited by Troels Engberg-Pedersen. Edinburgh: T & T Clark.

Malone, Andrew. 2009. "Burn or Boast?: Keeping the 1 Corinthians 13,3 Debate in Balance." *Bib* 90: 400–406.

Martin, Dale B. 1990. *Slavery as Salvation: The Metaphor of Slavery in Pauline Christianity.* New Haven: Yale University Press.

Martin, Dale B. 1995. *Corinthian Body.* New Haven: Yale University Press.

Massey, Preston T. 2018. "Veiling among Men in Roman Corinth: 1 Corinthians 11:4 and the Potential Problem of East Meeting West." *JBL* 137: 501–17.

Maston, Jason S. 2016. "Anthropological Crisis and Solution in the Hodayot and 1 Corinthians 15." *NTS* 62: 533–48.

McFarland, Orrey. 2017. "Divine Causation and Prepositional Metaphysics in Philo of Alexandria and the Apostle Paul." Pages 117–34 in *Paul and the Greco-Roman Philosophical Tradition.* LNTS 527. Edited by Joseph R. Dodson and Andrew W. Pitts. London: Bloomsbury.

Meeks, Wayne. 1983. *The First Urban Christians.* New Haven: Yale University Press.

Meggitt, Justin. 1998. *Paul and Poverty.* Studies of the New Testament and Its World. Edinburgh: T & T Clark.

Mihaila, Corin. 2009. *The Paul-Apollos Relationship and Paul's Stance toward Greco-Roman Rhetoric.* LNTS 402. London: T & T Clark.

Millis, Benjamin. 2010. "The Social and Ethnic Origins of the Colonists in Early Roman Corinth." Pages 13–36 in *Corinth in Context: Comparative Studies on Religion and Society.* Edited by Steven J. Friesen, Daniel N. Schowalter, and James C. Walters. Leiden: Brill.

Mitchell, Alan. 1993. "Rich and Poor in the Courts of Corinth: Litigiousness and Status in 1 Cor 6:1-11." *NTS* 39: 562–86.

Mitchell, Margaret M. 1989. "Concerning *peri de* in 1 Corinthians." *NovT* 31: 229–56.

Mitchell, Margaret M. 1993. *Paul and the Rhetoric of Reconciliation.* Louisville: Westminster John Knox.

Mitchell, Margaret M. 2001. "Pauline Accommodation and 'Condescension' (συγκατάβασις): 1 Cor 9:19-23 and the History of Influence." Pages 197–214 in *Paul Beyond the Judaism/Hellenism Divide.* Edited by Troels Engberg-Pedersen. Louisville: Westminster John Knox.

Mitchell, Matthew W. 2003. "Reexamining the 'Aborted Apostle': An Exploration of Paul's Self-Description in 1 Corinthians 15.8." *JSNT* 25: 469–85.

Moses, Robert Ewusie. 2014. *Practices of Power: Revisiting the Principalities and Powers in the Pauline Letters.* Minneapolis: Fortress.

Murillo, Herbert A. 1954. *Acts of the Pagan Martyrs.* Oxford: Clarendon.

Murphy-O'Connor, Jerome. 1978. "Corinthian Slogans in 1 Cor. 6:12-20." *CBQ* 40: 391–96.

Murphy-O'Connor, Jerome. 1979. "Food and Spiritual Gifts in 1 Cor. 8:8." *CBQ* 41: 292–98.

Murphy-O'Connor, Jerome. (1983) 2002. *St. Paul's Corinth: Texts and Archaeology.* GNS 6. Wilmington, DE: Michael Glazier; 3rd rev. ed.: Collegeville, MN: Liturgical.

Murphy-O'Connor, Jerome. 1988. "1 Corinthians 11:2-16 Once Again." *CBQ* 50: 265–74.

Murphy-O'Connor, Jerome. 1993. "Co-Authorship in the Corinthian Correspondence." *RB* 100: 562–79.

Murphy-O'Connor, Jerome. 2009. *Keys to First Corinthians: Revisiting the Major Issues.* Oxford: Oxford University Press.

Naselli, Andrew David. 2017. "Is Every Sin outside the Body except Immoral Sex? Weighing Whether 1 Corinthians 6:18b Is Paul's Statement or a Corinthian Slogan." *JBL* 136: 969–87.

Neutel, Karin B. 2015. *A Cosmopolitan Ideal: Paul's Declaration 'Neither Jew nor Greek, Neither Slave nor Free, nor Male and Female' in the Context of First Century Thought.* LNTS 513. London; New York: Bloomsbury T & T Clark.

Newberry, Julie. 2019. "Paul's Allusive Reasoning in 1 Corinthians 11.7-12." *NTS* 65: 43–58.

Oakes, Peter. 2009. "Contours of the Urban Environment." Pages 21–35 in *After the First Urban Christians*. Edited by Todd Still and David Horrell. Edinburgh: T & T Clark.

Økland, Jorunn. 2010. "Ceres, Κορή, and Cultural Complexity: Divine Personality Definitions and Human Worshippers in Roman Corinth." Pages 199–229 in *Corinth in Context: Comparative Studies on Religion and Society*. NovTSup 134. Edited by Steven J. Friesen, Daniel N. Schowalter, and James C. Walters. Leiden: Brill.

Omanson, Roger L. 2011. "Second Corinthians 8:4 and 9:1 and the Larger Context of Paul's Letters." *RevExp* 108: 307–11.

Oropeza, B. J. 2017. *1 Corinthians: A New Covenant Commentary*. New Covenant Commentary Series. Eugene, OR: Cascade.

Oster, R. E. 1988. "When Men Wore Veils to Worship: The Historical Context of 1 Cor 11:4." *NTS* 34: 481–505.

Paige, Terence. 1991. "1 Corinthians 12.2: A Pagan Pompe?" *JSNT* 14: 57–65.

Parker, David. 2008. *An Introduction to the New Testament Manuscripts and Their Texts*. Cambridge: Cambridge University Press.

Pascuzzi, Maria. 1997. *Ethics, Ecclesiology, and Church Discipline*. Rome: Editrice Pontificia Universita Gregoriana.

Pascuzzi, Maria. 2009. "Baptism-based Allegiance and the Divisions in Corinth: A Reexamination of 1 Corinthians 1:13-17." *CBQ* 71: 813–29.

Peppard, Michael. 2016. "Brother against Brother: *Controversiae* about Inheritance Disputes and 1 Corinthians 6:1-11." Pages 133–52 in *The First Urban Churches 2: Roman Corinth*. Edited by James R. Harrison and L. L. Welborn. WGRWSup 8. Atlanta: Society of Biblical Literature.

Perkins, Pheme. 2012. *First Corinthians*. Paideia. Grand Rapids: Baker Academic.

Perriman, A. C. 1994. "The Head of a Woman: The Meaning of κεφαλη in 1 Cor 11:3." *JTS* 45: 600–22.

Pogoloff, Stephen M. 1992. *Logos and Sophia: The Rhetorical Situation of 1 Corinthians.* SBLDS 134. Atlanta: Scholars.

Portier-Young, Anathea. 2005. "Tongues and Cymbals: Contextualizing 1 Corinthians 13:1." *BTB* 35: 99–105.

Ramelli, Ilaria. 2009. *Hierocles the Stoic: Elements of Ethics, Fragments, and Excerpts.* Translated by David Konstan. WGRW 28. Atlanta: Society of Biblical Literature Press.

Richardson, Peter. 1983. "Judgment in Sexual Matters in 1 Corinthians 6:1-11." *NovT* 25: 37–58.

Robertson, Archibald, and Alfred Plummer. 1963. *A Critical and Exegetical Commentary on the First Epistle of St. Paul to the Corinthians.* ICC 33. Edinburgh: T & T Clark, 1963 (repr).

Sampley, J. Paul. (2002) 2015. "The First Letter to the Corinthians." *NIB* 10:771–1003.

Sampley, J. Paul. 2004. "Paul's Frank Speech with the Galatians and the Corinthians." In *Philodemus and the New Testament World.* NovTSup 111. Edited by J. T. Fitzgerald, G. S. Holland, and D. Obbink. Leiden: Brill.

Schmidt, J. E. C. 1801. *Bibliothek für Kritik und Exegese des Neuen Testaments und älteste Christengeschicthe.* Bd 2.3. Hadamar.

Smit, Joop F. M. 1991. "The Genre of 1 Corinthians in the Light of Classical Rhetoric." *NovT* 33: 193–216.

Smit, Joop F. M. 2002. "'What Is Apollos? What Is Paul?' In Search for the Coherence of First Corinthians 1:10–4:21." *NovT* 44: 231–51.

Smith, Jay E. 2008. "The Roots of a 'Libertine' Slogan in 1 Corinthians 6:18." *JTS* 59: 63–95.

Smith, Jay E. 2010. "Slogans in 1 Corinthians." *BSac* 167: 68–88.

Stanley, Christopher. 1992. *Paul and the Language of Scripture: Citation Technique in the Pauline Epistles and Contemporary Literature.* SNTSMS 69. Cambridge: Cambridge University Press.

Still, E. Coye III. 2004. "Divisions over Leaders and Food Offered to Idols: The Parallel Thematic Structures of 1 Corinthians 4:6-21 and 8:1-11:1." *TynBul* 55: 17–42.

Tabb, Brian J. 2017. "Paul and Seneca on Suffering." Pages 88–108 in *Paul and Seneca in Dialogue*. Edited by Joseph R. Dodson and David E. Briones. Leiden: Brill.

Talbert, Charles. (1987) 2002. *Reading Corinthians: A Literary and Theological Commentary*. New York: Crossroad. Reprint, Macon: Smyth & Helwys.

Theissen, Gerd. 1975. "Die Starken und Schwachen in Korinth: Soziologische Analyse eines theologischen Streits." *EvT* 35: 155–72.

Theissen, Gerd. 1982a. "Social Integration and Sacramental Activity: An Analysis of 1 Cor. 11:17-34." Pages 145–74 in *The Social Setting of Pauline Christianity*. Philadelphia: Fortress.

Theissen, Gerd. 1982b. *The Social Setting of Pauline Christianity*. Philadelphia: Fortress.

Theissen, Gerd. 2001. "The Social Structure of Pauline Communities: Some Critical Remarks on J. J. Meggitt *Paul, Poverty, and Survival*." *JSNT* 84: 65–84.

Theissen, Gerd. 2003. "Social Conflicts in the Corinthian Correspondence: Further Remarks on J. J. Meggitt, *Paul, Poverty and Survival*." *JSNT* 25/9: 371–91.

Thiselton, Anthony C. 2000. *The First Epistle to the Corinthians*. NIGTC. Grand Rapids: Eerdmans.

Thompson, Cynthia L. 1988. "Hairstyles, Head-Coverings and St. Paul: Portraits from Roman Corinth." *BA* 51: 99–115.

Tsai, Luke. 2016. "Brothers in Dispute: A Socio-Economic and Legal Analysis of the Litigants in the Church of Corinth." PhD dissertation, Dallas Theological Seminary.

Ware, James P. 2014. "Paul's Understanding of the Resurrection in 1 Corinthians 15:36-54." *JBL* 133: 809–35.

Wasserman, Emma. 2017. "Gentile Gods at the Eschaton: A Reconsideration of Paul's 'Principalities and Powers' in 1 Corinthians 15." *JBL* 136: 727–46.

Welborn, L. L. 1987. "On the Discord in Corinth: 1 Corinthians 1–4 and Ancient Politics." *JBL* 106: 85–111.

Welborn, L. L. 2016. "Inequality in Roman Corinth: Evidence from Diverse Sources Evaluated by a Neo-Ricardian Model." Pages 47–84 in *The First Urban Churches 2: Roman Corinth*. WGRWSup 8. Atlanta: Society of Biblical Literature.

Westcott, Brooke Foss, and Fenton John Anthony Hort. 1882. *The New Testament in the Original Greek*. Vol. 1. Cambridge; London: Cambridge University Press, 1881–1882. (Abbreviated in text as WH)

White, Devin. 2017. *Teacher of the Nations: Ancient Educational Traditions and Paul's Argument in 1 Corinthians 1–4*. BZNW 227. Boston: De Gruyter.

Willet, Rinse. 2012. "Whirlwind of Numbers: Demographic Experiments for Roman Corinth." *Ancient Society* 42: 127–58.

Willis, Wendell. 1985. "An Apostolic Apologia? The Form and Function of 1 Cor 9." *JSNT* 24: 33–48.

Winter, Bruce W. 1998. "Puberty or Passion: The Referent of ὑπέρακμος in 1 Corinthians 7:36." *TynBul* 49: 71–89.

Winter, Bruce W. 2001. *After Paul Left Corinth: The Influence of Secular Ethics and Social Change*. Grand Rapids: Eerdmans.

Winter, Bruce W. 2002. *Philo and Paul among the Sophists: A Hellenistic Jewish and a Christian Response*. Cambridge: Cambridge University Press, 1997; 2d edition; Grand Rapids: Eerdmans.

Wire, Antoinette Clark. 1990. *The Corinthian Women Prophets: A Reconstruction through Paul's Rhetoric*. Philadelphia: Fortress.

Wiseman, James. 1972. "The Gymnasium Area at Corinth, 1969–1970." *Hesperia* 41: 1–42.

Wright, N. T. 2007. *Surprised by Hope*. London: SPCK.

Made in United States
Orlando, FL
10 February 2023

29751146R00104